THE PLEASURE OF STILLWATER FLY FISHING

THE PLEASURE OF STILLWATER FLY FISHING

PETER REEVES

SWAN·HILL
PRESS

First published in the UK in 1998
by Swan Hill Press, an imprint of Airlife Publishing Ltd

British Library Cataloguing-in-Publication Data
A catalogue record for this book
is available from the British Library

ISBN 1 84037 018 1

Typeset by Phoenix Typesetting, Ilkley, West Yorkshire
Printed in England by St Edmundsbury Press Ltd., Bury St. Edmunds, Suffolk

Swan Hill Press
an imprint of Airlife Publishing Ltd
101 Longden Road, Shrewsbury, SY3 9EB, England

Contents

1. The appeal and enjoyment of angling   7
2. Equipment   13
3. Casting   30
4. The private life of the trout   40
5. Moving stillwaters   52
6. Bank fishing – where to start   61
7. Fishing the lure   68
8. Small flies   81
9. Fishing the nymph   99
10. Boat fishing   112
11. Seasonal patterns   123
12. Fly tying   139
13. Tail piece   167

Index   181

Chapter 1

The appeal and enjoyment of angling

A ngling in its various forms appeals to a very wide range of devotees. This appeal reaches across differences of age, sex, class, culture and nationality. In Britain the awareness of the satisfaction which can be gained from angling has without doubt been on the increase and the sport has been gaining broader support – as the wide range of angling magazines now available shows. I am particularly pleased, for instance, to see many more women successfully taking part and enjoying the sport in its coarse, sea and game aspects, although a limited number of women have long been honourably associated with the sport. For example, Dame Juliana Berners, Prioress of an abbey near St Albans in Hertfordshire wrote the earliest British book dealing with fly fishing; her *Treatyse of Fysshynge wyth an Angle* gave information on how to make rods, hooks and flies for fishing plus instructions for their use, and was written as early as 1496 – over 150 years prior to Isaak Walton's celebrated *The Compleat Angler*. More recently the British salmon rod-caught record has been held since 1922 by another lady, Georgina Ballantine – an astonishing 64 lb (29 kg) taken at Caputh in Scotland.

Moreover, the occupations of those beaming individuals who are shown in the press proudly brandishing their catches for the camera show a burgeoning of interest at all levels of society. Angling provides a common interest and a great deal of fulfilment for a high proportion of the population. Why is this? What is the fascination of this sport, which has, over the years, generated vast quantities of words in books and magazines? The subject has been scrutinised and documented from every conceivable angle and still the words flow off the presses in an inexorable and eagerly awaited stream. The quality of some of the writing is truly exceptional.

Many themes have been investigated in this huge library, and many experiences shared with those who share angling's fascination. Perhaps inevitably, the most usual theme is 'how'. 'How to do it' is obviously a starting point of reader interest, with 'how I did it' appealing to those who may have passed this stage and seek to enjoy a taste of the philosophy of others, usually more experienced or enjoying better facilities. Further, of course, this rich vein of literature enables one to savour, albeit at second hand and with the use of one's imagination, the flavour of fishing otherwise denied one by reason of geography, cost or privileged opportunity. It also allows the reader to defy the normal restrictions of time and sample the circumstances of another era. The boundless treasures of angling literature is another area of discovery and delight which enhances the particular interest of the reader but also conveys the passion and excitement of angling in other styles, other places and for other fish than those one may have experienced. But whilst the committed angler will appreciate this window of experience, it is most unlikely that anyone not fully sympathetic to the sport will be able to identify with the experience of the author. The author may be able to build on an inner interest, whether recognised or not, but it is unlikely that any writer, no matter how persuasive, will be able to implant an enthusiasm in a reader who is unsympathetic or uninterested. A good writer will have the power to fan a spark into flames but the spark must be present.

So before looking in detail at various aspects of fishing in general and fly fishing in particular it may well be worth sparing a moment to ask not 'How?' but rather 'Why?' Why do so many people from such varied backgrounds take such pleasure in the sport? What is the motivating force which has generated so much passion for so many centuries?

Angling is of course a form of hunting and as such is a time-honoured means by which the human race has for thousands of years sought to add valuable protein, flavour and variety to its diet. In fulfilling this very basic requirement there is naturally a sense of satisfaction. The bigger and better the catch, the greater the sense of achievement on the part of the hunter. But the catching of fish has from the start been totally different from other forms of hunting. Water is not man's natural element, so even for a proficient swimmer, the pursuit of a wary quarry very much at home and elusively nimble in its environment is fraught with problems. Right from the very beginning, therefore, anglers have had to rely on guile, with observation, imagination and innovation playing a vital role. With this more cerebral and contemplative approach, it is not surprising that for many angling provides more pride in success and a greater degree of satisfaction than other forms of hunting. The hunting instinct which has been deeply ingrained by the experience of successful ancestors over very many generations is heightened in this rather more sophisticated and developed form of hunting.

Amongst the many other factors which make angling so compelling is curiosity. The lure of the unknown, the fascination of the mysterious, does not only appeal to the young, but can tantalise one and lead one on in search of understanding throughout life. To me the surface of a sea, lake, pool or river hides a world as alien as any planet in a far-flung star system, even in today's scientific world. The environment is totally foreign, the flora and fauna totally different and, except in very unusual circumstances, obscured from view and from one's awareness. For example, despite every monitoring gadget that science makes available to us, most of us are prepared to accept that beneath the surface of any large area of water such as Loch Ness there may be something – perhaps not the monster of legend, but something unexpected and hitherto unknown. Similarly, our major oceans have not yet revealed their full store of secrets. And, on a smaller but more relevant level, when an angler stands on the bank of a river, lake, loch, lough, lochan or reservoir he has no idea of what the surface conceals. The questions in every angler's mind – 'How many?', 'How big?' and 'Where?' – remain reliably and reassuringly unanswered.

Every angler is aware that on any cast, at any second, in any fishing day, he may experience the greatest thrill of his angling life – the ultimate personal experience, the most sharply etched and enduring memory. Very few sport anglers now satisfy their hunting instinct out of a need for food. Many, if not most, do not even consume their catch themselves but treat them as trophies of the hunt and get their reward in seeing others eat them – perhaps after they have languished as part of a 'trophy hoard' in a freezer.

In fact for the modern angler, whose nutritional needs are probably supplied overwhelmingly by local supermarkets and whose catch is not important as a food source, the reward probably comes from the intense feeling of success, whether it be an adult catching highly prized delicacies from sea, stillwater or river or a child taking minnows or sticklebacks with net or line. It is this sense of inner fulfilment that I am sure is the main motivating influence in sport angling and the foundation of our pleasures – and frustrations – in angling.

Like most foundations, however, there are subsequent structures built on which extend and refine (or possibly dilute) the original, early response. In an overpopulated society that has developed and used the ability to change the original environment, very little is 'natural'. The fields, rivers, woods and open ground are not there to be freely roamed at will. It all belongs to someone and is subject to controls. It is virtually all manipulated to achieve an effect or has undergone change as a result of earlier, or adjacent, utilisation. The area of totally unspoiled, natural countryside in the 'civilised' world is negligible and, if and where it exists, it can only be maintained by rigid protection – which is in itself wholly unnatural. Population pressures, together with personal and communal ambitions, are constantly changing our environment and it is usually only when features have virtually disappeared that their unique value is recognised and appreciated. Remnants may be artificially preserved, but as living museum pieces they are no longer part of an environment, merely a show giving insights into some aspects of the past.

We live in the shadow of water extraction, planned water storage and earlier and current pollution from industry, agriculture, forestry and our own lifestyles. Our inland waters therefore do not have free access, are not as nature intended and generally, if they support fish stocks, it is as a result of human intervention, protection or restoration, often commercially motivated. None of us is free to roam and fish at will, on impulse. We must furnish ourselves with rod licences from a body which appears to do little more than tax us for our pleasure without offering anything in return on stillwaters, other than freedom from prosecution. We must also gain permission from the owners for the facility they grant us in allowing us access to their water and to fish for their fish. In many cases, where water authorities have created reservoirs and stocked them with fish, there is a case for requiring payment, but some people will be unconvinced in the case of natural waterways with wild salmon and sea trout returning from feeding at sea, obeying their own instincts.

The 'unnaturalness' of our fishing need not inhibit our enjoyment of the sport, however, since we are in the main already products of and conditioned to an engineered environment, and our absorption in our activity will in any event hopefully help us forget that it is no longer 'natural'. But there is one aspect which may well affect our enjoyment, the modern principle of value for money. This presents an impediment to a full appreciation of the delights of angling – the lack of spontaneity in our approach. Very few anglers find themselves in a situation where they actually *need* to fish. For the overwhelming majority we do it because we choose to – and we choose to because it is enjoyable. When something ceases to be enjoyable the natural inclination is to stop. In angling this is not always quite so easy. Most of us have to make specific arrangements, in an otherwise crowded series of commitments, to fish. We have to travel to our selected venue – often several hours' drive. On arrival we purchase our day permit, which gives us the right to fish under the rules of the water, which will specify the number and minimum size of fish we are allowed to retain. We are committed; our day often does not allow us to change our minds after we arrive at our venue. Moreover, it is all too easy to misunderstand the nature of the day permit. With it, we purchase the right to fish with a maximum limitation on our catch. We do not buy fish, but the right to exercise our skills in angling for them. We may catch the maximum or nothing at all – although, if we have the skill, the conditions are appropriate and our judgement is sound, we should be able to expect a reasonable chance of leaving the water with something to justify our efforts.

But what do we do if after leaving home in pleasurable expectations and filled with optimism, driving for an hour or so, purchasing our day ticket at no small expense, tackling up and starting to fish, we find that our confidence is dispelled by a change of conditions and the enjoyment factor is dissipated altogether? The stillwater day ticket has made fly fishing of varying character and often excellent quality available to very many people who would not otherwise have had the opportunity. It has, however, also imposed a new philosophy and new pressures in that it does tend to encourage an emphasis on results, to the detriment of the carefree nature of the 'gentle art', where one would expect to fish for enjoyment and, once the enjoyment was no longer there, stop and do something else.

Some fortunate people can still fish with this attitude to some degree. Those who live close to the waters and expect to use the facility freely, often purchase a season ticket, allowing them to fish within the rules of the fishery without time limit. They can then fish selectively, at times convenient to them and the most conducive periods according to conditions. This certainly does allow a more relaxed attitude to fishing. Some time ago, I held an annual season ticket for Grafham Water for several years, which I then viewed, with a large measure of justification, as the finest water of its type in Europe. I fished on average three times a week and, even though a round trip was over two hours' drive, I would often be selective and arrive for the 'magic periods' of dawn or, more frequently, the evening approaching dusk. I felt I was fishing prime time and in the evening I was fishing fresh, in both mind and body. I thoroughly enjoyed these periods and as a result possibly fished better and fared better. However, not having just paid out for a day ticket, I was never under pressure to see my time out and if any of the periods lost its magic and I felt that I was no longer enjoying what I was doing, I had no compunction in packing up and leaving. It is noticeable that season ticket holders still have the same tendency to fish the times that suit them, rarely flog the water all day, and come and go with a very relaxed attitude.

I am not suggesting that a season ticket on a water is important in fishing for pleasure but it does give a different perspective – and that difference may need addressing. Day-ticket anglers, who will be the majority on most waters, should seek to minimise any sense of pressure inherent in the situation. If confidence is reduced to the level that anticipation and enjoyment are at a low ebb, try making changes. Changing flies and tactics are obvious remedies and likely to revive flagging confidence. Take a break and contemplate the chances of more interest and action elsewhere on the water. Move around the water and try other spots, exchanging experiences with other anglers (although this may only deepen your gloom!). Becoming desperate is sure to destroy your enjoyment so, if the immediate fishing prospects are not conducive, break off for a picnic, a chat, a spot of bird-watching, a nap or whatever. Conditions may change subtly and you may start fishing again with renewed confidence and enjoyment. That is, after all, what you are there for!

Confidence is important to an enjoyment of the sport. One does not want to be constantly struggling with one's technique, and feeling frustrated as a result. Fly fishing, like all forms of sport angling, should be fun and exciting. Having said that, we cannot catch fish consistently all the time – if we could then the excitement would surely pall. There are a wealth of books giving advice on techniques and approaches, and many give the impression that their advice is infallible and if it is followed it will result in reliable catches of better fish. Although such books are well-intentioned, and can be helpful in developing a more efficient understanding of techniques, they do tend to build up the reader's expectations of results which, if not achieved, can damage his morale and therefore his enjoyment. Few books currently combine the 'how to do it' aspect with the philosophy of 'how to enjoy doing it'. We all no doubt enjoy catching fish, but we should enjoy our fishing as well, and there is a subtle difference. By tailoring our approach we can be more successful in both!

It has been said in the past that the fly fisherman progresses through various distinct stages, according to his level of experience. The first stage is that of wanting to catch as many fish as possible. The next is wanting to catch as large a fish as is possible, and the final stage was said to be wanting to catch the most difficult fish (which clearly relates to fishing on running water as it is difficult in a reasonably sized stillwater to know just what is there, let alone which is the most difficult). On some days – perhaps too many for comfort – all fish seem to qualify for that description! My own feeling, however, is that an extra stage could be added: wanting to experience once more the delicious sharpness of the hand-trembling thrill and excitement that the first contact, playing and capture of one's early fish created and to be enveloped again in the vibrant, intense pleasure that suffused through one's entire awareness following these early successes. This is not to suggest that one necessarily develops a blasé or jaded approach, but nothing compares with the delicious excitement of those earlier successes.

Chapter 2

Equipment

E quipment for stillwater fly fishing should be selected with very great care and thought if the maximum pleasure is to be gained from the pursuit. In effect, equipment falls into two distinct categories: that which is designed for the well-being and comfort of the angler and that which is intended to establish and maintain contact with the quarry. Both are important to your success and pleasure.

Clothing

It is, perhaps, as well to start with your own situation. If you are to operate efficiently and to take pleasure in being where you are, you need to feel comfortable. This calls for clothing suitable for the occasion – and in Britain the occasion can vary from hour to hour, day to day and season to season.

Clearly, common sense in clothing does not relate solely to fishing. For any activity in the open we need to dress for warmth on cool days and try to keep cool on warm ones. There are some aspects, however, which do call for specific consideration. Remember first that you are at the water by choice and for pleasure. Comfortable clothing suited to outdoor wear can contribute considerably to your sense of well-being and help you to fish better. As you will often be out for a full day you should appreciate that conditions can change. Listening to the weather forecast for the area will be helpful but it does not pay to accept it without question – forecasts are not always fully accurate! So you need to take suitable clothing to cater for possible changes in the weather. Since there is often very little shelter from the wind on stillwaters – particularly the larger ones – you should always bear in mind that you will normally be cooler at the water than away from it and although you will be active you will not expect to be moving around very much. Further, wading in cold water or sitting exposed to the wind in a boat can make you feel chilled, so always take adequate warm wind- and rain-proof clothing. You do not have to wear all the clothes you take with you but it is as well to be prepared – the day can seem very long if you are cold and uncomfortable. While on the subject of being prepared with clothing, as one who occasionally forgets the advisability of maintaining sufficient freeboard to the tops of my waders, I can thoroughly recommend taking a spare pair of wading socks in your tackle bag, and also a spare pair of trousers in the car. The unmistakable sensation of a wader filling up with cold water on a cold day is, I can assure you, the prelude to hours of discomfort which dry socks inside plastic bags can eliminate.

Remember too that you will be active in casting etc. and clothes should therefore be loose-fitting, allowing for unrestricted movement. In addition, several lighter layers are more effective for warmth than a single heavy sweater, as well as being more flexible for changing conditions.

Although on the larger stillwaters you will often not be involved in stalking fish, it does not make sense to dress too conspicuously in very bright colours. You do not want to risk alarming the fish by signalling your presence and it is to your advantage to merge into the background where possible with drab tones of neutral colours. Drab brown, olive green and grey clothes may not express the personality of the more flamboyant angler, but they do make sense in your role of hunter and even if they do nothing more than boost your confidence level by making you feel dressed for the part, they perform a useful service.

In very warm weather light, loose-fitting clothing is clearly indicated. However, it should be remembered that the effect of the sun is intensified by the reflection from the water and some protection is advisable for those prone to sunburn. Baseball-type caps with large peaks which shade the eyes and face make for comfort, as do long shirtsleeves which can be rolled down to give protection from the sun. A handkerchief worn 'Foreign Legion style' under the cap may look mildly ridiculous elsewhere but anglers are essentially practical and this will save the back of the neck from becoming sunburned. For those who are sensitive to suggestions of eccentricity, sunhats with a peak at the front and a turn-down peak at the back to protect the neck are also now available. Effective sunglasses are a must to protect the eyes from glare from the water, and of course from the risk of injury from artificial flies due to casting errors. For this reason it is a good idea for those who do not normally wear spectacles to wear sunglasses during daylight hours, regardless of the light conditions. The polarised versions can be very useful in reducing glare from the water and allowing you to see the fish following or approaching your fly, which you may otherwise not be aware of. This in itself makes the fishing more exciting and enables you to fish with more alertness and confidence.

Rather more specialised is waterproofs. It is important that these are not just sold as waterproof but are actually capable of keeping water out during many hours of unrelenting, torrential driving rain. Every angler should make absolutely certain that his selection of waterproof clothing will do just that. There are some very satisfactory synthetic materials currently available which require little in the way of maintenance (e.g. Gore-tex etc.).

However, most anglers still opt for coats made from wax-treated, thornproof cotton. But be warned, although most brands look similar, they do not necessarily perform alike. From my own experience, and from discussion with others, I have come to the conclusion that the waxed-cotton coats from J. Barbour & Sons Ltd of South Shields, properly waxed and repaired as necessary, can be totally relied upon to keep wind and water out without causing a condensation problem by virtue of its ability to 'breathe'. But this reliability cannot be taken for granted in look-alike material from some other manufacturers. Barbours have a wide selection of styles in varying weights of material, and their experience has enabled them to produce reliably waterproof outdoor clothing with cut and styling that allows for the free movement necessary for outdoor sports. It is vital, however, to regularly rewax them with their own or similarly formulated dressing to keep water out and prevent abrasive wear causing holes, especially in areas such as elbows and the inside of the arms, where they rub against the body, and also creases in the sleeves etc. This can be a messy and unwelcome chore, but it is essential if one is to remain dry and comfortable in foul weather.

A stud-on hood in the same material is also essential for comfort in high wind and driving rain, and can give a measure of protection against high-speed flies which do not conform to expectations under adverse casting conditions. The larger hood allows more freedom of movement and is more suitable for this reason – it can also be worn more comfortably over caps, woolly hats and so forth.

The longer coats can reach down over the tops of waders and, with non-absorbent drip strips replacing the lower part of the lining, will be sufficient under some conditions. However, in windy weather, and definitely for boat fishing, waterproof and windproof over-trousers are necessary. (Remember to wear these over your waders or rubber boots!) As they will be in the water when wading, avoid the ones with cotton lining, which will draw water up over the tops of your waders. Also, remember that whilst slits in the side are convenient for access to your normal trouser pockets, they can also allow water to seep in. My choice is for over-trousers of PVC-coated light-nylon weave with an elasticated waist and no pocket slits, which are light and flexible, totally impervious to wind and water and can be waded in without problems and used in a boat without risking a wet seat. One aspect of wading in over-trousers is worth pointing out. The trousers come over the waders and it is prudent to have a clear idea of where the tops of the waders are, especially when wading deep.

Headgear is really a matter of common sense. For summer, there is a wide range of headgear to give protection from the sun. As I have said, a light baseball-type cap with a large peak to shade the eyes from the sun is ideal but there is a wide choice of sunhats with wide brims and big peaks. For wetter weather a truly waterproof cap is ideal, since this can be worn under the hood of your coat. Waterproof hats with big brims are all very well but can be a nuisance when the wind gets underneath them in very blustery weather and they cannot be worn under the hood comfortably.

There is one final item to be discussed before turning to the tackle itself, and it forms a neat 'bridge' between clothing and tackle, as it could be construed as either. It is the fishing waistcoat (or vest as the Americans call it). Although it is worn, it is in fact either an extension or an alternative to a tackle bag, depending on the degree to which you choose to encumber yourself. (What happened to that carefree image of freedom when a rod, spool of nylon and matchbox of flies were considered all that was necessary?)

A sleeveless coat composed of a multitude of pockets sewn together, the fishing waistcoat is a masterpiece of tailoring ingenuity and is an essential organiser, allowing us to carry all the clutter that we feel could be of some conceivable use. With so many confusing pockets, some cleverly hidden, it can also be a brilliant way of temporarily losing small items! Used sensibly, it distributes weight and makes items easier to carry and conveniently accessible. However, with all the many pockets stuffed with fly boxes, spare spools etc., simple tasks like bending down to pick something up can be challenging, due to the restricted movement. It does pay, therefore, to give some thought to the stowage plan when loading up this useful item. The smaller and more commonly used items should go in the front and in the more accessible pockets, with the bulkier objects stowed where they will not impede free movement. It goes without saying, that having arrived at a workable system of pocket loading, it is advisable always to return objects to the same point from which they came.

Tackle

Clearly tackle is important to success and enjoyment, and as such is worth some careful thought. There is an element of uncompromising functionality in fishing tackle, combined with the beauty of businesslike simplicity in design and craftsmanship. The rods, reels and other cherished impedimenta have a direct appeal which positively invites handling – they are not merely tools for a job but are perhaps like weapons, with a character and charisma of their own. I do not for one moment believe that I am alone in my pleasure at handling fishing tackle, even when there is no immediate prospect of using it for the purpose for which it was designed. In or out of season I will occasionally respectfully slide a rod out of its bag or lift a reel out and pull a few feet of line off purely for the pleasure of looking at and appreciating the feel of these objects, which seem to encourage tactile appraisal. In use, their efficiency and the needs of the job in hand can often obscure their intrinsic attractiveness, but this can be appreciated quietly when not in use, and it is a simple pleasure available to us at any time.

In selecting tackle, the procedure is often to decide on a rod as the main initial purchase and then add other items to suit. This is, however, not the most satisfactory method of kitting up. Time spent in considering where you will fish and what your main style of fishing will be can prevent frustration and save you the expense of purchasing tackle that is not totally suited to your requirements. However, you will never be safe from unnecessary expenditure; even with ideal tackle you will still be tempted to look at new or different items as the first step in deciding that you have been depriving yourself of an essential acquisition.

In assessing the relative importance of items of tackle it is as well to look at it from the viewpoint of the fish. For the fish, only the fly will be of interest and hopefully this will be all it is aware of until it is hooked. You will need to propel the fly to the fish for which, because of its low mass and high air resistance, you need a heavy fly line. But a heavy fly line tends to be very noticeable and fish are very observant, so we separate the two with a tapered fine translucent leader. To provide the necessary energy to propel all this out to the fish in the right order and with a semblance of control we use a rod, and the reel serves to store the line and release or retrieve it as required. But in all of this, although everything has a part to play, the humble fly is the main feature and all the rest of the expensive equipment merely the means of putting it into position as inconspicuously as possible.

So you clearly cannot make a sound judgement about a rod – which will be the main purchase in terms of cost – without first identifying which style or styles we will employ and the type of water we will mainly fish. For instance, on small waters, fish will generally be stalked from the bank using cover afforded by the bankside vegetation, and casting will usually be short-range and precise to visible fish, with a requirement for minimal disturbance from the fly line. Clearly in these circumstances a powerful rod requiring a heavy line to load it would be a liability, especially for short range casting. A medium/short rod capable of casting a lighter line (AFTM 6 or 7), which will land more delicately, would be more appropriate. However, many small waters have a stocking policy favouring large fish, so some backbone in the rod would be useful in subduing the larger fish.

The AFTM system is a scale which relates to the weight of what the tackle supply trade deem to be the average aerialised length of fly line, i.e. the first 30 ft (or 9.2 metres). It should be noted that these scale divisions are bands into which the weight of the front portion of the line falls and are not precise weights. This means that a particular AFTM 7 line could conceivably be closer to either an AFTM 6 or AFTM 8 rated line than to an AFTM 7 from another manufacturer. In fact this will often be the case, perhaps even in different line types from the same manufacturer.

17

Fortunately, these variations are not critical but they can make a distinct and noticeable difference in use – and there is no way of finding out the extent of this band variation until the line is on the rod.

On lochs, lochans, loughs etc. angling traditionally involves fishing small flies, usually from a boat. Delicate presentation is always helpful in not advertising the presence of something unusual to the fish, and as a consequence making him seek refuge. Accordingly quite a light line will be used probably in the range AFTM 5–7. If you are fishing from a boat, casting will invariably be wind-assisted, and as a drifting boat moves through the water to the fish long casts are rarely called for – especially where angling pressure is light. Accordingly a rod which will comfortably handle a light line is indicated and if most of your fishing is from a boat, perhaps a longer one than usual to help 'work' the flies (between 9 ft 6 in and 11 ft or 2.9 to 3.3 metres).

On the other hand if most of your fishing is to be with small flies from the bank with, against and across the wind, casting distance becomes more important so that a more powerful rod action, still handling a line in this range but more likely at the top end, would be helpful. To facilitate line speed to achieve distance, a slightly stiffer action and shorter rod is useful, perhaps 9 ft to 9 ft 6 in (2.75 to 2.9 metres). The same principle applies to fishing small flies and nymphs on reservoirs, when of course this type of fishing would mainly be employed. However, on larger and heavily fished waters, where fish are encouraged to retreat from the shore area, distance can be important for the bank angler, and some sacrifice to presentation is a normal compromise. Better to risk alarming the occasional fish by the use of a relatively heavy line than not being able to present a fly to him at all!

Fishing a lure again calls for some thought in tackle selection. Lures are bigger, heavier (especially when weighted to sink) and offer more air resistance in casting. Further, they are often effective when stripped in, i.e. moved quickly through the water, for some distance. Clearly the distance the lure can be moved through the water is related to the distance it is cast out. All these factors point to a heavier line to cast further (with less relative air resistance in relation to its mass), and with control for the sake of safety, which in turn calls for a powerful rod capable of handling the line weight (typically AFTM 8 or 9). Since the rod in this type of fishing will be required to handle a sunk line, which greatly increases its resistance on retrieve, this power is virtually essential.

Now, it is all very well to identify which outfit would be best for a single or main style of fishing, but what about the angler with a taste for variety? In effect, the fly fisherman on the larger reservoirs, which can offer some of the most demanding, frustrating and rewarding fishing, can, as the season progresses, expect to encounter all of these requirements. Most people will divide their fishing between bank and boat and will adapt their approach according to circumstances and the time of year. Does this mean three separate outfits for the varying styles? It can do, but very seldom does. Most will strive to achieve a happy medium with tackle which is not rigidly dedicated to a narrow application range; it is very important that our tackle matches our needs and these can vary.

My own tackle, which suits me ideally for perhaps 95% of my fishing – largely on the East Anglian and Midland reservoirs – is perhaps typical of the 'cover everything' compromise. But if I were to fish only from a boat with small flies, especially on Highland lochs or similar water where wild fish would be faster, smaller and more cautious, it would not be so suitable. I use two identical 9 ft 6 in (2.9 metre) reinforced carbon-fibre rods rated for lines AFTM 7–9. The manufacturer's line weight recommendation range indicates a tolerance range on my own rods of AFTM 7, 8 or 9. Optimum weight would be an 8 line for most comfort-able performance. A size 7 perhaps rather light unless more line is aerialised or higher line speed employed to load the rod, and a size 9 tends to overload the rod and produce a slower and less crisp performance. In effect I use all three in one form or another. Normally I use an AFTM WF7 with high line speed for a crisp delivery with more control (a lighter line is – or should be – thinner and offers less air resistance), an AFTM 8 for heavier wind conditions, and a shooting head of slightly shorter length than usual cut from an AFTM DT9 line for distance casting with lures and, if need be, any other type of fly. There are advantages in each line configuration for given circumstances which will be dealt with later.

Having seen how different tackle ranges relate to different stillwater circumstances, you will hopefully be able to start to identify the tackle set-up most likely to suit your needs. We can now take a look at individual items. As I have said previously, the fly is of paramount importance and as such merits particular attention and will be dealt with in detail later.

Leaders

Working back from the fly the leader is an important item of terminal tackle. The leader connects the fly to the fly line and transmits the energy conveyed by the rod through to the fly. It is made from nylon, either level or tapered. It also separates the rather obvious and necessarily heavy fly line from the fly – and as a result, hopefully, from the awareness of the fish. As a general principle the distance of separation should be as much as can be comfortably handled, particularly when using a floating line. This will clearly vary according to conditions. Nymphs with little air resis-tance and fished largely down and across the wind will turn over well on leaders from 18 to 22 ft (5.5 to 6.75 metres) in length, although it is unwise for a novice caster to start with this length of leader – approximately 14 ft (4.25 metres) is suggested as a starting point. On the other hand, punching out a bulky but light Muddler minnow into a stiff breeze on anything much over half this length will invoke intense frustration and possibly the darker side of one's vocabulary.

There is no doubt that for small flies and a smooth turnover a tapered leader is beneficial, with supple monofilament from about 18 lb (8 kg) breaking strain down to about 5 lb (2.25 kg) for small flies and nymphs or 8 lb (3.5 kg) for lures covering most situations. Do not fish over-light where large fish or weed-beds are likely; it may be broken by a fish, leaving a hook in situ and trailing nylon. The leader can be a factory-produced knotless tapered type, one tied at home from various reducing breaking strain (and thickness) monofilament, or a combination of both. Within the last few years a useful additional option has become available in the form of braided leaders which are tapered, hollow, braided monofilament. Even though these do taper down to quite low breaking strains, they are not as translucent as normal monofilament and are therefore much more noticeable. Consequently a tippet of monofilament is added to the end to conceal its presence. The advantages are that the braided leaders are available in different densities and can be obtained as floaters, slow sinkers, or with different sinking rates. I find the heavier versions turn over well but my tippets of monofilament can be tapered down and up to 20 ft (6 metres) long – I do not want that visually obvious piece of braid anywhere near my fly!

The loop-to-loop system generally employed with braided leaders (see figure 1) offers a flexible and very fast means of changing terminal tackle from floating or slow-sink to fast-sink and thus of varying the depth at which the fly fishes.

It is usual to fish with tapered leaders for good turnover, even though for boat fishing downwind, a level section in the appropriate diameter is almost as good. Whatever leader system is employed a selection of spools of monofilament nylon in appropriate breaking strains for running repairs and replacements are essential. Alarming tangles can appear as if by magic, especially in swirling, gusting wind or when fish are known to be in the vicinity. You should also check for wind knots (spontaneously appearing overhand knots caused by casting faults) regularly. If they become tight and cannot easily be unpicked, discard and renew that section, because the breaking strain will be reduced dramatically and the

Figure 1   The loop-to-loop joining system

odds stacked heavily in favour of any lively fish which is subsequently hooked escaping.

During the course of most fishing days there will be many changes of fly. Tying knots reduces the strength of nylon due to surface stress on tightening, so cut off the end when replacing a fly. But remember: it is surprising how this can shorten a leader during the course of a day.

There is now a choice of nylon monofilament for leaders and tippets: the traditional type, usually a limp form, and now the so called 'double strength' which is very fine for its breaking strain. This has a clear advantage but it does tend to be very shiny indeed and to reduce this element of visibility I would suggest rubbing with a degreasing blend of fuller's earth and liquid detergent, which acts as a mild abrasive, until the shine is gone. This is of particular importance when fishing near the surface.

Another feature is that in use, this type of monofilament can develop a tendency to springy curliness, especially after a tangle has been sorted out, which refuses to straighten out. Despite this disadvantage, it is ideal for fishing nymphs and small flies particularly, as it is much thinner, it has a higher degree of natural movement because of its greater flexibility for its strength and the reduced water resistance makes for better fly movement in the water. For fishing heavier flies the traditional form offers a better degree of control in turnover and I am sure reduces tangle and knot problems.

Lines

Ingenuity and inventiveness seem to be boundless in this area of the tackle market, and the available options seem at first sight unnecessarily complex and confusing, and disproportionate to the market size. Basically, fly lines are a central core of strong braid, classified according to stretch characteristic, over which is coated a shaped plastic covering of varying density and profile.

One of the first properties to look for is lack of 'memory'. In a fly line 'memory' is the tendency to hold the shape of the coil it assumed in the manufacturer's box or on the fly reel. The straighter it hangs when it is unrolled from the coil or pulled from the reel, the better it will fish and cast. Some of the newer constructions I have tried have been dreadful in this respect and have resembled coiled springs both in casting and on the water. This is not at all what we want; the straighter a line lays on or in the water, the more direct the contact we have with the fly and the fish and the more we are aware of what is happening to the fly. Whilst it is unlikely that a line, no matter how good, will unroll immediately into a straight line after weeks or months coiled up, most will straighten up after a pull – if a line does not, have nothing to do with it as it will only be an aggravating feature and detract from your future enjoyment. This quality will probably be reflected in the price, but not necessarily. I have had some really excellent and cheap 'mill ends' which have performed flawlessly and durably and branded makes which have left much to be desired – but there is an element of luck, particularly in the unbranded sector of the market.

As mentioned, fly lines are shaped plastic over a core. They are relatively heavy and bulky compared with other forms of fishing line. If you take a hackled wet or dry fly and try to throw it, you will begin to appreciate why this is so. Its principal function is to carry a fly, with relatively high air resistance to its mass, the required distance from the angler to the fish. It has, accordingly, to be able to use the energy imparted to it by the rod and tow the fly with it. The front taper profile of the line is to encourage turnover and the transmission of this energy to the leader.

Virtually every fly line has this front taper (level or non-tapered lines seem to have disappeared completely from the market). However in other respects, there are three distinct types of fly line. The double-taper line usually has a longer and more gradual front taper and is entirely symmetrical, like a very stretched out cigar shape. As such it can be loaded onto the reel from either end, as there is no difference. In fact it is claimed that once one end becomes worn or damaged, usually with numerous cracks in the coating, it can be taken off the reel and reversed, and the other end will be as good as new. Perhaps this depends on how long it has been on the reel, the conditions of storage and how much of the line was normally aerialised in casting the other end. The advantage of the double-taper line is claimed to be delicacy and accuracy in presentation. This is evident in the lighter line weights and on smaller waters, especially from boats for small flies with lines rated AFTM 5 or 6. However, I find that the bulkier mid-sections on heavier lines show a frustrating disinclination to 'shoot', adversely affecting control and presentation. My own feeling is that the comfortable control of the other profiles can allow at least as good a presentation without the disadvantage of the high bulk and reduced flexibility of the double-taper line above size AFTM 6. In essence, at the risk of outraging successful and dedicated users of this line type, apart from small-water or specialist boat angling, the double-taper line has limited application on stillwaters.

The alternative full-length profile is the weight-forward or 'torpedo' taper as it has been referred to. The principle here is to have a short fine tapered section at the front, behind which it tapers quickly back to the thickest and heaviest section of the line, then a longer, less steep taper back to the end of the front 30 ft (9 metre) section, where the running line starts, which is thin and level. In casting the heavier front end aerialises well and the thin running line offers less weight for it to drag out behind it and less friction to slow it down in running through the rod rings. Longer casts are therefore possible, timing is aided by the profile differences and less effort is involved. In addition the thinner line is easier and more pleasant to handle in retrieving. One disadvantage is said to be less delicate presentation, but truly delicate presentation is rarely achieved with a heavier line anyway, regardless of profile. In addition, control of the line is difficult with the thin running line, and lifting off with much more than the front 30 ft (9 metres) from the water to recast to moving fish is inviting problems; one has to hurriedly strip in line to get the thicker part into the top rod ring to do so with safety and dignity. The weight-forward is the usual choice of full-length line for medium and large stillwater fly fishing.

There is one variation on the weight-forward profile which should be mentioned. This is the long belly line, which has a longer than usual thicker front section, created, we are advised by line manufacturers, for the benefit of the 'more proficient' caster who has a tendency to aerialise more line than usual and more than is good for it. The theory behind this is interesting, but personally I find that I do not get on with these so well, possibly partly because the extra length of thicker front section creates more air resistance, reducing line speed.

The third profile type, the shooting head, is really a progression from the weight-forward with the principles enhanced to take it a step further into an outright committed casting tool. I am surprised that this line form, once so ubiquitous on the larger Midland reservoirs, appears to be falling out of favour and is becoming less commonly used than the weight-forward line.

The shooting head or shooting taper is merely the front 30 ft (9 metres) or so of a double-taper or weight-forward line – and the weight being equal, I prefer the latter – joined to a light, low-friction backing. The line rating of the shooting head is normally at the top of or slightly higher than the normal line loading for the rod. Some anglers have advocated a lower-rated line with extra length for better distance and presentation but I find the reverse is more effective. A heavier line cut off shorter is easier and therefore safer to manage, especially in a boat where there are often several people in a confined space, and also where a minimum of false casting is an expression of good manners to your boat partner.

Although shooting tapers can be purchased, it is usually more satisfactory to use either an old line which is cracking behind the front taper (the running line) or buy a cheap double-taper (or weight-forward) mill-end line to cut up. This allows the shooting head to be custom balanced to both your rod and your own casting style. Simply thread the line through the rings – it does not have to be on a reel – and briskly aerialise it over water (or long grass, which reduces the danger of line damage) until the length being false cast feels to be loading the rod comfortably – not overloading it. This will be something like the normal 30 ft (9 metres). Once you have determined the optimum length cut off the line at about 3 ft (1 metre) down the rod from the top ring. This then just needs to be attached to the shooting line to complete it (see section on knots).

The choice of shooting-line backing can make or mar the pleasure of this line system. Originally 20 to 30 lb (9 to 13.5 kg) nylon monofilament of the sea-fishing type was used. This type of nylon can have a 'memory' which would put an elephant to shame. This character, plus the high speed at which a shooting head can pick up the shooting backing meant that any slight disarrangement resulted in an immediate tangle, which took much patience and valuable time to unpick. Then new monofilaments came onto the scene, such as oval-section limp nylon and 'memory-free' prestretched monofilament. These improved matters, although handling, especially with wet and cold hands with stiff fingers, was always a problem. The distance achieved, however, when the backing went through the rings without a problem was magical!

The final answer to date has been found in a rather expensive hollow braided nylon monofilament line developed for spinning. This is a revelation. It is virtually memory-free, it is beautifully supple, it shoots divinely and it rarely tangles – and if it does it is very easily sorted out. As if all these features were not enough, it is easy to attach and for floating work will accept the old-style grease floatant Mucilin (from the red tin without silicone) rubbed into it. With the Mucilin rubbed well in and allowed to dry on the surface the shooting backing does not absorb water, it floats so that contact with the floating or slow-sinking shooting head is better, it is drier and therefore easier and more comfortable to handle, and it is lubricated so that it shoots even better! I even dress the shooting backing for sinking shooting heads very lightly in this manner for improved handling and it does not seem to affect the sinking rate of the shooting head itself.

In addition to the line weight groups covered by the AFTM system and the varying profiles, there is another consideration, that of the specific gravity of the coating. By varying this the manufacturer imparts different performance characteristics. The most common line in general use is the floating line, which will float naturally without any aids. However, to position the line and leader at different depths and reduce the tendency to rise to the surface on retrieve, a variety of lines of different sinking rates are available. These offer a wide range, from the very slow to the ultra-fast for deep fishing. All of these sink rates are usually available in nearly all of the line profiles and in all of the most usual line weights. In addition there are hybrid lines. Some have floating coatings for the most part with a sinking coating on the tip section, which are called 'sink-tip' lines. Others have the reverse for fishing off the bottom: a fast-sinking coating for the main line and a short front section with floating coating. The permutation of line possibilities therefore becomes potentially more than mildly confusing. Most anglers would view a floating line as essential and some will use nothing else. Many, however will add a slow- and a fast-sink line and feel they are ready for anything, but there will always be the occasional 'collector' seeking to emulate a mobile tackle shop.

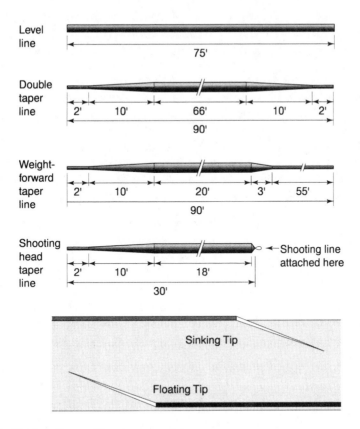

Figure 2   Various line profiles. (not to scale)

Rods

I suggested earlier that to some extent the rod selects itself, depending on how and where we will fish. You should have given some thought to the line size and type you will use before looking seriously at rods. This will narrow down the confusing range of possibilities offered in the catalogues. The style to be employed will further reduce the choice with regard to action and length, and practical considerations such as the amount you are prepared to spend will also restrict the range of possibilities. You will thus start to develop a shortlist of potentially suitable rods – which in fact may not be very short!

How does one get closer to that final, satisfactory decision? Manufacturers' or retailers' descriptions may offer an exercise in imagination (sometimes excessively so on the part of the copywriter too) but it is most unwise to be solely guided by these. They are artfully designed to sell their goods, not to assist you in your selection. If you know someone whose opinion will be soundly based on experience, seek their advice;

perhaps even try their tackle. Even if you do not know someone, but see an angler casting well under conditions which you will relate to, ask them what they use, how they feel they get on with it, whether they would make the same choice again and what they would recommend. Fly fishermen are by and large naturally extremely helpful and normally pleased to chat and give advice. We all had to start some time and were grateful for help and advice. Tackle dealers also are happy to give advice but it should be remembered they will quite reasonably be biased towards what they have available in stock for sale. Remember also that, whilst we all do it, waggling a rod about in a tackle shop is not going to tell you much about what it will be like to fish with. Always try to cast with a rod, prefer-ably with the lines you intend to use, before making a purchase. Most dealers will be pleased to arrange for you to try a rod out first. Be prepared, too, to try any rod they suggest may suit you.

But whilst it may be helpful to gain impressions from others on how specific rods perform, always remember that it is how it performs for you, under your circumstances and with your lines and your casting style, that is the only thing that matters. The power and line ratings will have narrowed down the selection, but you now have to come to grips with different lengths, actions and constructions, most of which will currently be variations on carbon-fibre, or graphite as it is sometimes called. There is no single best choice and only by trying them out can you know how they will suit you – but be sure you try from the range of types you have identified as relating to the style of fishing you will be doing. Do remember, however, that if, for example, you have identified long-distance casting as necessary, this can only be achieved at the expense of delicacy in presentation and will require heavier lines, which in turn need more powerful rods.

Rod designs and materials change rapidly, virtually seasonally, and it would be imprudent to mention any specifically. However, as fishing conditions also change, and in order to be in a position to capitalise on opportunities as they are presented, many anglers, especially on the larger reservoirs, carry two rods. These are usually set up to take account of different approaches – one rod with a floating line and nymphs, for example, and one perhaps with a sinking shooting head and a lure or 'booby' nymphs. One rod is really sufficient but two can save valuable time in changing lines. Further, dusk, when fish can become active, is the time when for some reason the most testing tangles occur – no doubt through lack of co-ordination because of tiredness and changing con-ditions. As this more promising time is very precious it is comforting, and can save one's sanity, to have a similar rod/line/fly combination set up to turn to immediately.

When carrying two rods, it does make sense to ensure that they are identical. You will not then have to adjust to different weights and actions and all your tackle will be fully compatible with either rod.

Reels

Reels can be most exquisitely engineered and many are truly works of art in fine alloys, rivalling items of jewellery in concept, design and execution. Not inconsiderable sums can be spent on some of these very highly prized gems but in essence, and to be practical, the role the reel fulfils, whilst important, is a very simple one, and, this is an area where one can safely decide whether to spend or save money.

The reel is employed purely in the functional role of line storage and control. It stores the line, or part of the line and backing, when not in use. It releases the line in a controlled fashion when required and retrieves and stores it again as necessary. There are those, principally in the tackle-supply trade, who assert that the reel 'balances' a rod. In some contexts this may be so, but if you try casting a line without a reel on the rod you will see that this argument is unconvincing – although the line becomes something of a handful!

There is nothing at all wrong in using a beautifully engineered reel; pride in its ownership and pleasure in its use can give an added dimension to your satisfaction. The important features, however, are reliability in action and adjustments, allied to light weight combined with strength. But remember that if two identical rods are used, two identical reels plus fully interchangeable spools will be required and the expense mounts. If the reels are not identical and the spare spools are not totally compatible then problems are certain to arise when your lines cannot be mounted onto your rods because they are loaded on non-compatible spools.

The requirements for reels are:

(a) Adequate capacity for the range of lines used – not forgetting fully adequate backing. Better a larger reel and extra backing line than a small one which can lock solid when reeling in quickly and untidily, with line jammed against the cage. A large-diameter central spindle to the spool, or a smaller one effectively made larger by ample backing, will not only make for faster line recovery but will cause less 'memory' problems, i.e. a less curly line.

(b) A good adjustable and reliable 'check' system which will prevent over-runs when line is taken off quickly. This can, and usually does, cause the reel to jam, with potentially grievous consequences. Set the check with this purpose, and only this purpose, in mind.

(c) Strength. It is amazing how much inadvertent abuse a reel can be subjected to, including dropping onto rocks or hard surfaces, or into mud etc. When the reel is of a metal-cage construction, it may be bent enough to prevent the free rotation of the spool, again inviting unhappy results.

(d) Ideally a fully exposed, smooth rim. This will allow the hand to be used to provide a sensitive braking effect to slow down the run of a large fish.

(e) The lightest possible weight without compromising strength. Forget about balancing; more weight means more energy, and day-long distance casting, especially with powerful rods throwing heavier lines, can be very tiring.

Over a number of years of fishing I have amassed a number of fly reels, some from a highly regarded (and expensive) manufacturer which have always behaved impeccably as their pedigree would suggest, and others rather more utilitarian in nature with excessive manufacturing tolerances. My fishing bag bulged with an assortment, which were only partly inter-changeable, and much frustration resulted when I wanted to use lines which were on spools which fitted only one reel, which was already in use on another rod. To overcome this I re-equipped and standardised on a single reel model made from composite graphite with easily changed plastic spools. The reel is from the Leeda LC range, amply meets all the essential listed criteria, visually complements modern carbon-fibre rods, has no polished metal to flash in the sun and possibly alarm fish, and is very good value for money, especially for the spare spools. In use so far I have found it totally reliable and, more importantly, as pleasurable to use as reels costing four times as much. I understand that this range may soon be replaced by a similar reel where the cage and frame is in alloy. Since this is heavier, my preference is for the original version.

Other items

Nets are essential items when needed but tend to be a nuisance when not in use. They should be strong, capacious, light and long enough in the handle, particularly for boat use. A knotless, rotproof mesh which will not terminally trap droppers when netting fish is useful. This is another item where the options are considerable, running from cheap and useless via cheap and practical to beautifully produced versions with sometimes too many elaborate engineering details for their own good. I find my turnover in nets is quite brisk, as they are so easy to leave behind on the bank, especially when packing up at night. A simple metal alloy spiked-handled net, which can be thrust into the mud when wading, is particularly useful but not easy to find in the tackle shops these days. For the wealthy, ultra-lightweight fibreglass versions of this simple and prac-tical design are available in sizes that can safely accommodate the fish we all dream of – but at a price.

Nets are probably not used as often as we would all like, but when they are used they should be deep enough to take a reasonable fish, have a good-sized and strong frame and, if they are the folding type, not be prone to catching itself in its own meshes when it is unfolded. A good-length handle is also very important. If you are wading frequently, a net head which sinks and a handle that floats are very useful, as the net is handy when it is needed but in the way when it is not.

Blunt-nosed scissors or nail clippers are useful for trimming nylon and may save on dentists' bills! A floatant for flies and degreaser (fuller's earth and detergent mix) for leaders is essential. Almost essential is a hook-sharpening device – a diamond file or a small section of fine carborundum stone. This aids hook penetration and boosts confidence. A small piece of wax candle to rub on spigot rod ferrules to prevent sticking (and wear) takes up little room. A marrow scoop, or plastic equivalent, to check on your catch's last meal can be very helpful and educational.

As for fly boxes, a large box may make for an undemanding filing system but the portability of some monster multi-layer creations is minimal. For the 'travel light, walkabout' approach, a few small, pocketable and colour-coded boxes with Ethafoam, Plastazote or similar lining, made of bright colours to aid visibility in long grass and moulded plastic for lightness and floating ability, are quite adequate. A good-quality waterproof torch is also a very useful accessory.

If a fish is being kept it should be despatched as speedily as possible with a sharp blow to the back of the head with a suitably weighted priest before unhooking. This should be done efficiently and without delay, so keep the priest handy. Fish keep well in submerged or wet basses or fabric bags. They do not keep well in sunny conditions in a plastic carrier bag! If the water regulations allow and you want to return the fish, they should be handled as little as possible and with wet hands, unhooked quickly and carefully and gently returned to the water and supported until they swim off.

Finally, this collection of essentials needs a method of transportation in the form of a fishing bag. The angler is again spoilt for choice in this area. Providing the following basic requirements are met it does not matter unduly which type you choose. It should be:

(a) waterproof
(b) capacious enough to accommodate all your tackle, spare clothing, and food and drink for the day comfortably
(c) robust and with a broad shoulder strap.

Chapter 3

Casting

T his chapter will be the most difficult from both the reader's and the author's point of view. Just as it is virtually impossible to learn to swim without getting wet, so it is less than ideal to attempt to learn casting from a book. The principles and individual actions may be gleaned, sequences may even be put together, but it is extremely difficult, if not impossible, to learn to cast with the essential rhythm and timing without a rod in your hand and the benefit of practice, preferably guided.

Casting is a co-ordinated set of sequences which are critically interlaced by precise timing. Although relatively simple once grasped, the acquisition of this skill can cause intense and even depressing frustration – but one day it all comes together in the way that learning to drive does and one wonders why it seemed so difficult and why it took the time it did. Without doubt it takes time to learn – there is no instant way to get the 'feel' of the action or the vital sense of timing. The time it takes is obviously reduced if you have a competent instructor to point out and correct your faults. Practice is also important – but practising faulty technique merely ingrains bad habits and creates doubts about your ability to triumph in the struggle with seemingly hostile or recalcitrant tackle.

This frustration is not helped by observing more experienced casters at the water, apparently effortlessly and impeccably laying long, controlled lines on the water. It may be a crumb of comfort to those who feel they have not yet achieved satisfactory levels of performance to know that there seems to be a universal optical illusion that suggests, from sidelong glances, that one's neighbour's casting is better than it actually is – because of this illusion they may well be forming the same impression of your casting!

Most anglers are sensitive about their casting ability and although they may claim to be adequate, they would like to improve. Few will have had any formal casting tuition from a qualified instructor. There are, however, a few exceptionally good casters who are a joy to watch. At this level of proficiency their actions are akin to a graceful aerial ballet and their languid actions, seemingly devoid of effort because of their immaculate timing, magically propel line and leader across a prodigious distance to land as gently as a moonbeam kissing a still silver pool. It all looks so deceptively easy – until you try it!

Stillwater fly fishing imposes the most demanding requirements of 'fine and far off' casting, particularly when one is bank fishing. There is a lot of water in front of one on the larger lakes and reservoirs and one naturally assumes – sometimes correctly – that there are no fish conveniently close. If you cannot achieve those extra few metres when required you are doomed to disappointment. Of course, no matter how far you get there will always be an extra few metres separating you from the fulfilment of your dreams. Nevertheless, unless you have some very radical problem you can confidently expect to develop a good working casting ability which you will refine into a better one with the benefit of experience and critical analysis and observations. Very soon you will joyfully feel your ability has become elevated to a higher level, and in experiencing the pleasure of achievement you will temporarily forget your reason for being at the water – until some misguided fish has the temerity to interrupt your celebration of your accomplishment by hijacking your fly!

The simple overhead cast

In casting the rod will play the more common of its two functions (the other being the somewhat less used 'playing' of the fish and absorbing shocks through sudden movement). In casting mode the rod absorbs the energy imparted by the movements of the caster acting on the inertia of the line, and then transmits this as required to the line, acting rather like a spring. The simple overhead cast is the core sequence on which the double haul – the normal long-distance cast – is constructed. It is often employed for short-distance casts and for shorter line work in boat fishing, where the casting is usually wind assisted. In essence the action is similar to using a whip, although you should never, ever allow it to crack. The whip cracks because the lash is propelled forward whilst it is still unrolling backwards and the subsequent turnover speed becomes exceptionally high, causing the report and very high stress on the end of the lash. Whilst it is perfectly possible to 'crack' fly line and leader in the same way, for normal terminal tackle the material will not cope with the stress and part of the leader, plus flies, will part company with the rest and be lost, necessitating a fresh tippet and flies. This impatience is probably the most common first failing of the beginner – always allow the line to unroll and straighten before changing direction.

The simple overhead cast is executed facing the direction the rod is pointing and in which the line will travel, with the front part of the line (normally less than 30 ft or 9 metres) lying on the water or with a short length suspended from the rod tip ring. A few metres of line should be on the water and not in a heap under the rod but pointing towards the place at which the cast is to be made. If it is in a heap (perhaps because a boat drifts onto it), a simple *roll cast* (see page 37) will set it out.

Bring the rod up with your elbow close in to your body, accelerating smartly, from a position parallel to the water surface. Check this movement typically at the 'one o'clock' position. Do not think for one moment that on your first, fifth or even fiftieth attempt you will actually stop at one o'clock. Many anglers, while not realising it, will go closer to three o'clock (or even later) and cause immediate problems. All will vehemently deny that they went one minute past the twelve o'clock position, but they will be wrong. This back cast is not only the first step towards a forward cast but a vital part of it; if this goes wrong the whole cast is doomed. The rod has a very pronounced tendency to drift back much too far and this is the most common cause of problems and frustration for the novice caster (and some who have progressed well past this point!). Very experienced casters will often allow a rod to drift back but it is not recommended and they need to call on their experience to make adjustments in order to maintain control of the line. The novice caster should bear in mind that with a longer drift back, causing a wider arc of rod movement, the rod will open up too wide a loop, with increased air resistance and an attendant loss of line speed. Moreover this allows the line to drop below the horizontal, where you risk losing control and the flies are more likely to snag in the landscape behind you than to be propelled gracefully forward over the water. Try initially not to allow the rod to go past the perpendicular, i.e. not to allow the hand holding the rod to travel back past your ear. Nevertheless, however careful you are it is virtually certain that the rod will still drift too far back to start with.

With the rod checked in the vertical position (with an inevitable drift to one o'clock or so) the line is propelled back and unrolls behind you. At the point at which the line has straightened out (not earlier), and before it starts to drop, commence the forward cast with a sharp and accelerating push forward of the forearm from the elbow and then a downward rotation movement (as though using a hammer) and a follow-through by the wrist to a position between ten and nine o'clock. This will send the line forward briskly. Try to aim for a point about 3 ft (1 metre) above the water surface for the line to straighten out in front and then drop lightly onto the surface. The whole exercise takes quite a few words to describe, but it is a relatively simple and quickly performed sequence of actions. This should all be done with the hand which is not holding the

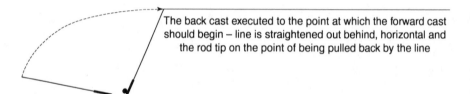

The back cast executed to the point at which the forward cast should begin – line is straightened out behind, horizontal and the rod tip on the point of being pulled back by the line

Figure 3   The simple overhead cast: the back cast

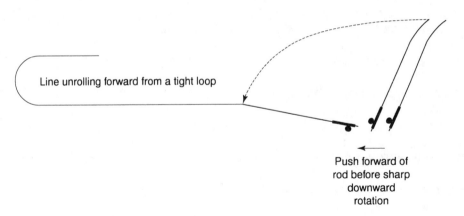

Line unrolling forward from a tight loop

Push forward of
rod before sharp
downward
rotation

Figure 4   The simple overhead cast: the forward cast

rod (the left hand for right-handed casters) holding the line firmly at a point below the bottom rod ring.

Any problems you encounter will usually relate to the back cast, which is the foundation of a good cast. Remember, check the backward movement of the rod at the upright position – not later – and *do not* start the forward movement until the line has straightened out behind you. To start with it is generally helpful for a novice caster to turn his head and body at the waist to see what is happening to the line until the timing becomes ingrained.

This description assumes that the line started off laid out in front on the water (or on grass for practice with an old line). However, it needs to get there in the first instance and this will usually be done by an earlier cast. The principle is the same but starts with line being pulled off the reel and 6 to 10 ft (2 or 3 metres) of the line (in addition to the leader) pulled through the tip ring of the rod and laid on the water or the ground in front of you. The hand which is not holding the rod holds the line. The full sequence of the simple overhead cast is then followed, except that when the line is cast forward the aiming point is higher (about head height) and whilst the line is being propelled forward, the hand holding it is opened slightly, allowing it to travel through the hand, being pulled out by the momentum of the cast portion of the line. This will lengthen the line by a few metres. If more line distance is required then close your hand on the line again after 'shooting' extra distance through the rod rings and before the line starts to drop in front. Repeat this sequence as many times as is necessary until sufficient line is aerialised to reach the desired fishing point or until your current casting abilities are at their limit.

This is termed false casting, and it is generally necessary to build up aerialised line and speed for distance to be covered. It will be noted that as more line is aerialised it takes longer for the line to straighten out in front and behind so that the time needed for each false cast becomes progressively longer as more line is being aerialised. There are, however, other considerations to take into account. For line control to be maintained on weight-forward profile and shooting head lines no more than 3 ft (1 metre) of the thinner running line or shooting head backing should be released out through the tip ring in false casting, as line control will otherwise be lost and you could well end up wearing rather than casting the line! Another point to bear in mind is that a narrow loop of line in the casting action has less air resistance and therefore moves faster and further through the air for any given effort. A narrow arc in the casting action produces a narrower line loop and a wider arc in casting action produces a wider loop with less efficient casting properties through greater air resistance.

The simple overhead cast is the starting point for the stillwater fly fisher; in fact it is the only type of cast used normally by some river anglers, small stillwater specialists and boat loch-style fly anglers. It is effective and, with suitable tackle, can present the fly very delicately and precisely. It does, however, have limitations in its distance range and to overcome this the double-haul technique is commonly used as an additional sequence. For a beginner I would earnestly suggest that, if you are not receiving casting lessons, ensure that you have achieved the timing, distance and presentation of the simple overhead cast comfortably and confidently before moving on to the double haul.

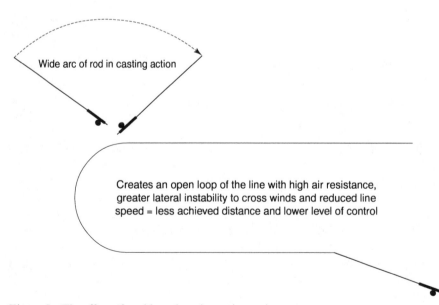

Figure 5   The effect of a wide rod arc in casting action

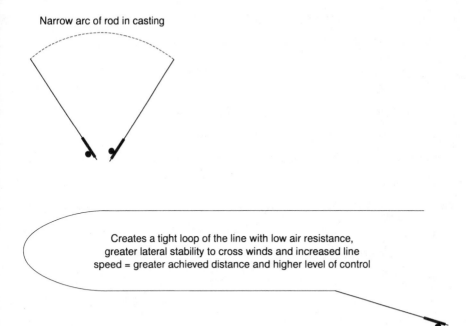

Narrow arc of rod in casting

Creates a tight loop of the line with low air resistance, greater lateral stability to cross winds and increased line speed = greater achieved distance and higher level of control

Figure 6   The effect of a narrow rod arc in casting action

The double-haul technique

Before describing the double-haul technique for increasing line speed and with it distance, it is helpful to consider the mechanics of the rod's absorption and transmission of energy. If we appreciate what we are doing and why we are doing it, then it is more likely that we will do it better. If you were to try casting with a rod which was not loaded with a line (do not do this as you may damage the rod), you would find that the only resistance to the rod would be air resistance and its own initial inertia, which because of its low mass would be negligible. Very little energy would therefore be stored for release. However, when loaded with a fly line, the lift-off into the back cast puts a bend into the rod (thus storing energy) as it meets the resistance of the mass of the line, which is normally increased by the surface tension or friction of the water.

When the rod is checked at its upright position the rod will recover and transmit the stored energy to the fly line causing it to be sent out as an unrolling loop behind you. If the rod were put into a forward cast whilst the line loop was still travelling back there would be minimal reloading of the rod with energy due to lack of resistance and it would only serve to accelerate the turnover of the loop, causing a crack and probably losing the flies and part of the leader. However, if the line is allowed to straighten

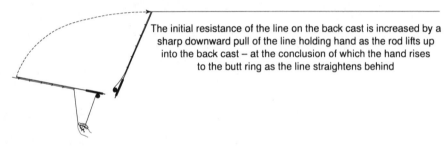

The initial resistance of the line on the back cast is increased by a sharp downward pull of the line holding hand as the rod lifts up into the back cast – at the conclusion of which the hand rises to the butt ring as the line straightens behind

Figure 7   The single-haul (the first part of the double haul)

out fully, its momentum will pull the rod tip back, transmitting energy to the rod ready for the forward cast.

This resistance is increased, and the stored energy with it, if the rod is moved forward at this moment, before it has an opportunity to recover (i.e. straighten) and lose the energy. Quite clearly moving the rod on the forward cast whilst the line is imposing maximum loading on the back cast causes the rod to bend more under the extra pressure – storing more energy which is released by transfer to the line when the forward rod movement is checked and the left hand (for a right-handed caster) releases the line, allowing loose line to shoot through the rod rings.

This of course merely describes in more detail what happens in a simple overhead forward cast; it does not increase line speed or energy stored in the rod. However, if you allow the hand holding the line (not the rod hand) to increase the resistance of the line to the rod on the back cast movement by pulling line in (by moving it sharply down whilst the rod is moving back), this will put a bigger bend in the rod (i.e. store even more energy). This would be a single haul and in itself will add precious distance, providing the forward movement is made at a moment when the extra energy is reapplied without loss.

However, what you did on the back cast to increase stored rod energy you can do again on the forward cast. After applying the single haul on the back cast with the left hand (right hand, of course, for left-handed casters) move your hand back up to the region of the rod handle and, as you move the rod forward, loaded by the enhanced momentum of the fly line, bring it down sharply, pulling the line with it. This will further increase the rod's stored energy. The total sequence can be repeated several times to build up even more line speed to achieve more distance.

This process inevitably seems rather complex and confusing when described on paper, but it is fairly simple in practice and is soon achieved without thinking about it. It is not necessary or desirable to wear yourself out trying to apply repeated violent actions with the rod – better effects by far are achieved by precise timing of the smooth but brisk movements, otherwise energy is wasted.

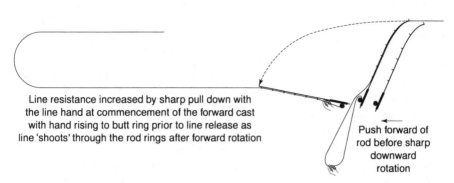

Line resistance increased by sharp pull down with the line hand at commencement of the forward cast with hand rising to butt ring prior to line release as line 'shoots' through the rod rings after forward rotation

Push forward of rod before sharp downward rotation

Figure 8   The double-haul cast: the forward cast

Casting as such is a matter of 'feel' and timing, and if the tangible indications are exaggerated the learning process can be speeded up. So if you have difficulty appreciating what is happening and when to start the next movement, I would suggest that you employ a shooting head line one AFTM rating heavier than normal for your rod, but cut shorter to compensate. If you remember that whilst casting, you should have no more than 3 to 5 ft (1 to 1.5 metres) of the shooting backing outside the tip ring, you will find it much easier to feel the rod loadings with this tackle and to determine the timing for each part of the sequences. This line need not be wasted, as it is also useful for fishing in windy conditions, with heavy flies or from a boat where your action may be restricted or inconvenienced by the boat's movements or the presence of others.

There will be many occasions when you will not want to cast out to the same point from which the line was finally retrieved. This may be because of wind line drift, to cast to a fish you have seen moving within range or simply as part of systematic water coverage. It is worth pointing out that where the arc of direction change is significant, that is to say 20° or more, in the interests of safety it should not be attempted in one back cast – use the false-casting technique to move in the desired direction at about 20° at a time.

The roll cast

The simple overhead and double-haul casts will be the ones you use most of the time on stillwaters, and there will only be limited call for other casting techniques. But one other style which can be useful on occasions is the roll cast. This is a simple movement which requires the line to be cast to be on, or in, the water. This is because the rod movement is limited and to be effective it requires maximum line resistance immediately – not just the mass of the line but also water tension. It merely consists in the rod being brought briskly up from a position roughly parallel to the water in front of the body to an upright position – no further back – then in one smooth continuous action, being snapped sharply forward and down in the direction the line is intended to travel, at the same time describing a small arc. The line will follow the direction of the rod tip, a loop will roll along the line and the leader will roll and straighten out.

With the fairly light lines and short rods used by trout anglers the distance one can achieve with this method is very limited, compared with salmon rods and lines. However it can be useful where short casts and minimal disturbance are called for. Since the line does not travel behind the angler at all, it is useful when there is an obstruction such as a wall, tree or hedge close behind. Additionally, when one is fishing from the bank or a boat there are occasions when a fish will be seen following the fly. One can try to quicken its interest but, if this does not work and the fish is still very close, a roll cast is ideal to re-present the fly and offer the fish a second opportunity to attach itself. In fact, if the fish has shown an interest in the fly, having it suddenly disappear and equally suddenly reappear, it will often respond more positively, presumably because it recognises that it may suddenly disappear again for good. Many fish are taken in this manner, especially from boats, and the roll cast is unquestionably the fastest method of re-presenting the fly under the circumstances.

Another use for the roll cast is when the line for an overhead cast is lying in loose coils in front so that the rod will not lift it from the water in a back cast. This can happen for a number of reasons but is common in a drifting boat, which moves down onto the line. A roll cast under these circumstances does not achieve much distance, but it does set the line out nicely for a crisp lift off for a normal back cast without the need to retrieve the slack line by hand.

Fly casting is a fascinating subject in its own right. An ability to cast adequately on a stillwater, which generally means sufficient distance with reasonable accuracy and presentation under wide-ranging weather conditions, is important in order to gain confidence and gain the most enjoyment from the pursuit. The art can be taken to a higher degree but it is not, thankfully, necessary to become highly accomplished or expert in this area to catch fish on stillwaters and to enjoy doing so.

There are, however, some further points which it may be helpful to mention. Wind knots, from simple overhand knots to complex and wholly unbelievable tangles are certain to bedevil you. They are intensely frustrating and much more likely to occur when you feel the chance of a fish is good. This is because they are a result of poor technique or being too ambitious; sober line control is less likely when one becomes excited. It is vital that these knots are removed as they occur by unpicking if possible or else by replacing the affected section of the leader.

One major reason they occur is poor rod control in the overhead casts. The rod tip should travel backwards and forwards in the same plane; imagine that your rod tip cuts a path or slot through the air in the back cast which is to be used on the forward cast. There is a tendency to make a circle with the rod tip; this is poor technique which will cause wind knots. The rod tip should move forward in precisely the same path in which it moved back; if it does this problem, and that of the flies hitting the rod, should not occur. A further point to bear in mind is that the rod should not be allowed to twist in casting. The front edge of the reel should face the front all the time and not be allowed to turn to the side on casting.

When casting directly into the wind, which can often be a very frustrating but occasionally a rewarding exercise, this becomes increasingly important. In a stiff wind, cast directly into it if possible, with a tight vertical loop from a small rod-movement arc; a brisk, snapping final wrist action can be helpful in these circumstances. What is most unhelpful is attempting to cast across a strong wind or allowing the rod tip to follow a circular path, opening up a lateral loop. This is tantamount to inviting the wind to take control of your line. It is also not advisable to use a very long leader when casting into a strong wind, since it is most unlikely to turn over and more likely to be blown back at you, making all your labours in vain. It can be very hard work struggling to cast effectively into a stiff wind, but it can be well worthwhile on occasions. At least the back cast will be wind-assisted, and a good back cast is a good start for a successful forward cast.

In very high winds, the shooting backing of a shooting head, being much lighter than a full line, can become totally uncontrollable, creating tangles in casting and intense frustration. A line tray (a fabric netting tray surrounded by raised nylon fabric worn at the waist) may help up to a point but there may come a stage when the only thing to do is to change to a full-length conventional line or move to a more comfortable position. The same problems apply in a boat in a following high wind, when the shooting head backing is picked up from the floor by the turbulent wind and blown out in front of the boat. This is a problem if the boat is drifting at speed in the conditions and drifts over it. Very high wind conditions and shooting heads rarely go well together. A bulky, floating fly line can also be a problem when one is attempting to punch it out into a strong wind and changing to a higher-density, lower-wind-resistance slow-sinking line may enable you to maintain action in a 'fishy' position. If the position is not promising after a fair trial then move to another, possibly more sheltered spot.

Chapter 4

The private life of the trout

To fish successfully for trout with a fly, it is not strictly necessary to know more than what range of flies to use, how to present and fish them and how to react in the event of fish showing a positive interest. These are the essential requirements of every novice, but the question is how to use this information to meet every changing set of circumstances we are likely to meet. And if we did know exactly what to do in every situation, it would not make our angling nearly as rewarding and fulfilling.

The angler is a predator in pursuit of predators and has the advantage of far superior intelligence, with reasoning power and rapid, constructive learning patterns. This means that only in the most dire and unpromising situations do we even approach anything like a mechanical, repetitive response in our sport. Our nature as a super-predator makes us not merely observe and react instinctively, but also ask questions like 'What if . . . ?', try alternative approaches, seek to explain why things have happened the way they have and predict future responses. And of course we know that the more information and background knowledge we have about our quarry, the better equipped we will be to make better, bigger and more reliable catches. This translates simply as more knowledge equals more involvement, equals more confidence, equals more enjoyment.

From a situation where we only want to get to grips with the trout (on our terms if possible) we naturally move on to a desire to accumulate as much useful knowledge as is reasonably practical. We understand that at some time, in some place, under certain circumstances, some fragment of knowledge of the nature, habits, background, history or motivation of the trout may provide the clue which becomes the key to success when conditions become extremely difficult. An angler's 'need to know' quickly becomes a broader 'wish to know'. From a position of sound knowledge we can justifiably feel we are making progress. Even the awareness that we have this knowledge and understanding, whether it is immediately relevant or not, brings an extra interest to our fishing.

Parentage and origins

The indigenous European form of trout, the brown trout (*Salmo trutta*) has long been recognised as a highly prized fish, both from the sporting angle and for the table. It is considered to be a relatively long-living fish and one which exhibits slow growth and development, although these features are greatly affected by other circumstances such as ready food availability.

A member of the salmon family (Salmonidae) its natural distribution is wide; it occurs in both still and running waters throughout Europe, including Scandinavia. It has also been introduced into countries as far apart as New Zealand, the U.S.A. and the higher altitudes of Kenya and Nepal, where its sporting and culinary qualities have become readily appreciated. In many cases it has found the new locations very much to its liking and prospered, quickly reaching very large sizes and rapidly developing self-sustaining populations.

The brown trout needs good water quality (free from polluting contaminants) and a high oxygen content. Possibly for this reason it is not to be found where summer water temperatures are high – cooler water is capable of retaining a higher concentration of dissolved oxygen than warmer water. Summer water temperatures in the range of 10°C to 18°C seem to suit it well. Very low temperatures are not beneficial since they have a limiting effect on the food supply – but this aspect is unlikely to affect anglers in the British Isles.

Without question a remarkably handsome fish, the brown trout adopts a markedly different appearance according to its habitat (particularly the nature of the bottom in the water in which it is found) and to a lesser extent its diet. In the British Isles these local marking adaptations and behavioural differences have given rise to considerable confusion; it was previously believed that the various adaptations were in fact different species. As a result, a plethora of common (local) names and even erroneous 'proper' (i.e. scientific) names have been applied to what is basically the same fish exhibiting different marking and other environmentally or diet-linked characteristics. For instance older books will carry reference to common trout, bull trout, slob trout, black-finned trout, Loch Leven trout, gillaroo trout, sea trout, Loch Stennis trout and others, all of which are now possibly recognised as one species with markedly different appearances. I say 'possibly' since the debate appears to be continuing and in some scientific quarters there is a view that there are three distinct forms. These being separated into the oceanic form (the sea trout, *Salmo trutta trutta*), the lake form (the Alpine lakes rather than British stillwaters), *Salmo trutta lacustris* and the common form, *Salmo trutta fario*. It is very easy to understand how the confusion arises. A typical fish from an acid loch will go from bronze/green on top through rich brown to a cream belly, liberally splashed with brilliant red spots.

The same fish from an alkaline reservoir will be largely silver with a darker back and with black spots. Brown trout in southern, alkaline lakes or reservoirs will rarely show any trace of brown coloration.

Happily, any finer form of classification is outside the province of all but the most pedantic of anglers. It is sufficient to be aware that within the same environment, with due allowance for individual responses and very localised conditions, all brown trout can be expected to be similar. Decisions by zoologists to burden them with one scientific name or another will not change matters one iota for either the fish or the anglers.

The brown trout will be the dominant game species in waters which hold natural and self-sustaining stocks of trout. Where spawning facilities are poor, stocks may be augmented from a hatchery programme or transfer from other waters.

The other main species to be encountered in stillwaters is a 'recent' import from the U.S.A., the rainbow trout, generally given the scientific name *Salmo gairdneri* but sometimes also referred to as *Oncorhynchus mykiss*. The original distribution of this species was from the northern tip of Asia to southern California along the Pacific coast. Like the brown trout, it has been introduced very widely internationally where the climate is suitable. This certainly includes the British Isles, and it is very widely stocked in fisheries where spawning facilities are limited or non-existent – which means most of the Midland and southern English reservoirs. Stocking is necessary regardless of the spawning opportunities since, with only very rare exceptions, the rainbow trout does not breed naturally or successfully in British waters and therefore does not produce self-sustaining populations. For this reason small juvenile rainbow trout are virtually unknown to British anglers.

The rainbow is a very striking and attractive fish. It is shorter-lived and grows and develops faster than the brown trout. The back has a deep blue/greenish coloration becoming lighter to silver through the flanks and belly. The back, sides, dorsal fins and tail are freely covered with small black spots. The flanks frequently have a distinct iridescent magenta sheen, although this is not always seen. Like the brown trout, the rainbow also has varying forms; some, like the sea trout, demonstrate a migratory, sea-going habit, and are known as 'steelhead' trout in the U.S.A. and Canada. In addition 'strains' denoting the origin of various naturally occurring forms may be encountered, such as 'shasta', 'kamloops' and others.

Whilst the natural incidence of maintained local forms of brown trout are of interest since they continue to be encountered so long as breeding stocks remain self-sustaining and free from outside interference, this is not the case with the rainbow. At the time of its original introduction into the British Isles, the differing characters of the various forms – their migratory tendencies, spawning periods, feeding and growth habits etc. – may well still have been distinct. However, those that were released into our running and stillwaters, almost without exception, failed to breed. Accordingly as the original fish met their end such specific characteristics died with them. The rainbows' presence in British waters relies virtually exclusively on artificial hatchery productions. In addition to sporting interests, their faster growth habit and tolerance of high-density populations endears them to the commercial fish farming world for table use. As the 'deep-litter broiler' of the fish world, they have justified considerable investment in breeding and selection for optimum food conversion and growth rates. These are also characteristics which fishery managers are also unlikely to ignore; publicity from bigger fish being caught regularly from their waters will attract other anglers in numbers to try their luck. It is most unlikely, therefore, that any examples of the original different forms of rainbow trout which may have been initially introduced will remain in the British Isles or Europe; selected, faster-growing hybrids from these original fish, with currently little or no variation, will have replaced them.

Apart from the rare occasions when stillwaters are part of a river system and salmon and sea trout have access, these two species, the brown and the rainbow trout, form the overwhelming bulk of stillwater game fish which will be encountered by anglers in the British Isles. There will be a few 'exotics', mainly introduced as a novelty to draw attention to specific, generally small, stillwaters as a commercial gimmick. Not all of these will strictly be trout. For instance American 'brook trout' (*Salvelinus fontinalis*) have been stocked in some waters in recent years, but in reality this is not a trout but a form of a closely related species, the charr. We do have our own naturally occurring native forms of this species in a few northern waters but they are not normally encountered extensively enough to warrant specific attention, although they do sometimes turn up as a bonus when trout fishing.

Spawning and breeding

For angling purposes, the indigenous brown and the immigrant rainbow can more or less be classed together when considering spawning. They are both winter-spawning species. The brown trout breeds naturally and extensively in the British Isles, where conditions are suitable – a supply of clean, well-oxygenated water running over the fertilised eggs. These conditions occur in shallow streams with coarse gravel bottoms (called redds), where the hen fish 'cuts' an indentation by the action of her body and tail. Positioning herself upstream she is joined by a cock fish and there is a virtually simultaneous release of ova and sperm-containing milt, arranged to fall into the area of the indented gravel. The hen fish will then, again by the use of her body and tail, disturb the gravel upstream so that it rolls down in the current, covering the fertilised eggs. Clearly there will be extensive losses in this process, with loose eggs carried in the current to feed other fish, many or most of them other trout. During the spawning period several thousand ova may be released by hen fish and both sexes may lose up to 30% of their pre-spawning body weight. The fertilised eggs, protected from being carried away by the current by the gravel covering but benefiting from the flow of oxygen-rich cool water filtering through it, develop into alevins. The gravel is essential, as silt would clog the gaps and prevent the essential flow of water with vital oxygen from reaching the ova.

Once hatched the young alevins will be in running water (winter is usually a time of plentiful rainfall so that the water flow is generally assured), and protected for the first few days by coarse gravel. Initially attached to a yolk sac the young fish will receive nutrients from it and gradually learn to intercept small organisms brought to it by the current. Then as it develops the ability to hunt actively and fend for itself it will grow in the stream environment until it drops downstream into the still-water which its parents left to spawn. None of the actual spawning can occur in actual stillwater, of course, but natural lakes, lochs etc. will generally have suitable small feeder streams or burns which are often dry in summer months, save for deeper pools, but flow in the wetter winter months.

In stillwaters with self-sustaining populations these small trout (now called parr) will inhabit the margins, especially around weed beds. They will be of no immediate interest to anglers, but will seek to feed safely on food items of suitable size and avoid predators such as herons, cormorants, grebes, fish-eating ducks – and other, larger fish. Since brown trout are slow-growing, by the time they reach a size to interest an angler (which will vary greatly according to the feeding potential of the water) they will have served a long apprenticeship in survival and will have these very special qualities of wild fish.

Brown trout stocked in waters that do not have natural populations, and all rainbow trout, have a very different background from natural-history and angling viewpoints. Artificially inseminated and brought up in a totally synthetic, antiseptic, protected environment, hatchery fish are not automatically subjected to any process of natural selection. Worse still from a purist's viewpoint, for their formative years they experience only their own peer groups, have no experience of evading predators and may even associate man with the appearance of food.

With automatic feeding systems with no obvious human involvement, an unvarying diet of floating trout pellets does nothing to inculcate a natural seasonal feeding pattern. Moreover, high-density stocking in rearing ponds creates anxious, unquestioning, competitive feeding and the timing of feeding may be wholly unrelated to that of their wild brethren. It is small wonder therefore that recently stocked fish are disoriented, easy game, and avoided by experienced anglers – at least until the going gets tough! I do appreciate the realities of life – and some waters do seek to overcome some of these problems by introducing new fish in small batches after having acclimatised them in floating cages in the water in question – and I have no wish to criticise the system; artificially reared fish are much to be preferred to no fish. But it is necessary to mention these factors, as they affect fish behaviour from an angler's viewpoint. What is utterly amazing though is the rate at which recently introduced stock fish do adjust and, despite their previous wholly artificial existence, learn and become part of their environment, with the survivors rapidly assimilating the feeding patterns and survival skills of wild or virtually wild fish. A 'stockie' may be a long way removed from a natural fish, but a stocked fish that survives for a year or even a few months is a vastly different and much sharper individual and worthy of considerable respect. Natural feeding patterns are very quickly absorbed in open, large waters, where presumably more experienced fish serve as role models.

In artificially constructed reservoirs, there will normally be no spawning facility. The metabolism of fish introduced into such waters, however, even if they have been artificially reared, will not be affected and will follow a normal life-cycle. For such waters, stocking is usually with mature or semi-mature fish. These will be hatchery bred and produced where natural breeding losses are probably reduced at least tenfold. This has important angling implications. Because of sporting considerations, in addition to close season protection in the case of brown trout (the more recently introduced rainbows not being included in older legislation), we do not fish for them over the winter months. Brown trout would appear to come into spawning condition earlier than rainbows and accordingly can be expected to be in better 'mended' condition when angling for them commences in the spring. Sexually mature hen fish of both species may manage to clean themselves of ova in stillwaters where normal spawning facilities are not available, with any ova retained being reabsorbed. Certainly fish, especially rainbows, containing ova and milt may be taken by anglers well into May. In any case, the fish are not at their best in early spring, as considerable physiological changes are taking place. With the lower winter temperatures and fewer hours of daylight slowing down their metabolic rate, and with less food available, they are geared to return to condition slowly during the early part of the year except in areas of abundant food and in early, warm springs.

With relatively less food naturally available, early-season fish are generally less selective and at this time are much more inclined to take nondescript lures. This may be as a result of an urgent need to rebuild themselves following winter and the problems of spawning, whether frustrated or not. Equally, of course, any memory of unpleasant experiences or dangers associated with the observation of anglers' lures will be less clearly recalled following several months free from any angling pressure, and with only other predators to watch out for. Many fish taken at this time will be naive younger fish, not sexually mature, but some over-wintered mature fish will also find the prospect of a larger potential food item appealing, although more often than not they will be out of condition – darker and duller in colour, often very lean. These fish are of no value at this stage for either sporting or table purposes and should be returned to the water carefully and as quickly as possible. Within a few weeks they will recover out of all recognition.

Seasonal feeding patterns

During the very early part of the season fish will usually be found in deeper water which may be warmer than that at the surface, which is chilled by cold winds. On warmer days with sunshine, however, the shallower water of the margins will warm up under the rays of the sun, giving a more comfortable environment for the fish as well as possibly stimulating some food activity. Shallower water is therefore well worth prospecting under such conditions.

As the days become longer and water temperatures start to rise, food becomes more abundant and widespread, and from mid-May through June there will be an increase in insect hatches. Fish will feed on these throughout most of the water, and especially where they are sheltered from cooling breezes. During the early part of the season, however, they will be restricted to smaller food forms, typically nymphs of Ephemeroptera (upwing flies similar to mayflies), bloodworms (larval form of the chironomids or 'buzzers' as anglers generally call them) or the free-swimming pupae of these flies (usually referred to with questionable accuracy as 'buzzer nymphs'). There will also be other food forms – crustaceans such as freshwater shrimps, water lice and water fleas (daphnia) – but all of these are relatively small and, at this time of the year anyway, not likely to be found in convenient high concentrations. With cold winds often blowing, which are no help to weakly flying creatures, terrestrial insects will be carried out onto the water and these will also feature in the trout's diet at the beginning of the season. The early part of the spring will therefore see the fish in need of replenishing their body resources and becoming more active, with water temperatures starting to slowly rise and hours of daylight lengthening but with food not plentiful and probably well distributed. This spells mobility with a purpose – good news to the angler.

As we will see in chapter 11, when we look at seasonably variable food items, by a happy coincidence the period when the hours of daylight reach a maximum and water temperatures are comfortable – i.e. ideal conditions for prolonged feeding – food not only does become more diverse and more plentiful but individual food forms also increase in size. This is the period where any residual winter loss of condition is not

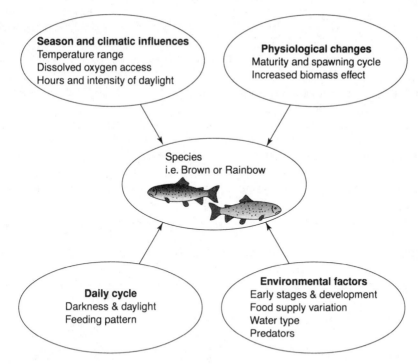

Figure 9   Some key factors affecting trout feeding behaviour

only made good but improved upon, with greatly increased insect life and larger insects – sedges now make their appearance, as do the large damselfly nymphs, and some waters also have hatches of large mayfly.

These are great months for the angler, with the fish more obliging and feeding harder, especially in the upper water and surface areas. They are also now fully restored to prime physical condition and give a much better account of themselves – and of course their culinary properties are much improved. This applies particularly to the rainbow trout, which although it would normally spawn later than the brown has a faster growth rate supported by a bigger appetite. In addition the rainbow shows more mobility within the water, being much less territorial by nature, combined with increased surface or near-surface activity and a greater propensity to shoaling – all features which make it easier to locate and which are readily taken advantage of by anglers fortunate enough to fish during this period.

As summer brings higher water temperatures (large water masses take some time to change) the drop in oxygen content suppresses this un-restrained appetite and the fish tend to lie deeper in the water, closer to the thermocline (the level at which the warmer surface water and the cooler, deeper layer meet) and in many waters possibly also at the level of

47

the daphnia (water fleas), which feed on algae whose depth is to some degree influenced by the intensity of light levels. Fish do of course feed on daphnia – at times, irritatingly, to the exclusion of other food forms. However, whilst anglers can find this period (July and early August) exasperating, the fish will often also feed selectively at the surface on hatching chironomid and sedge pupae when light levels and temperatures at the surface are low – at dawn and dusk. Whilst such activity is very welcome and can be intense but short-lived, with good quality fish often contacted, there is one practical problem for the angler: they are sometimes unreliable and in any event up to nineteen hours apart!

Towards the end of summer and into autumn the hours of daylight shorten and the angle of the sun drops, causing lower daytime temperatures. This has the effect of once again boosting the trout's appetite and particularly the earlier-spawning brown trout need to build up their physical resources. As trout are carnivorous, their diet is naturally high in protein, but at this time of the year there is an item in many waters which offers particularly high levels of protein, enabling the fish to build up their resources rapidly for spawning (whether or not this can effectively take place). This takes the form of large shoals of coarse fish fry, which by now are approximately 2 to 3 in (5 to 7.5 cm) in length. These shoals, which represent a good meal and, where available, abundant, are often managed by being 'herded' in shallow water by a group of large fish and present an easy target. Fish which have been feeding on fry are often stuffed with them.

As the hours of daylight continue to shorten and the temperatures ease back again to cooler conditions into and through September, feeding activity in general declines, although there are days of late-season interest which continue to the end of September (the end of the angling season for brown trout) and beyond for rainbow, which on some waters may be fished for until much later in the year.

This feeding cycle is of particular relevance to anglers. While humans have personal food preferences, which will vary from one individual to another, this does not seem to apply to trout. As far as one can tell, individual preference as such does not enter the feeding pattern. If there is a choice it would seem to be related to relative food availability; if there is more of it available, then it is automatically first choice. Autopsies confirm that most trout caught within a given area at approximately the same time will have been feeding almost exclusively on a single food item, subject of course to high availability – although there will usually be a few examples of very different food items consumed at presumably the same time or very close to it. This would seem to indicate that trout are conditioned to accept, within limits, what is most conveniently available in quantity at any given time. This does not rule out the element of curiosity at an unusual occurrence. An unusual or immediately unrecognised object, which is perceived not as a danger but as a possible food form, may be investigated. If visual examination is not conclusive, the trout has only its mouth with which to investigate the object.

Within this seasonal feeding pattern cycle there are other factors which affect the trout's response to food. There would seem to be a largely unpredictable – to us at least – response to climatic conditions. Sudden weather changes, very turbulent conditions and marked changes in wind direction seem to have the effect of unsettling fish and changing their feeding habits whilst prolonged, settled periods of high atmospheric pressure can often provide days of good feeding and as a result good angling opportunities.

Maturity and behavioural changes

The ages of fish, like their weights, become talking points and form the basis of legends which are not to be trusted unless they are reliably authenticated. However, as a slow developer, the 'brownie' can be expected to be longer-lived than the faster-developing rainbow. Ages in excess of ten years would seem to be credible, but whether the same credence can be given to ages running into a second decade and more, as has been suggested remains a moot point.

The rainbow trout is generally acknowledged to be much shorter-lived, at least in our waters, where it is an introduced species. To some extent its more obliging feeding habits contribute to a much lower survival rate in any event. Moreover, we should remember that commercial selection processes have centred around fast growth rates to large sizes, and this does not contribute to longevity. Accelerated growth rates to a possibly unnatural size adds an extra strain to the body, and will take its toll on any creature.

Both species will shoal as younger fish and of course a shoal has many mouths to feed. It must therefore be prepared to move around freely in search of an adequate food supply, pausing to take advantage of suitable concentrations when they are found. There is no doubt that the rainbow displays this shoaling tendency more strongly than the brown trout, and the shoals would appear to accommodate mixed sizes (presumably mixed age groups) more frequently. Little research appears to have been carried out on shoals and their behaviour – how long they exist for, why they form, why they break up, whether fish continually come and go, whether the shoal divides into smaller units or amalgamates with others in still-waters are questions which are still largely unanswered.

From the angler's standpoint, however, the shoal is generally good news for sport. Whilst a particularly large fish, the fish of a lifetime which anglers dream of, is most unlikely to come from a shoal, the shoal, especially if it is composed of rainbows, can contain very acceptably sized fish – although the majority will inevitably be of smaller fish. When a shoal is feeding, the fish are usually very visible, and the angler will be sharp and alert, watching confidently for any sign of fish taking his offerings. Takes from fish under these conditions usually leave no room for doubt, as they are unmistakably positive. Your flies will probably be seen by a number of fish in the shoal. As they move to investigate it, they will become competitive, and are likely to lunge at it and take quickly, fearful of losing a prized food item to other fish in the very close vicinity. So, soft or questionable takes are much less likely to occur when fishing to a shoal.

Providing a fish does not make a mistake and become a casualty to an angler or other predator, and given freedom from disease and access to adequate nutrition, it will grow in size and find that its peer group has greatly diminished to the benefit of otters, ospreys, anglers, mergansers etc. A larger fish will obviously require more energy not only for its normal life processes but also in moving through the water. Whereas a small fish with little water resistance would find an energy gain in moving through the water to take a small nymph, a considerably larger fish might end up expending more energy in reaching small food items than it gained from them. Charging about through the water in search of small food items when they are well dispersed would be counter-productive. The widely held view is that such fish respond by developing a diet of generally larger food items. Anglers believe that in the case of trout this means that fish is on the menu more frequently, although autopsies of such fish do not necessarily vindicate this view. However, if a trout is inclined to take larger fish into its diet on a regular basis, quite clearly it does not have to feed so regularly, so lack of corroborating stomach content evidence does not necessarily disprove the anglers' view. And the fish diet does not have to be exclusive, of course. With such highly nutritious meals a trout can well afford the luxury of occasional 'recreational' feeding on smaller, familiar food items which do not add up to much on the calorie balance sheet. They can still therefore be caught by normal fly-fishing tactics but clearly less often by virtue of their greater experience and fewer numbers.

The fact that their meals are larger and not taken so frequently means that the fly fisherman sees less of the larger fish and assumes that they have gone lower in the water and become bottom feeders. This does make sense if a fish has changed feeding habits; it will no longer be necessary for it to stay in a high-risk area. Also, food items associated with lower water – snails, freshwater shrimps etc. – can be harvested with less effort. Where the best fish are to be found in any large water is a perennial topic of discussion that torments anglers, but there is some evidence that they are generally in deeper water.

Some years ago, before the rules were amended to ban it, the use of lee boards on Grafham Water became very popular. These are a form of drift controller and were very simply stout planks of wood which were fixed with G-clamps to the gunwale of the boat on the lee side. This has the effect of changing the drift of the boat from the direction of the wind to across the wind. The advantage of this was that a fast-sinking line cast out in front of the boat was not overtaken and run over by the drifting boat but allowed to sink – and fish – deeply for extended periods. This resulted in unexpectedly high numbers of large fish being taken during the course of that season (and incidentally a reduction in the following seasons). The ban on the use of this device did not, I feel, result from the loss of the larger fish, which would be an invisible resource anyway, but more from the alarmingly high stress it placed on the structure of the boats, a stress which they were surely never designed to withstand, and as a result was a potentially dangerous practice. It was doubtless also expensive, since the life of the boat would be reduced. I did experiment with this method myself but was alarmed at the extent to which the fibreglass shell and gunwale of the boat flexed under the pressure. But the season did appear to confirm the anglers' view that as fish increased in size their diet changed and they moved to the bottom, more particularly since this style of fishing (virtually wind-powered trolling) was invariably conducted with the largest lures available – designed to emulate fish.

Another angler's theory is that the larger fish, being predominantly brown trout, move towards the shoreline to feed after dark, but this remains difficult to prove without fisheries lifting their embargo on fishing after dark. The few brave souls who do manage to fish at daybreak in the summer nevertheless generally manage a better than average weight for their catches – but they do remain largely unwitnessed!

Chapter 5

Moving stillwaters

Whilst we refer to waters such as lakes, lochs, loughs, tarns, reservoirs etc. as 'stillwaters' to distinguish them from the running and sometimes tidal waters of rivers and estuaries, it is something of a misnomer. These waters are very rarely 'still', being subject to movement as the wind stirs up the surface as well as to currents associated with the wind and convection currents caused by temperature changes in conjunction with the topographical features of the submerged terrain. In these water conditions fish can be found behaving in a similar fashion to their river counterparts. In a river a fish will have to 'swim' with its head upstream to maintain station in the current whilst waiting for food items to appear in the flow of water. Similarly in stillwaters fish will often swim upwind (against the surface or subsurface water flow) looking for food in the water being pushed along towards them by the wind or other factors. Clearly the area of water they scan in this way is significantly greater than they would cover by merely maintaining station in the water and waiting for the movement to bring food items to them. This activity requires energy output on the part of the fish and since this precious resource is not to be squandered, it is a good sign that the fish are likely to be on the feed and, therefore, more likely to show a positive interest in the angler's flies.

Water stratification

Some stillwaters can have areas of surprising depth and in the deeper parts the water will stratify into definite layers of different temperatures, with little inclination to mix. The upper layer closest to the surface, which for most of the year will be the warmest and most oxygenated, is termed the epilimnion. The hypolimnion is the lower or deeper part, which will be colder, except in winter, and less well oxygenated. The difference in winter is due to the fact that water has its highest specific gravity at 4°C; when it reaches that point it will sink to the bottom through the warmer, lighter water. This warmer water in turn will be sent closer to the surface where it will be cooled and sink in its turn, until the surface becomes colder than 4°C. At that point the specific gravity

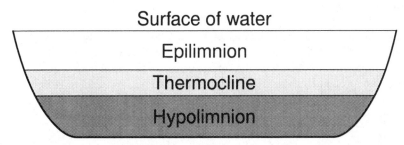

Figure 10   The stratification of deeper stillwaters

becomes lower and the colder water, or ice as it will eventually become, 'floats'.

The layer which divides the epilimnion and hypolimnion is called the thermocline. There can be marked differences in temperature between the two, and it is in the thermocline that the temperature range is widest within a limited depth range. This is a significant feature for the fish as a comfortable level can be found within minor variations in depth when high summer temperatures affect the upper water levels. The level of oxygenation will also vary between layers and at different times of the year.

When the water is stirred by winds and produces waves the overall surface area is increased. In warmer weather this provides a greater cooling effect at the surface, and as cooler water will absorb more oxygen and the air contains more than the water, there is a greater area in which oxygen can be transferred from the air to the water. As a consequence the surface level will become relatively more highly oxygenated than those layers below. Higher oxygen levels stimulate greater activity and, since more activity requires more energy, this calls for the replenishment of physical resources, which requires more food. Whether fish actually experience the sensation of hunger as we know it is open to conjecture but by and large high oxygen levels promote increased feeding interest and probably also a greater sense of alertness, well-being and interest in food.

In the hot summer months, when wind levels are often minimal and the air temperature rises, the temperature builds up in the epilimnion and as a result this area of the water is unable to hold the same quantity of oxygen. Trout are not well adapted to warmer water and consequentially reduced oxygen levels, and under these conditions they are frequently found at the thermocline level, which can be quite a narrow layer, where they are much more comfortable. They can often move to the surface as the sun goes off the water in the evening and the surface becomes cooler and richer in oxygen. Since there is often a hatch of fly at this time there is a double incentive for this upward migration.

Fish populations

There are thankfully still areas of mainly natural stillwaters where the populations are self-sustaining and entirely natural. They are likely to be remote from heavily populated or industrial areas with their attendant pressures and pollution. Such waters can be very abundant in remote areas of Scotland, where the lochs and lochans can support indigenous populations of totally wild fish. These will typically be waters with feeder burns or streams offering spawning facilities for natural regeneration – although not exclusively so, since birds and winter floods may redistribute a few fish into otherwise deprived waters.

In the areas where peat abounds the waters are stained brown and become acidic and the trout may provide the only resident fish population. A similar situation of course exists in the loughs of Ireland, the llyns of Wales and the tarns and lakes of the English Lake District. The sheer proliferation of fishing waters in an area such as Sutherland or the Western Isles leaves the angler spoilt for choice. Many of these waters contain only brown trout or brown trout as the only species of game fish. Although there are some very notable exceptions, many of the acid waters lack the fertility to support strong food chains and there are often few natural predators to the trout – other than perhaps ferox or cannibal brown trout! Populations are accordingly often too high to be conducive to a high average size, in a species which has a relatively slow growth rate. Because of this there is sometimes a tendency for those who normally fish richer stocked and less natural waters, containing only relatively large specimens, to dismiss the pursuit of smaller fish in remote, wild areas as being of little interest. It amounts perhaps to a matter of choice, preference and personal experience.

I was fortunate enough to start my own fly fishing many years ago in the rivers and lochs of Sutherland. My memories of those early days are cherished ones and whether the 'brownies' ran one (most unusual), two (with luck) or three (all too often) to the pound, these exquisite living jewels, totally creatures of their wild environment and caught in truly inspiring and fully natural settings were always a thrill to catch – and still will be when I am there next! Their colours, fresh from the water, are breathtaking and their fight for freedom, on light tackle, utterly belies their size and inspires respect and regard. Even though the normal size may be smaller than in the stocked 'put and take' waters, each day's fishing can often provide undisputable visual evidence of the presence of much larger fish in residence. Nowhere else will the angler be in greater touch with the true spirit of the sport as a whole or closer to reality with a capital 'R'.

While fish from the more remote stillwaters are totally wild, and their takes can be lightning fast, they are not intensively fished for, especially when some walking is required to reach the water in question, and as a

54

result they can be unsophisticated in their awareness of the angler and his ways. They are not normally demanding – your flies will possibly be the first artificials they have come across – and this is really fun fishing at its best. Do not, however, make the mistake of underrating these fish – they can be as difficult and frustrating as any.

The northern waters are also likely to offer bonus additions to the ubiquitous 'brownie'. There has been some limited stocking with rainbow trout in some, usually more accessible, waters. However, the more natural additions, in a few waters, will be charr, with their more colourful appearance and perhaps disappointing sporting qualities. These fish will only usually feature when they venture out of their normal deeper water, and even then only irregularly in the few waters in which they exist. When waters are linked to river systems, some can offer that super athlete of the water, the sea trout, which is a migratory form of the brown trout. This fish rejoices in a wide variety of local names (whitling and finnock, which are normally reserved for the juvenile fish, as well as white trout, peal, sewin etc.). The sea trout can be extremely shy and, when freshly arrived from the sea, where most of its life is spent on rich feeding opportunities, rather soft-mouthed. This feature, combined with the usual dazzling display of energy and heroic agility when hooked, means the ratio of fish hooked to those landed can be more than mildly frustrating.

Waters with a link to the sea may also offer salmon, which can be caught in stillwaters and which are often stocked as fingerlings from hatcheries into their local habitat to supplement the normal wild stocks or, in a few cases, stocked into stillwaters with no outlet, as grown-on fish. Salmon and sea trout are of course migratory and spend most of their adult lives feeding in the rich larder of the sea, returning to freshwater for the sole purpose of breeding. They are, accordingly, only temporarily available in stillwaters as they travel from sea to headwaters for spawning; they may be 'resting', or waiting for suitable water levels for the next stage of their journey to the redds. They are only of interest on their journey to the spawning grounds – and then usually in the earlier stages. After spawning they lose body weight and condition and become kelts, which are emaciated and would be of no sporting or culinary interest, even if they were not properly protected by law on their return journey to the sea.

It is well documented that salmon do not feed on their return to freshwater; authenticated instances of food discovered in their stomach contents on this journey are rare or dubious. However, they will rise to flies and take artificial flies, spoons, spinners, worms etc. The fact that they do so apparently without any intention of swallowing would suggest that this action relates to habit or memory from the time at sea when, judging by their weight gains, their feeding would have been voracious. Alternatively it could be an act of aggression, possibly to safeguard the chances of survival of their eventual progeny by eliminating potential predators or competitors for food supplies in waters often not abundantly rich in nutrients. We do not know exactly why they should take these offerings but often the flies and lures employed are very noticeable in the water, if not positively gaudy – consciously or unconsciously appealing to the rapacity of the species. Whilst it may be disconcerting that we cannot establish the reasons why flies are taken by non-feeding fish, we can take comfort from the fact that they are.

Whilst the sea trout displays many similar aspects of life style, it does not fast totally on its return journey to rivers and lakes and can be taken on flies and lures which may be reminiscent of food items related to its life in either the sea or freshwater.

The stillwater pursuit of these migratory fish (on their passage through lake, loch or lough systems) is, regrettably, a relatively fringe area of still-water fly fishing and can therefore only be given passing mention in a book of this kind. For those fortunate enough to have the opportunity to sample this rather specialised area, specific local knowledge and experience is highly recommended. Whilst it is not always easy to obtain such knowledge in advance, the letting agents or the local tackle dealers serving the area may be able to give details of the normal dates when migratory fish are available in lake or loch systems, and advice on preferred tackle and tactics. But the nature of the quarry is often unpredictable so do not be too reticent at trying other fly fishing tactics – providing of course that any local rules governing the fishing allow them. Sometimes tradition denies locals their full chances through a reluctance to give other methods or flies a try. The stranger is no slave to tradition and may fare better as a result.

Reservoirs

There is another type of stillwater which is relatively new and is offering the opportunity of game fishing in highly populated areas to anglers who would otherwise have very little, if any, local opportunity, and which has been instrumental in creating a new cradle of culture in game-fishing. The waters in question are water-supply reservoirs. These were created or developed primarily to supply water for cities and industries in their area and as a consequence they are often convenient to populated areas.

The game-fishing potential of the earlier reservoirs would not have been viewed as a matter of consequence, except possibly as a potentially interesting private resource for the water companies' management. It is not clear how some of them came to be stocked with trout and become the foundation of a new angling culture, but I do recall reading that the residents in the area surrounding Hanningfield Reservoir in Essex were plagued by the very heavy hatches of mosquito-like chironomids (or 'buzzers' as most anglers would term them), which were viewed as a serious nuisance. It was said that trout were introduced as a form of biological control and, since the younger, faster-growing fish, would be more effective as feeders on this food form and tend to feed on larger food items near the bottom as they approached maturity, angling would be necessary to cull the grown-on fish, and a restocking policy would have to be introduced because of the lack of spawning facilities. Whether this is correct or not and whether the residents saw a reduction of the chironomid fly hatch nuisance in the vicinity of the water as a result is not really important, except of course to those directly concerned. What is important to the rest of us is that reservoir fly fishing became available to a new and, at that stage, unprepared group of anglers.

On more fertile agricultural land, the water has often tended to be much more alkaline and with a higher content of soluble nutrients encouraging plant growth, which offers both protection and food for organisms in the food chain. In particular the alkaline levels are very important in providing the calcium required for the body-shell and skeletal development of food forms as well as for the trout. Where the alkalinity is high food also tends to be more abundant, and this can create very high differences in the growth rate of the fish in the water. Comparing acid (pH 5.0 to 6.5) and alkaline (pH 7.0 to 8.5) waters, the fish in the latter can grow to double the length in two or three years. This will of course equate to a corresponding difference in body weight. Alkalinity is not the only cause however; recently constructed reservoirs in agricultural areas also have the benefit of fertilisers, which are leached out by rainfall from the fields and into the streams and rivers which supply them.

Another factor in water fertility is daylight, which is required for the growth of plant and phytoplankton (small organisms). This is needed for photosynthesis, which of course can only occur to the depth at which sunlight can effectively penetrate, the sun's rays being absorbed by the upper water layers. In lowland situations with gently contoured landscapes, greater areas of flooded land are likely to be within this productive depth range than in hilly areas with precipitous fall-offs and steep gradients which lead quickly into water too deep for good light penetration. These circumstances give unprecedented growth rates in richer alkaline waters of overall moderate depths.

Some of the early reservoir anglers would have been established fly fishers more used to lakes or lochs in less fertile areas or to brook or river fishing. Their earlier experience would have done little to prepare them for the new situation. Their existing fishing tackle and styles were perhaps a necessary starting point, but rapid readjustment would be called for. In very fertile waters and with little early competition from other fish species, growth rates were startling by any standards and the pioneer anglers on these waters would have been astounded at the size and strength of the fish stocks.

This was a totally novel situation and of course attracted numerous new followers, many without previous fly fishing experience but excited by the unique opportunities on offer. With no traditions, and with enthusiastic newcomers who had a lot to learn and were unfettered by earlier concepts, a new culture in angling was rapidly forged. Whilst it would not be accurate to suggest that other methods of fly fishing were not examined, from both the U.K. and elsewhere, they were subject to close examination as to their relevance to this new situation and the best and most appropriate tackle and techniques were distilled from the established order. Where they did not exist or fell short of requirements, many eager and enquiring minds were applied to producing acceptable answers. Reservoir stillwater fly fishing was – and still is – an area where older views are under constant challenge and new technology and concepts always welcomed for critical examination relatively free from prejudice. It is true to say that, for the U.K. generally, the development of reservoir fly fishing has extended and revitalised the interest in freshwater game angling and has had very far-reaching implications throughout the sport generally, bringing in new participants, new tackle concepts, new techniques, new philosophies, new understandings, new enthusiasm and new appreciation to benefit all its branches.

Modern stillwater fly fishing reservoirs tend to fall into two very distinct types, each with a decidedly different management philosophy. The larger public-supply reservoirs (Grafham, Rutland Water, Hanningfield etc.), with large quantities of water, have tended to develop a strategy of providing an environment which is as natural as possible under the circumstance. The fact that trout are in the water in the first instance, without spawning facilities to enable them to maintain a natural population, is in itself of course unnatural, but apart from their introduction to the water little is done to upset the natural course of events – with the exception of sometimes reducing the level of coarse-fish competition by trapping or netting.

The introductions, in virgin waters, have been fingerlings or very small fish in large numbers (usually rainbows, with a smaller proportion of brown trout), to grow on in the nutrient-rich waters. After a while of course stocking with very small fish such as these is not practical. If the water is open to angling, small fish which are not wise to the ways of the world would be a nuisance to anglers, who in handling undersized fish to return them could cause unacceptable damage. In addition, the more established waters would have a well-established population of larger fish, many of which would be potential predators of the small fingerlings. It is therefore necessary to stock with fish which are at least large enough to be relatively safe from other fish predation and also of a size which does not require the angler to return catches to the water, with the attendant risk of injury. The tendency is therefore to restock on a regular basis – in relation to catch estimates – with fish at, or slightly above, the typical 12 in (30 cm) minimum size.

With faster-growing rainbow trout, normally the greater proportion of stocked species, fish of this size are relatively young and become 'street-wise' quite rapidly. In addition, from this size, their growth in open water containing a rich food supply can be very rapid in summer conditions. The water companies which control large waters are therefore obliged to make concessions to practical circumstances in their stocking policies, but they adhere to the provision of fishing which is as near as possible natural and stocked fish which escape the initial hazards do become very quickly effectively 'wild', often with vast areas of water in which to seek refuge and education. The stocking density in large reservoirs is usually quite low and from a game-fish point of view, unlikely to put natural food supplies under any serious pressure.

The second type of water is smaller stillwaters which have proliferated in recent years. They obviously have to maintain a higher population relative to their size, otherwise they would find it difficult to attract sufficient anglers to be commercially viable. Their turnover of fish per acre is inevitably much greater in both numbers and weight, and as a consequence the potential for the unsupplemented rapid growth of stocked fish is much lower. Inevitably, therefore, in order to attract anglers, many of whom are honest enough to admit to being attracted by the possibility of large fish, the stocking policies have to be different from those of the large reservoirs. Significantly larger fish are stocked in these waters; indeed many of them compete for anglers with the prospect of very large fish indeed – at appropriately very high prices.

Many anglers appreciate this facility, whilst others say it is not for them; it is a matter of personal choice. It certainly stimulates the rapid growth of fish-farming techniques. The popular fishing press has an apparently endless succession of photographs of self-conscious captors struggling to support slippery fish of well over 10 lb (4.5 kg) – often known to have been introduced to the water only a day or so previously. I suspect that devotees of one type of water will make only rare appearances on the other. The skills and techniques required will differ, and so will the basic philosophies in their approach to and expectation from their sport.

As I have said, the rise in the provision of stillwater trout fishing has established the rainbow trout as a major sporting resource in British angling. Originating from North America it has several differing forms and is an extremely well adapted and obliging addition to our waters. From the producer's point of view it is a rapid-growing and early-maturing fish which greatly facilitates quick and economic productions for stocking. Cash is not tied up too long waiting for a saleable product, and with high conversion rates food bills are reduced which, with the shorter time scale, gives less opportunity for disease problems to occur.

From the fishery's viewpoint, the speed and relatively low cost of production makes the rainbow a viable proposition, and this is greatly enhanced by its popularity with their customers. It is much less prone to the dourness that the brown can exhibit, especially in the more mature stage.

It is, however, the views of the angler which have made the rainbow such a resounding success on the British stillwater scene. Whilst all anglers are aware of the naturally inherent and oft-displayed ability of all fish to be perverse and unco-operative enough to drive them to the point of despair, the rainbow is usually (but alas not always) the least moody in this respect. Whilst it is stocked in larger numbers and can therefore be expected to feature more frequently in catches, there is more to the rainbow than this! Anglers find that it is more gregarious in its habits for more of its life than the brown. All small fish tend to live in shoals, but the rainbow shows a positive tendency to remain in this social group up to a larger unit size – although even they will show an inclination to more isolationist existence when older and larger. On occasions rainbow shoals can include fish of 3 or 4 lb (1.4 to 1.8 kg) and sometimes more, and when these are encountered in a receptive mood the fortunate angler is in for a period of highly memorable activity!

On a large reservoir well frequented by anglers, the progress of a feeding shoal of rainbows can often be identified by a tight concentration of boats in a small area in the case of a static or slowly moving shoal, and by the 'Mexican wave' effect of bent rods along the bank in the case of a shoal moving with more determination and pace. The shoal effect is helpful to the angler in eliminating the need for fine tuning or precise requirements in selecting a fly. A single fish will swim to a fly, investigate it and either take or swim away. In a shoal the interest of one fish will be noted by several others and this interest will not be leisurely and detailed but competitive. Precise fly selection in terms of dressing, colour and size therefore becomes less critical and the odds of seeing the rod bend into another fish are increased.

It is no surprise therefore that rainbows, which shoal more at higher average weight (but possibly of similar age because of faster growth rates), feed more at or close to the surface, and feed more reliably than browns through the season, are greatly appreciated by the mass of stillwater fly anglers. As an added bonus the rainbow, once hooked, will be most likely to give a highly visual and exciting performance of long runs and athletic jumps out of the water in its attempts to get free. This is in distinct contrast to the rather sulky tug-of-war from the depths (often referred to as 'jagging') which takes place with a hooked brown trout.

Chapter 6

Bank fishing – where to start

For many anglers, the arrival at the water for a day's fishing involves a complex mix of emotions and concerns. There is the excitement of anticipation of the day's sport, which is heightened in our minds by the glorious uncertainties of what the day may hold. One day will produce the most memorable event in our angling career, be it the biggest fish of our life or the most difficult, the greatest number, the greatest bag weight – who knows? One day it will surely happen; will this be it?

Unless the weather conditions are extremely poor and depress our expectations, most of us approach the water with the awareness that the day is one of virgin opportunity. 'Mr Big', who has successfully frustrated the attempts of other anglers (and perhaps ourselves) in the past lurks in his deep, murky environment, blissfully unaware that his immunity may be about to come to a spectacular end. I find that as I travel to my selected venue my optimism gradually increases as I preview the day's events in the mind – that is until I am 2 or 3 miles from the water! Perhaps I associate the familiar objects on the final approach with the results of previous trips, but optimism gives way to realism and minor anxieties tend to creep into my mind in the form of doubts – small ones yes, but doubts nevertheless! Odd thoughts tend to drift in like, 'Is the water fishing well? Perhaps another day would be better.' These doubts are of course quickly dispelled, but most of us will arrive with an air of contrived nonchalance, beneath which our emotions are in a state of mild turmoil.

The excitement of fishing is a very personal and ever-changing blend of satisfactions and anxieties. Very occasionally I find myself arriving at the water in a relaxed and blasé state of mind. This may result from concentrated periods of fishing, tiredness or other factors which may have made me preoccupied or distracted. When this happens I feel cheated and miss the stimulating maelstrom of feelings which usually accompany tackling up and starting the day. I think that all of us have imprinted on our memory the excitement of our first successful day's fishing, the throat-drying and hand-shaking thrill of the first contact with our quarry, followed after an apparent eternity of doubt by the incredulous confirmation of capture – the fish in the landing net, gleaming with vibrant sheen and colour, violently spraying water droplets in all directions with its powerful muscular body contortions.

Finding the right area to fish upon arrival, having acquired a permit for the day, we turn to the water for the business in hand. On very large waters this in itself necessitates the first decision. Do you drive to another point on the water or do you start fishing within walking distance of the lodge or hut? If you have fished the water before you will have some previous experience to call on, and other factors such as wind speed and direction will guide you. But if you have no previous experience of a very large water and no clear idea of the local geography, what can you do?

You can always take the bull by the horns and wander off to start building up your experience for the future. Some people are very independent and prefer to find out for themselves. However, most prefer to benefit from the knowledge of others. It is usual for large waters to have fishery wardens in attendance at civilised hours, someone dispensing permits and often a shop or counter selling angling requisites such as spools of nylon, lines, flies etc. These people will normally have up-to-date knowledge of the water and will be prepared to give advice on what areas are fishing well, which flies and techniques have been found to work best and so on, and if you are new to the water or visiting it after a long period of absence, it is certainly worth while seeking this information. If nobody associated with the fishing management can provide it, other anglers in the area will virtually always respond sympathetically to such a request, particularly from a newcomer. I personally derive as much pleasure from seeing another angler succeed from advice or flies I have supplied as I do from my own attainment – always providing that this success is kept within respectable limits!

If you are given advice on your position and tactics, you will have to decide whether to accept it or not. The novice may not appreciate this, but experienced anglers who are in the habit of chatting to fishery staff will know that the quality of advice can vary, and under some circumstances it can also be disturbingly inconsistent. However, if you are totally new to the water you have nothing better to base your decision on – unless of course the conditions make following the advice inadvisable. For instance if your informant suggests fishing in a wholly unprotected spot direct into the teeth of a howling gale, it is wise to take the ensuing problems into account. But assuming that there is no apparent reason to doubt the advice and it is practical to follow it, then it makes sense to make for the suggested area. *En route*, or even before you set out, other factors can give you clues as to where it would be prudent to begin, or perhaps to try next. The wind direction and strength will have a major effect. It will be helpful and less tiring to have it working with you than fight against it all day – although you should be prepared for this if necessary. If you can see the water, concentrations of other anglers in specific areas would normally suggest that these places may be fishing well. If you cannot see the water but the car park areas are well filled you could make the same assumption about the adjacent areas. This assumption could

Above: Bank fishing, even on a big water, can be intimate in character.

Below: Small stillwaters call for a more stealthy approach.

Above: Fishing the summer evening rise at Rutland Water. *(Peter Gathercole)*

Below: A heavy rainbow from the bank. *(Peter Gathercole)*

Above: Playing a good loch trout hooked at range. *(Peter Gathercole)*

Below: Last stages of an exciting tussle. *(Peter Gathercole)*

Above: Good day, good surroundings and good sport. *(Peter Gathercole)*

Below: Playing deep at Rutland Water. *(Peter Gathercole)*

Above: Boat action in the North Arm at Rutland Water.

Below: The extra dividend of remoter areas is freedom from crowds and impressive scenery.

Above: Loch style fishing from a boat – Rutland Water. *(Peter Gathercole)*

Below: Playing a big brownie caught deep

Above: Playing two fish from a boat can present welcome problems.

Below: Nearly there – a well conditioned rainbow comes to the net.

Another good rainbow succumbs to a black lure.

prove erroneous if large groups of friends have driven to the water in convoy and prefer not to separate, but generally there is a reason for anglers to group together, and success breeds success.

Having arrived at your chosen location, you have to decide where precisely to begin. You will rarely be treated to the sight of fish rising with feverish abandon in an obvious feeding frenzy. The water itself will be rather featureless and not unduly helpful. On most days however you will note that the 'stillwater' is not actually still. Under the influence of the wind, the surface will be moving, with waves which clearly indicate the direction and speed of the movement. Once you cast out the line, it will be subject to these forces and you should make an assessment of what the effect will be and whether, for the equipment and style you intend to employ, these effects will enhance or diminish the chance of agreeable and rewarding sport. As a result, some adjustment to your original ideas (based on your observations at your last visit when appropriate) may be called for.

In addition you should take account of the physical characteristics of the area. Although the subsurface features of the water will be obscured, those of the surrounding terrain will not. The contours and slopes of the ground that run down to the water from the surrounding land are unlikely to change dramatically at the water's edge and can be expected to continue, to some extent at least, below the water. Even on an unfamiliar water, therefore, you can begin to build up an understanding of the likely subsurface configurations of deeps and shallows and start to take these into account so that you fish at depths that are likely to be productive. These depths, of course, will vary according to circumstances, but on waters where fishing pressure is high, very shallow water is unlikely to hold confident, taking fish except at dawn or possibly dusk.

In artificially constructed reservoirs, where previous land areas have been flooded by the construction of dams, the dams themselves can give interesting fishing depths, depending on their style of construction. Where fishing is allowed from the area, the depth of water off the dam face is usually obvious. However, in the raising of levels and subsequent flooding, fish-holding areas can be created by submerged features such as roads and tracks, hedges, avenues of trees, drainage ditches etc., which may run right down to the water's edge and continue into the water. The effects of these features can persist for very many years and they are well worth investigating. Other locations of advantage are points which separate small bays and other promontories which protrude into the water and allow greater coverage and access to water of more variable depths.

Time and experience will give you an instinctive awareness of the more comfortable and potentially most productive spots to start. Comfort may seem to be secondary to productiveness but when you are fishing for a whole day, under late spring or early autumn conditions, it can be a long time from first light to the end of the evening and you may get greater pleasure from working with, rather than fighting against, the prevailing conditions.

The novice may have a suspicion that the best spots are those already taken by someone else, and this may well be perfectly true. However, it should not be a cause for despondency since conditions will invariably change during the course of a day and with it the behaviour patterns of the fish. 'Hot spots' may develop well-deserved reputations but they can cool down rapidly under some conditions, and the fish will become accessible from previously less favoured areas.

It should be clearly stated at this point that, whilst there may be indications as to the most promising available starting point, the fish themselves may have different ideas about where the conditions they need at any given time can be found. Never, therefore, be bound by predetermined ideas or rooted to an unproductive spot. Be prepared to experiment and find out for yourself where the best chances of success for the style being used are to be found. Only the fish know the full story of what is happening in their own environment. The angler's experience, logic and reasoning is fine and often very helpful, but sometimes simple trial-and-error elimination techniques are called for. One of the things that make angling pleasure so enduring is that our build-up of experience and confidence also includes an awareness that we do not, and can never expect to, know the full picture in the face of so many complex variables and features that are invisible to us.

Having said that, most anglers believe that their chances of success are increased by a reasoned approach to the job in hand, and quite rightly so. If your reasoning is well founded and you draw the right conclusions, then you will generally arrive at places where fish, or concentrations of fish, are present in above-average quantities and more fish will be covered by your flies. This being the case the chances of acceptance should be better. The awareness of this fact has a further effect. If you feel that you are fishing better water, it will intensify your alertness and reasoning on what to offer and how to present it, as the confidence that you are in one of the right spots will avoid the distraction of wondering where you should be moving to next.

The two main reasons why trout will be found in a particular spot, as far as we can tell, are shelter from uncomfortable conditions – very bright sunlight, the level of oxygen in the water or adverse temperatures (too hot or too cold) – and the availability of or the search for food.

When you are bank fishing, you are restricted to covering the water you can access by casting from the shore – or close to it if you are wading. This offers very few options when fish seeking shelter from uncomfortable conditions take to deeper water. Clearly in such circumstances you must assess where deeper water is fishable from the bank. Steeply sloping dam walls are an obvious option where fishery rules allow angling from them, which is not always the case because of safety considerations. Where it is allowed always remember that the area near the water's edge can be very slippery with wet algae. Losing your footing on the hard concrete can in itself damage both you and your tackle, but scrambling back up the wet slippery slope is also very difficult, especially without studded soles. Apart from the dam, other options include the areas which shelve down to deeper water more sharply than others. Look at the steepest slopes entering the water and work on the assumption that they will continue beneath the surface; this is not always the case, but it is more usual and in any event it is worth a try in the absence of other information.

With regard to the search for food, you are somewhat more in control of the situation and your powers of reasoning can be called into play more profitably. The diet of fish on most stillwater locations will be mainly of aquatic origin and relatively small. This diet will, at times, include small fish, which will be fairly strong swimmers. Other food items will include insects at differing stages of development, molluscs, crustaceans etc., which will not be strong swimmers and at times will be carried through the water wholly or partly at the mercy of currents. These currents will very often be created by wind action on the water surface. The wave action will clearly indicate the surface movement direction but, since it cannot pile up the water on the shore onto which it blows, there will be other, less obvious, compensating movements of water at or below the surface, which will be governed by the configuration of the shore line, the wind and the bed of the lake in the area of the shore. These currents within the water will clearly carry along with them food items which are suspended, or swimming weakly, in them. Where the effects of these currents become concentrated, as by shallowing water or current convergence, so will the number or rate of incidence of subsurface food items carried by them. This effect is of great consequence to feeding fish and, as a result, to the angler, who will always be searching for areas in which feeding fish congregate.

There are, of course, other very direct visual indications of the presence of fish, such as their movement. These movements will generally be caused by fish taking food items at or just below the surface, disturbing the water in a whorl on the surface which can be seen or heard, or the head, back or tail arching through the waves or ripples. These feeding movements which disturb the water surface are called rises and are an indication of the presence of feeding fish. It is clearly worth covering these areas. Even if no fish are actually observed, if there is strong evidence of aquatic flies hatching from a spot it is fair to assume that the fish are aware of this and perhaps feeding slightly deeper on the nymphs or pupae as they rise to the surface to hatch. It is very important to remember that fly fishing is not simply surface oriented; it is very much a three-dimensional exercise. One can be in the right spot but miss out by fishing at the wrong depth. And the 'right' depth is not fixed; it can change, moving either deeper or higher in the water, at any moment. One aims to be in the right place, at the right depth, at the right time, with the right fly in the right size and fished in the right way – quite simple really!

Setting up

Having arrived at a likely starting point on the water, you will be keen to get into action as soon as possible. If you can see fish moving, you will be desperate to get amongst them before they 'go off'. There is nothing unduly complicated in setting up but it is worthwhile being methodical about it to avoid possible frustrations later. In putting the rod sections together it helps to ensure that the rings are in line before the ferrules or spigots joining the sections are pushed together. Most modern anglers use carbon fibre (graphite) rods with spigot joints which, like the older style of brass ferrules, can bind or stick on occasions. They are also subject to wear and some form of lubrication may be helpful. For brass ferrules, the time-honoured method is to rub them quickly in one's hair; the transfer of a minute amount of oil from the hair was sufficient. This does not work for everyone of course and the follically disadvantaged will have to apply more conventional lubricant. For spigot joints many people carry the stub end of a candle; an occasional light wipe with this will keep the spigot from binding and help reduce wear.

With the rod set up the reel is fixed to the handle with either screw fittings or sliding rings. It pays to ensure that the reel is fixed securely to the rod – I can assure you that having the reel fall off whilst playing a fish is very disconcerting indeed. Ensure that all retaining rings are securely fixed over the reel fittings. If they are not secure, make them so with adhesive tape, rubber bands, string, wire or whatever is available to prevent the reel from working loose. Draw off some of the line, or leader if in situ, from the reel and make certain the adjustment of the check mechanism is set correctly to allow the reel to give line freely, but not so freely as to overrun when line is pulled briskly off. This will cause a bird's nest or tangle which will prevent the reel operating and cause breakage and the loss of the fish. Remember to set the reel tension or check mechanism in such a way as to prevent spool overruns, not to apply pressure to the fish. Avoid setting it so that there is any risk of breakage through very sudden pulls on the line. Any pressure you need to apply to a fish can be applied by controlling the line through the hand with light pressure from your fingers or using the palm of your hand as a brake on the exposed rim of the reel, assuming that your reel has one. If it does not then you are at a small disadvantage in fish control.

When setting up and initially drawing off line or leader from the reel, make sure that the length drawn off is longer than the rod. Then carefully thread the end through *all* the rod rings, making sure that the line does not become wrapped round the rod and being careful not to stand on it in the process! It is also better not to lay the rod out on the ground when setting up as you risk treading on it as well. With the leader threaded through all rings, pull the fly line itself up and through them so that the end is well outside the tip ring, otherwise the weight will pull the lighter leader back through and out of the rings. Then either attach the leader or adjust its length and tippet (end section) strength as required and select and tie on the flies – the usual method is the tucked or untucked half-blood knot (see figure 54). When the flies are tied, check that they are secure and that the knot does not slip – avoiding impaling your fingers on the hook in the process.

Before you start fishing remember that a leader straight off the reel can display 'memory' (i.e. remain in curls) and be reluctant to cut through the surface film. So stretch it if you did not do so before fixing the flies. Degreasing by rubbing the leader with a mixture of fuller's earth and a liquid detergent will also be helpful. The front part of the fly line itself will also generally benefit from a stretch. In addition be prepared and make sure the landing net is conveniently placed to hand and ready for immediate action.

Having arrived at a starting point, if you have continuing success there, there is clearly no reason to move on unless you are catching only small, obviously recently stocked fish. Whilst we are all grateful for the attention of 'stockies' at times, better fish have much more appeal. However, if you do not meet with success at your starting point it does not make sense to take root there. If after a fair trial without contact in one area, look around to assess how others are faring or where the chances of action may be better. Constantly moving round the water cuts down on actual fishing time, but moving intelligently will increase your chances of contacting feeding fish and there is no point in remaining at an unproductive area, as your confidence will suffer. Arriving at a fresh likely spot, on the other hand, will immediately increase your confidence and consequently your enjoyment. This means fishing with your mind in gear rather than in neutral – which itself increases the chance of engagement and the likelihood of reacting quickly enough when the opportunity arises to set the hook.

Chapter 7

Fishing the lure

U nless they have gravitated from other methods of fly fishing with which they initially feel more comfortable, most anglers on reservoirs will probably start fishing with lures. Perhaps because of this, experience often eventually leads them away from this style and for some reason they begin to look on it as an inferior or less respectable approach. This view is very difficult to justify. Regarding lure fishing as the sole approach and ignoring other absorbing and rewarding methods will be less fulfilling than a more flexible attitude. But equally, disregarding this method in favour of other styles is also needlessly limiting. All methods have their place and if they fit comfortably into the regulations and philosophy of the water in question there is no merit in arbitrarily excluding any particular approach without good reason. Most of us will have our own preferred methods of fishing and it is only natural to pursue them with more conviction, but in so doing we should resist any tendency to disregard other forms when they may be more productive. Seeking to pass on our own particular enthusiasm to others is fine but if in so doing we also manage to relay our personal prejudices, which may impede the pleasure of others, we will be doing them no favours whatsoever.

How lures work

Technically all artificial flies should be regarded as lures. However, lure fishing, in the current fly fishing context, is generally taken to mean fishing with a fly designed to attract the attention of a fish, not exclusively by representation of a known food item. Lures often are large, distinctively coloured and incorporate a degree of mobility. This mobility is not just the result of the high speed at which many are pulled through the water. Lures are constructed in such a way as to present a fluttering or throbbing movement as the water pressure acts on the materials, which sends visual and vibratory messages to the fish, inviting it to investigate further. Whilst many lures, by virtue of their size and coloration, will not (to us at any rate) resemble anything found naturally in the environment in which they are employed, it would not be true to say that no lures represent food items. Some, such as Appetisers, Muddler Minnows and various white and silver lures, are deliberately or coincidentally constructed to create the impression of fry or small fish, especially in distress. Others, such as black lures, can be representative of leeches and, with some imagination, others can be seen to have features in common with other items on the trout's diet. How any lure is actually perceived by the trout is of course another matter and, happily, likely to be a mystery to us for all time.

Essentially, lures are most successful when moving through the water, often quite quickly, although this is by no means always the case. We may like to think that the lure is taken by the fish because of the impression that it is a welcome, larger than average, food item, but considering the unusual constructions and psychedelic colour schemes of some lures, curiosity must also rank as a motivation. Moreover, as some fish may become territorial, aggression can also be a reason for the responsive take of a lure.

We do not usually know when a fish is interested in our flies, although we fish at our best and derive most pleasure from fishing when we can convince ourselves that this is likely at any moment. You should therefore operate the lure in such a way that it is tantalisingly attractive to the fish we believe are always there. Since lures are a very imperfect representation of the real thing – where a natural counterpart actually exists – an element of caution on the part of the fish is natural. Your task is to overcome this caution by skilful manipulation of the lure, using the line to impart natural and enticing movements to it, in order to increase its attraction to following fish. This may in itself be enough to create sufficient interest in the fish for it to seize the lure in its mouth and turn away, thus advising you of its presence by the pull you will feel on the line. All you have to do is then set the hook by striking. This is not the violent action which may be suggested by the word, but involves quickly tightening into the fish before it recognises its error and ejects the lure. When lure fishing this hooking is often obligingly done by the fish itself by turning away from the direction in which the fly is travelling. This self-hooking is more usual when the lure is being retrieved briskly through the water.

It is not, of course, always that simple, and a fish will often follow a lure, interested in it but not actually taking. It may signify its presence by quickly nipping or plucking gently at the lure. We can feel this brief resistance through the fly line on retrieve but you should always assume that in the absence of a solid take or other contact, a fish is there and needs its interest quickened. You can make any following fish feel that it may lose its prey by simulating evasion tactics in the lure. This can be done in several ways: by speeding up the retrieve, by modifying the angle of retrieve by changing the angle of the rod, or by stopping the retrieve and then restarting. This last method can be very effective as a fish following close will come onto the lure quickly and be obliged to react positively – either take it or avoid it. Also, stopping the retrieve will take pressure off the lure, which will then sink as though it is diving to escape and trigger a positive take by the fish. This is especially true when lures are weighted at the head with small quantities of lead (Dog Nobblers, Tadpoles etc.), and the efficiency of these lures suggests that they are a very potent weapon for the angler to exploit.

There is some similarity between lure fishing and playing with a kitten by pulling a length of wool in to tease its hunting instincts into play. The difference with lure fishing is that we usually cannot see the lure at the end of the line and must use our imagination to make the terminal tackle irresistible. Personally, I have little confidence in fishing with lures that have no mobility incorporated in their construction and feel much more confident using ones which wiggle and pulsate enticingly through the water on retrieve at varying speeds. An inert item pulled through the water does not convey the illusion of life and accordingly I am drawn to using lures which respond to passage through the water with the maximum movement of their parts (fur or feather) and an undulating course through the water conferred by slight weighting. One problem with fluttering elements is their tendency to become caught under the bend of the hook and cause the lure to spin in an unappetising and unnatural fashion. One type of lure which is not prone to this annoying tendency, and which includes many desirable features, as well as being very easy indeed for even a novice fly tyer to create is the Tadpole. This is a smaller version of the Dog Nobbler,

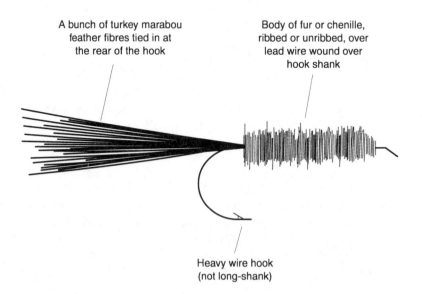

A bunch of turkey marabou
feather fibres tied in at
the rear of the hook

Body of fur or chenille,
ribbed or unribbed, over
lead wire wound over
hook shank

Heavy wire hook
(not long-shank)

Figure 11   A simple Tadpole lure

which has a pronounced heavy metal ball at the head and is often painted with 'eyes'. Being only very lightly weighted, the Tadpole is much safer to cast and more pleasant to fish with, and I recommend it.

Lure fishing technique

To fish the lure, cast it out and draw it enticingly through the water by retrieving the line, with the object of teasing a fish into taking it or following it with the intention of taking it. If a fish is interested enough to follow, it is your job to induce it to take by convincing it that the lure is of interest – and likely to get away. The best type and speed of retrieve depends on circumstances. On some days only a constant, uninterrupted retrieve is likely to be of interest. On others only erratic retrieves, with the lure diving and darting around, will work. Similarly some occasions demand only slow retrieves whilst on others only fast retrieves result in a firm connection. It is up to you to decide the best technique on the day, and constantly to monitor any change in the fish's requirements during the course of the day; your fickle quarry can change their requirements very often and very quickly.

Another variable factor is the depth at which to fish. This variation depends on two factors: change of retrieve speed (the faster the retrieve the greater the pressure on the line and the higher in the water it will ride) and the specific gravity of the line itself. A floating line with a fast retrieve will keep the lure close to the surface whilst a slower retrieve will allow the lure to sink lower in the water. A slow-sinking line will take it deeper for the same retrieve speed and medium-sink, fast-sink and very-fast-sink lines will all tend to take the lure progressively deeper for the same retrieve speeds.

By now, anyone who considered that lure fishing was simply a case of 'chuck it and chance it' may be thinking that perhaps there is more to it! Thoughtful and imaginative lure fishing can be both exciting and rewarding. With a lure there is normally much more movement through the water; more water can be systematically covered and on many days even when fish are reluctant actually to take the lure and so indicate their presence, they are often inclined to follow it in. They can be seen, if the lure is high in the water, by the disturbance they make or possibly by their dorsal fins or tails breaking the surface or the flash of their flanks as they turn back for the safety of the deeper water. In the case of lures fished more deeply it is often possible to see the dark shape of the back of the fish below the surface, turning away and making for deeper water when the lure approaches you ready for recasting. Wearing polarised sunglasses will help you to see the fish, and is highly recommended in any event to protect your eyes from the mirror effect of glare from the water and, perhaps more importantly, from the hook of a fly that is out of control.

71

The importance of eye protection cannot be overstated, but when it also benefits our fishing efficiency it really cannot be ignored.

The effective coverage of the water through the use of lures can be very useful in determining whether the water you are fishing actually contains fish, since they are likely to betray their presence in their reaction, one way or another, to the lure. Unless they are very confident in other methods on the day and water concerned, many anglers choose to start their fishing with a lure to determine where the fish are and what they may respond to. A lure can save you time by revealing the presence of fish, although a negative result should not be construed as indicating absence of fish – they may be preoccupied with natural food items which the lure cannot represent.

In the search for fish, and for optimum fishing depth and speed, it is helpful to develop a system of 'combing' the water – although such a system should not be applied too rigidly as intuition or instinct can be a potent force. This systematic approach is illustrated in figure 12. From a given spot on the bank (position A) you can fish on an arc, gradually increasing the distance and varying the depth and speed of retrieve, and then either progress along the bank to repeat the process (position B) or wade in and repeat it (alternative position B). Either way you should cover new water, varying your depth and retrieve rate until you find one that is successful and worth repeating – always remembering that one swallow does not make a summer!

It goes without saying that, having found a successful combination of depth and speed and style of retrieve, that particular combination should be given more attention. But always be aware that the fish are fickle; they

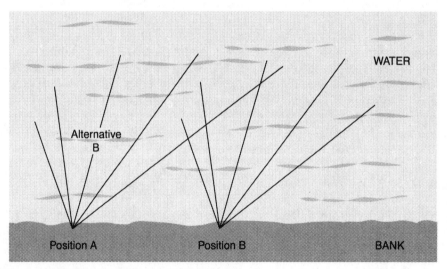

Figure 12   Covering the water systematically

may not all react in exactly the same way and they can all change their requirements at any time. So always be alert to possible alternatives and do not assume that having found a system that works it will bear fruit all day – be prepared to keep on the move and to try different tactics. Remember also that the more experienced and bigger fish did not get to be that way by responding in the same way as their less fortunate companions. Sometimes to get the better of individual fish you have to employ individual methods. Other variable factors in lure fishing involve the lures we use, especially their size, colour and construction.

Size

This is generally related to the size and type of hook on which the lure is tied. It normally ranges from a standard size 10 to a 4× (4 times normal) long-shank 4, single or double hooks, tied singly or in tandem. The size of a lure is perhaps not as critical as that of a fly tied to represent a specific food item, but it is an important feature in determining whether or not your offering is accepted by the fish, so experiment with the size as well as with other factors.

Colour

Another critical factor in fish response is the colour of the lure. Fish will often confine their attention to, or heavily favour, specific colours on a given occasion. Colour sensitivity is probably secondary to size in angling flies generally, but for lures it is often of greater significance. Many tend to incorporate a wide range of garish colours in an attempt to attract attention, but experience suggests that black is overwhelmingly the most regularly successful colour, followed by white. For situations where fish are difficult to attract, such as those feeding mainly on daphnia (very small water creatures which are virtually impossible to represent by artificial flies), hot-orange or lime-green lures can sometimes throw the most preoccupied fish off balance. These brighter colours are generally associated with higher summer temperatures, but are worth a try in difficult conditions at any time of the season.

Single colours will frequently work satisfactorily but for 'prospecting' work against varying underwater backgrounds, two contrasting colours will ensure greater visibility. My own favourite for the early season at Rutland Water, for instance, is just such a lure, a simple lightly weighted Tadpole I call the Ferret (for no other reason than that it is successful in searching for naive early-season fish). It has a body of blood-red seal's fur loosely teased out, ribbed with silver, and a 'tail' similar to the body length, or slightly longer, of a good bunch of mobile pure white turkey marabou plumes. I fish this with immense confidence as it invariably works like a charm in early season for me – and others to whom I have passed on copies. I do not think it has any special properties other than enticing movement and strong colour contrast, in colours that are reasonably natural – blood red in particular suggests food, either as wounded prey, or as the colour of fish gills and bloodworms (the larva of the chironomid) which are the mainstay of a trout's diet for much of the year in most waters.

Many people find that, overall, black lures bring results very reliably, particularly fished slowly and deeply in shallower water in early season or faster and just subsurface in warmer weather as the light fades in the evening during summer and autumn. In bright sunshine and warm summer conditions, especially in water coloured with algae, hot-orange or lime-green can also be effective, while in late summer and autumn, when fish are feeding on coarse fry and small fish, white lures can suggest the trout's preference. These are only guides, however, and it must be stressed that any colour is worth a try on any day if you are hard pressed to make contact, or even just to experiment – without trying something one can never be sure what the result would be.

On some days – not too many, so appreciate them when they come – virtually any colour will do, but it is more likely, if other factors are stable, that the fish will demonstrate a distinct preference for a specific colour. This colour preference can last for a number of days or just for part of a day, and on larger waters it may even be restricted to part of the water. Seasonal food availability may often give some clue as to a likely colour. For instance, when fish are clearly feeding on fry, white is a useful colour to try, especially when ribbed with silver because the lure then more closely resembles the food item that is currently available and favoured. Under such circumstances a lure can be considered as matching the dish of the day just as much as any other fly offering.

Construction

Anglers by and large are very resourceful and inventive, and it is inevitable that those with access to them will apply materials which may have been developed for a wide variety of other purposes to their hobby. As a result the basic range of lure construction materials is enriched by others from various technologies, which in turn give rise to new possibilities. Whether or not lures are viewed as 'traditional', the range of materials, both natural and synthetic, has been greatly extended for fly tying generally and more particularly for lures. These in turn have widened the range of construction techniques and the resultant water actions available.

Indeed, some constructions have got to the stage where it is highly debatable whether they conform to the spirit of fly fishing at all. A fish fry imitation carved from floating closed-cell plastic foam and glued to a long-shank hook, embellished with spirit-based marker pens and without any fur or feather fibre involved would seem to have very little in common with traditional fly tying – it is more like a plug. However, such a lure can be, and is, cast with a fly rod; is it really radically different from a lure laboriously created from spun deer fur, clipped to shape and similarly coloured to represent a small fish? The only difference is the basic materials, the techniques and the time and effort involved. Neither version uses truly traditional materials; does the fact that one is a natural material make a difference? There are moral issues involved here which have not been, and are not likely to be, universally addressed. Each water issues specific rules and regulations which the angler is obliged to conform to, and each angler subscribes to his own philosophy. The regulations vary, often inexplicably, from one water to another, and they are not always obviously logical or consistent. And within the framework of these rules each angler must decide what additional limitations, if any, he wants to apply. The temptation to make moral judgements, unasked, on behalf of others should be strongly resisted.

In general there are no rules or restrictions as such for fly fishing lures, but the expectation is that the end product will be fashioned from fur, feather, tinsel and silk (or their modern synthetic counterparts). Further, that the construction is expected to follow the techniques of the traditional dresser, updated as necessary, and not those of the blacksmith or plastics injection moulder! There are ethics of sporting behaviour involved which relate to but do not, except in formal stylised organised competitions, slavishly follow the past. There are also pragmatic considerations; the lures must be cast, in safety, with a fly rod! This fact alone is a limit on ingenuity, but it does not prevent further development. Early lures would have developed from representational wet flies, with the bodies extended on long-shank hooks but constructed of traditional materials such as seal's fur, wool, chenille, tinsel etc., and the wing tied longer and made of feather fibres or whole trimmed hackle feathers, in pairs or bunches, to give both movement in the water and a profile. (Hen hackles, which are softer, have more 'web' and give a more solid appearance as well as absorbing water more quickly for faster penetration of the surface film.) These lures are still in use and often also still incorporate throat hackles as a further throwback to small wet-fly origins.

Other materials and construction styles have now come onto the scene, together with new ways of using both old and new to bring fresh approaches to lures. One of the handicaps of long lure wings in feather is their tendency to wrap themselves round the hook and catch under the bend. This causes the lure to become unbalanced and to rotate or spin on retrieve through the water. Hair wings were one early innovation. Polar bear (once highly regarded but now as politically unacceptable as seal's

75

Figure 13   A 'Blond' style multiple wing

fur), squirrel tail, calf tail, buck tail etc., in a riot of colours, have all been – and still are – employed. These materials do not have much movement for small lures but for larger lures they are fine, although they are not easy to tie in securely and again have a tendency to lodge under the hook bend in vigorous casting. This is avoided to some extent in the 'blond' style of construction (see figure 13), where a second (or even a third) shorter wing tied further back down the body supports the main wing for more controlled movement. This style of dressing also gives more profile (a stronger silhouette), which may be helpful, especially in water coloured by disturbed mud particles or with algae in suspension.

Other relatively new materials to the U.K. scene have been deer and elk hair. These are interesting because the individual hair fibres are coarser and hollow. As a result they have natural floating tendencies, very much enhanced when the fibres are coated and sealed with modern floatants. This makes for better floating qualities when flies with such character are required, for instance adult sedge patterns, where the fibres can form dense floating wings, and daddy long legs, where the coarse fibres can be fashioned to form a body with good floating properties.

The advent of these newer materials from the U.S.A. also introduced a fly which originated there but which has established itself as a remarkably effective lure here under many circumstances, the Muddler Minnow. It was developed from a pattern originally dressed to represent a small fish with a pronounced, flattened head. To emulate the shape, bunches of deer hair were tied to a hook, without a base of wound thread, with a couple of turns of tying thread which was pulled tight. This had the effect of splaying the flared fibres round the hook shank like a collar. The process was repeated and the splayed material compressed to form a solid, untidy ball of deer hair. After being tied in, this was trimmed to the required size and shape with a pair of sharp, pointed scissors. The result was a seemingly solid but very light 'head'. The British version originally had a flat gold tinsel body with gold wire rib, a tail of short bunch oak turkey wing feather with a wing of grey squirrel's tail fibres over which was tied oak turkey wing-feather slips. Out of the water the result is unprepossessing but when floatant is applied to the clipped deer hair head and it is drawn through the water on a floating line in a good wave in summer conditions, the fish can go mad for it. Drawn briskly across the water it creates a disturbance which makes it easy to spot, but the bow wave caused by a good fish following it is even easier. When the retrieve is quickened the Muddler dives temporarily below rather than through the surface, causing a stream of air bubbles in its wake which can on occasions prove an irresistible trigger to following fish. Often if a fish follows for some time and does not take, this increase of pace will quicken its interest, as will stopping the retrieve and quickly restarting.

When the fish are onto the Muddler, it can sometimes be productive to ignore the usual rules of discreet fly presentation and advertise its presence by deliberately slapping it down on the water more vigorously. This is done by not just arresting the progress of the line through the rod rings but by giving a sharp tug to the line at the end of the cast, thus creating a quick turnover of the leader and lure. This can be a very exciting and addictive form of fishing, though physically tiring, and possibly nothing makes time pass faster than Muddler fishing on a good day. The early versions of the Muddler Minnow are still doing good service but its style of spun and clipped deer hair is now to be found on very many different types of flies, not all of them lures.

Perhaps the material which has done most to influence lure fishing since the post-war development of reservoir trout fishing is the discovery of the wonderful light, mobile, white turkey marabou feather. These long, down-like, fluffy white plumes are a by-product of commercial food production and when dry they are difficult to control; every slight air movement or disturbance sends them writhing about as though they are alive. They are easy to obtain, easy to dye, easy to tie in (especially when drawn through slightly moistened fingers and given a slight twist), and quite durable in use. When dry many marabou-based lures look more like a day-old chick than a fishing lure but when wet and drawn through the water the material condenses and pulsates in an extremely lifelike and enticing manner, even at low retrieve rates – in fact really fast retrieves cancel out the advantages of this material. It is now possible to have a small lure which will have an enticing action even when retrieved through the water at very slow speeds.

My own favourite form of Muddler uses this material in a very simple form (simplicity is something I favour). It is basically an unweighted Tadpole version of the Muddler with spun, clipped deer hair replacing the fur or chenille front body portion. The marabou tail is in white, black or brown and the deer-hair head in an appropriate matching colour (see figure 14). One has to ensure that the size and shape of the clipped head does not impede the hooking qualities of the gape of the hook.

The Muddler's appeal to the fish is not absolutely clear but there may be a clue in the fact that sick fry, with fungal growth around the head, making their distressed progress along the surface sometimes look remarkably similar to a slowly retrieved Muddler. In addition the similarity to the disturbance of hatching sedge flies skittering across the surface as they try to become airborne may evoke some compulsive reaction. Perhaps it is just a predator's response to a potential quarry seeking to escape, or the additional vibrations from the higher water resistance and turbulence of the head which may explain the fact that it can also be very successful fished on sinking lines at all depths. I particularly associate the Muddler, however, with summer fishing in a good breeze on the surface where the action is all visible.

One suggestion I would make, particularly during the summer months, concerns the end of the activity associated with the evening rise, once the sun goes off the water. Most anglers at this point elect to fish small flies or nymphs, and when darkness proper begins to set in, the fish appear to 'go off'. When this happens it is normally time to pack up, but before doing so try a few casts with a black lure pulled briskly across what is by then usually an unrippled glassy surface – it can very often have surpris-

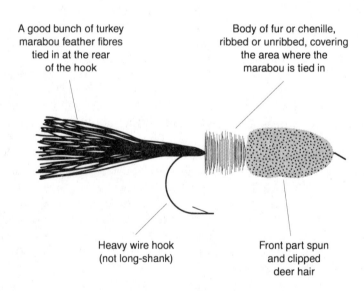

A good bunch of turkey marabou feather fibres tied in at the rear of the hook

Body of fur or chenille, ribbed or unribbed, covering the area where the marabou is tied in

Heavy wire hook (not long-shank)

Front part spun and clipped deer hair

Figure 14   A simple Tadpole Muddler lure

ingly effective results. I find that a black Tadpole Muddler is particularly effective and quite often produces the best fish of the day. Whatever the size it can be memorable, as playing a lively fish in the gathering darkness, not being entirely sure where it is, can certainly be tricky and gets the adrenalin flowing.

One aspect of fly fishing that is seldom applicable when lure fishing, is deciding when to strike. (As I have said this term is dangerously misleading, as the action is merely that of quickly 'tightening' into a fish to set the hook.) Because the lure is often (although by no means always) travelling quickly through the water, a fish taking will not only register its presence but quite frequently hook itself, especially if it is also turning away.

A lure may be taken by a following fish, however, which may maintain the same forward pace and not send such obvious signals to the angler. When that happens, the advice on when to react and tighten into a fish has to be the same with a lure as with any other form of fly. You should tighten whenever you feel there may be a reason to do so. This will not only be in response to obvious plucks and tugs but also to 'heaviness' on the line, any sense of something unusual or even sometimes untoward water movement in the vicinity of where you think your fly is. All experienced anglers will admit that they take many fish when responding to nothing physical at all – nothing seen, nothing felt, just a sense that it would be right to do so at that precise moment.

There is no doubt whatsoever that, whether the lure is one's favoured method or not, it can be very exciting indeed and is a fully legitimate means of fishing. There is no reason to feel that it is less acceptable than other methods, or to feel in any sense shy at using it. Most of us will have our favourite methods of taking fish at different stages in our angling development, but the fish are in the driving seat. I must admit that, like most anglers, I am drawn to representational small flies and nymphs fished delicately on light tackle, and I like to catch fish this way when there is an option. However, I basically like to catch fish and if my initial methods fail to work I do not give up, I adapt and try something else. This to me is the true essence of the sport. To subscribe arrogantly to the view that fish will be taken in a predetermined manner and in no other way despite any other circumstances seems wholly inconsistent with an activity where careful deliberation and a constructive and educated approach is what brings success.

I do not seek to promote the lure over any other method, but most strongly support it as an option, on the grounds that it is legitimate, revealing and rewarding, that it can be responsive to intelligent application and above all that it can be effective, exciting and great fun. It can be, and usually is, more disturbing to the water and fish than other methods, and for this reason it would be extremely discourteous to use it too close to someone who is already quietly fishing small flies or nymphs, with the risk of spoiling their sport. 'Too close' can be determined by common sense, and defined as where there is even the slightest risk of causing disturbance within or immediately adjacent to the area cast to by another angler. This basic rule of courtesy applies equally of course to any other style of fishing – always respect others' right to fish without undue disturbance.

Chapter 8

Small flies

Wet flies

Historically fishing with wet flies predates other methods and originated from very early techniques based on a visual awareness of the fish's feeding – i.e. at the water surface. Attempts were made to emulate their food items from materials then available. Practical difficulties such as the unavailability of modern silicone floatants, frustrated attempts to create a floating fly; as the fly imitations absorbed water they would start to sink. When this happened the early anglers would have been gratified to discover that the attractiveness of the fly to the fish was often not diminished.

To many anglers, fishing small wet flies is the essence of stillwater fly fishing. There is a definite charm to using flies which normally relate directly to aspects of the trout's current menu with regard to size, colour and shape, and which can be fished to good effect at or below the surface with a high degree of delicacy on relatively light tackle.

The small fly fishing which is employed widely today is often referred to as loch style and is derived from the traditional form of fishing, which has not changed radically since very early times. There have inevitably been changes, even on remote lochs, due to advancements in tackle design and construction materials. When one realises the problems of yesteryear, with heavy and cumbersome rods of lancewood, greenheart, bamboo etc., heavy brass reels and lines of silk with tacky dressings which absorbed water and had dreadful 'shooting' properties, it is a wonder the anglers' enthusiasm remained undiminished.

My own introduction to fly fishing was in fact through traditional loch fishing with small wet flies. Even though the tackle I employed then was nothing like today's products (a split-cane rod with a tapered silk line, soon replaced by a level plastic 'floating' line – which did actually float on a good day), I was an instant convert. To this day very light tackle on a remote Scottish loch, either roaming the banks or drifting in a boat – typically of very suspect safety standards – remains to me the quintessence of true fly fishing. Today many people, especially in England, start fishing on carefully managed lakes or reservoirs and are at the same time spoilt by the size and number of the fish available to them and deprived of a dimension of satisfaction in pitting their wits and reaction speeds against small, lightning-fast and very wild 'brownies'. The sheer delight of these fish from waters which are normally peat-stained and acid in breathtakingly beautiful and isolated surroundings more than compensates for their lack of size, as they leave the water revealing vibrant colours and markings which are quite exquisite but which unfortunately fade some minutes after capture.

The basics of small wet fly fishing remain generally the same today as a century ago. Usually three flies (although it can be one, two or four) are fished using a leader with short droppers – small spurs of nylon approx 4 in (10 cm) long made by leaving one end of a blood knot or water knot untrimmed or trimmed to the desired length. They are traditionally fished either from the bank or wading, but more usually from a drifting boat, on a short line. The short line gives one control over the bob fly – the fly nearest the rod, which is generally a bushy fly selected for its disturbance factor as it is dribbled across or through the surface in a mildly bouncing action. The reason for this action is to advertise its presence to fish, which will have their attention on the surface in their search for food. Apart from the attention-grabbing disturbance of the surface, it also simulates the struggle of an aquatic fly trying to break clear of the restraints of the surface film and disappear into the air, out of the reach of a hungry trout. It is therefore a positive challenge to a trout to secure a mouthful before all hope is gone and it is a form of an 'induced take', where the fish's interest is quickened by fear of loss. The attractive 'bobbing' action is more effectively achieved with a light line used in conjunction with a

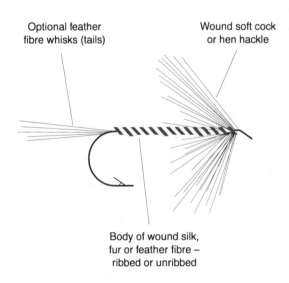

Figure 15   A simple hackled wet fly (Spider)

longer sensitive rod. Although 9 ft or 9 ft 6 in (2.7 or 2.9 metre) rods can be used, specialists prefer ones up to and even exceeding 11 ft (3.4 metres) for greater control.

Most anglers who fish this method will confirm that most of their fish will fall to the bob fly itself. There will be occasions, however, when fish drawn to investigate the disturbance caused by the bob will instead prefer one of the other flies which may be on offer, usually lower in the water and of different types. On occasions, of course, they may decline all the flies, but at least the bob fly will normally draw them to investigate the offerings. If you see fish investigating but not taking, you should give some thought to why. When this happens – or indeed, if nothing happens – it pays to change the flies for a different size, pattern, style or colour in the hope of finding something acceptable through a process of elimination, aided by experience and a knowledge of the food item that is likely to be in vogue. Variation in the retrieve rate or depth in the water may also bring rewards.

There will inevitably be days, parts of days, or areas of a water in which nothing appears to attract the fish. On other, more memorable days whatever you choose to offer will be accepted with regularity. Some flies can be fished with confidence all season, others may only be expected to be successful at particular times.

Wet-fly types

Wet trout flies will fall into groups or categories according to construction, and with the plethora of patterns available and the confusing array of fanciful and uninformative names attached to some of them, it will be very helpful to understand the basic constructions and where as a result of the construction and style, the different types may be fished on a multi-fly wet leader.

The simple hackled fly, or Spider as it is called, is simplicity itself to dress, but is nevertheless a potentially very effective fishing fly (see figure 15). It is extremely versatile in its representational properties and can be fished anywhere on a wet-fly cast. In the confusing conditions of reflected light in the surface mirror as the fly is drawn either in or just under the surface film, the circular wound hackle fibres at the front will effectively represent either the legs or the wing of a hatching or adult fly, according to colour selected. In fact it is possible, indeed not unusual, to suggest both with a bi-coloured approach. This is simply achieved by winding two hackles separately, one in front of the other, and selecting one colour, such as red game (a fox-like red/brown), for the legs and a lighter colour – cream or pale iron blue (a smoke grey) – to represent the wings. Enhanced visibility is another advantage of this style of tying – both for the fish and the angler! This style of fly can be used anywhere on a cast, but it is more conventional to use the more lightly dressed versions, with a consequently higher degree of mobility and less water disturbance, as

Body wound of tinsel,
silk, wool or fur,
ribbed or unribbed

Optional 'tail' of
feather, wool or
fur fibres

Tapering soft cock or
hen hackle wound
along the hook shank
towards the bend

Figure 16   A Palmer (or Buzz) fly

the tail fly (furthest from the rod) and the more heavily dressed or bushier flies as mid- or top-droppers.

The Palmer fly (shown in figure 16 without wings, but these can be added) is more fully dressed and can be used successfully as a bob fly on the top dropper. With its ability to cause more surface disturbance, it may also be used to suggest the skittering of a sedge fly across the surface in an attempt to take off. The Palmer differs from the Spider in that the hackle (or hackles, more than one generally being necessary) is wound down the body, tapering towards the hook bend, rather like a bottle brush. The 'busy' nature of the fly's general appearance, with more translucent hackle fibres seen against the light, helps in suggesting more movement by a fly, trying to struggle free of its pupal shuck or the surface film in an attempt to become airborne and away from hungry trout. Although it is dangerous to be too dogmatic or to even generalise too freely (there are always exceptions), nevertheless the 'busy' nature of this style, when fished as a wet fly, does seem to be more effective when used in busy water conditions such as in a big wave when the water surface is particularly disturbed and the fish's ability to study it in detail is more limited.

Because of its ability to suggest 'come and get me' confusion, the usual tendency is to fish a Palmer as a top dropper or bob fly when the disturbance in the surface film is created in order to attract the fish's attention. They may well take the bob fly but if they do not, they will have the oppor-

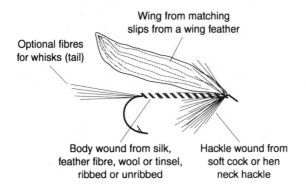

Wing from matching
slips from a wing feather

Optional fibres
for whisks (tail)

Body wound from silk,
feather fibre, wool or tinsel,
ribbed or unribbed

Hackle wound from
soft cock or hen
neck hackle

Figure 17   A winged wet fly

tunity to inspect the other flies on the cast more closely, which may well be more to their taste at that time.

The winged wet fly (see figure 17) differs from the Spider and the Palmer only in the addition of slips of feather fibres to represent wings. These will invariably be tied sloping back over the body rather than carried upright, as is seen in the hatched adult (sub-imago) stage of up-wing flies (Ephemeroptera). This is done for purely practical reasons, since a wet fly will normally be fished subsurface and this style will assist the fly to cut through the surface film in order to fish below it. Of course mature flies do not normally have a sub-aquatic existence, but they can be 'drowned' by waves etc. or be unable to break free from the surface film, and they may be found at or below the surface. The trout will appreciate the helpless and easily secured food item, which is powerless to escape.

Although we refer to our offerings as 'flies', this term can be something of a misnomer as far as some deliberate representations are concerned. Whilst many wet flies do have counterparts in nature as either individual species or groups of species of aquatic flies – or indeed terrestrial flies which may find their way onto the water and onto the trout's menu – wet-fly representation can go beyond this objective. For example some flies are tied to represent other food items. Small fish fry can be effectively suggested by metallic tinsel body dressings and wings of mottled black and white barred or iridescent wing feather tied thin and low over the hook shank to suggest their darker back and scales. Such flies, like the Teal, Blue and Silver, Peter Ross or one of the Butcher variants are well used and exceedingly effective. Representations of other food items can be found in the range of very useful wet flies such as beetles (the corixa or water boatman, the gammarus or freshwater shrimp) and terrestrial flies (the Bibio or hawthorn fly, crane flies, daddy long legs, etc.).

In addition to the attempt to emulate nature, imagination has come into play in the range of wet flies, and some creations employ colours and colour combinations with no natural counterpart. These 'fancy' flies are generally designed to attract attention by means of a high degree of visibility (shock tactics, although some do contain generic features that are similar to natural flies) and perhaps evoke curiosity. On their day they can indeed take fish when the normal range of food-suggesting flies fail. However, they should not only be regarded as a last resort when nothing else will work.

Because of their obvious appearance due to their striking colour, often with bright tinsels, these fancy flies can have a valid role as 'attractor' flies by grabbing the attention of any fish in the vicinity and inviting closer scrutiny. Once the fish has come closer, it may find a more conventional fly fished on the same cast more attractive and take that. There may indeed be something in the old adage, 'Dull day, dull flies – bright day, bright flies', but it does no harm occasionally to mix them.

Tackle for wet-fly fishing

There are a host of different approaches open to the angler in the area of small wet-fly fishing and many people prefer to use this method for most of their angling. There is a growing interest in competitive fly fishing (as though competition with the elements and the fish were not demanding enough!), and many of these competitions – and certainly the protocols for international fly fishing competitions – are based on wet-fly, loch-style fishing. The rules and regulations appear to be drawn up to preserve this basic philosophy, which has certainly stood up well to the test of time, equipment development, locations and lifestyles.

Fly fishing generally and stillwater fly fishing in particular has been given a major boost by the availability of stocked water reservoirs, which has opened up opportunities to those without earlier knowledge or experience of the traditions and culture that may have existed for many years. Inevitably this new culture will develop along more pragmatic lines and with different circumstances, different styles and attitudes will develop.

On a Highland loch, for example, bank fishing would have been – and perhaps in many areas still is – viewed as idiosyncratic. The traditional rods and lines would be suited to short-lining but incapable of distance casting as we know it today. From a boat all the water could be covered, but from the bank only a very small part would be accessible to someone with tackle unsuited for distance casting. To some extent this would not have mattered too much. There would be exceedingly little likelihood of pressure from intense use on a remote loch and the fish to be found in the margins, mainly smaller fish, would not be too familiar with the angler. A large reservoir in the English Midlands, however, may have very heavy bankside pressure. With the attendant disturbance, especially from incautious wading, the fish will inevitably be encouraged to withdraw from the shore area, and out of reach of those with limited casting range. Distance casting therefore becomes important, but that calls for heavier lines. Heavier lines mean more water and fish disturbance and, to compensate for the effects of this, longer nylon leaders are used. And longer casting with longer leaders departs to some extent from the principle of short-lining and the control of the bob fly. In effect a bob fly can only be dribbled through the surface film in the final stages of retrieve, and even then not too well if long leaders are used – perhaps to entice a fish which may have been interested enough to swim behind a fly on the retrieve but lacks the confidence or motivation to seize it.

This difference in approach is reflected in the tackle configuration throughout. To achieve distance, the rods are more powerful and the lines heavier, with differing profiles. The leader set-up also tends to be different for reservoir or larger lake fishing. Traditionally the leader (often referred to as a 'cast', which can be confusing when one also refers to the action of propelling the line with a rod as 'casting') for traditional short-lining would be 9 ft (2.75 metres) in length, with the flies from droppers spaced about 3 ft (1 metre) apart. With rather slow-action rods of 9 to 10 ft (2.75 to 3 metres) and unambitious distances being sought, there would be few problems in fishing three or four flies to a leader, although most anglers could be relied upon to generate a number of frustrating tangles during the course of a normal day's fishing. This set-up will still work very well but a leader of only 9 ft (2.75 metres) would now probably be regarded as rather short, even in remote areas. On English reservoirs, with a compelling reason for achieving greater casting

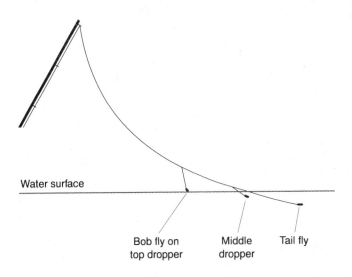

Water surface

Bob fly on top dropper   Middle dropper   Tail fly

Figure 18   A typical traditional wet-fly leader layout

distances, whilst multiple-fly leaders will still normally feature, the problems of major tangles with longer leaders and more vigorous casting actions will usually result in a reduction in the number of flies fished at any one time; two flies per leader will be more usual except for stylised fishing from a drifting boat.

Clearly, for a longer leader with droppers the actual construction presents a greater range of options. The top section and greater length may be of a braided or solid monofilament tapering down in thickness or level. The lower part, which will carry the flies, will be graduated and tapering to the tip, with decreasing thickness and breaking strain. Wet-fly fishing will often include at least one dropper, normally between 6 in (15 cm) and 3 in (7.5 cm) depending on prevailing casting conditions or the number of fly changes since the leader was originally tied. These options will be guided by the style of fishing and the size of flies you will be using. It is impractical to use heavy nylon tippets with flies dressed on very small hooks – the nylon will not go through the eye! Equally it is inadvisable, if not totally inexcusable, to use very low breaking-strain nylon to tie on large hooks, which will require more pressure to set over the barb and which will invite breakages.

In order to fish correctly, that is to say to have a natural manner and movement in the water, the tippet strength and diameter should be appropriate to the hook sizes used. In addition some thought should be given to the spacing of multiple flies on long leaders. The use of leaders more than twice the length of the rod is not only practical but commonplace, and multiple flies spaced further apart than the length of the rod can be expected to provide an interesting problem when the top fly catches in the tip rod ring and the fish on the tail fly is still too far away to be netted! It may be possible to overcome this by beaching the fish – backing away up a gently sloping bank and keeping gentle pressure on it to keep its head pointing up the line to the rod and leading it out of the water, where its own movements will help bring it up – but this is not always an option. It is better to be alert to the possible problem and to space the flies where the top fly will not impede safe netting.

Owing to the fact that unpicking tangles takes vastly longer than creating them, and that the time spent plucking away at impossible knots, often with cold, stiff fingers, does nothing whatsoever to increase one's enjoyment, it is best to try to avoid them. This is easier said than done. The tangles arise from faulty techniques in casting – but who can use perfect techniques all the time, with the distractions of tiredness, wandering attention, changing conditions, sudden excitement when the fish moves etc.? It helps to try to keep the rod tip moving to and fro in your casting actions as though it were locked in a slot in one plane, rather than allowing it to describe an oval path which will open up a horizontal loop and cause tangling problems. If you find your flies hitting your rod on the forward cast you can be sure you are guilty of this and should pay more attention to your rod-tip control on casting, otherwise you will be creating problems for yourself.

However, with the best will in the world, good intentions are not always enough, and tangles may appear. Two tangled flies and droppers are easier to deal with than three, and two flies are significantly less likely to tangle than three. Moreover, fishing two flies rather than three does not usually seem to reduce takes noticeably, even without allowing for time taken out for untangling. So my suggestion is that you restrict yourself to two flies. It does not totally eliminate the problem but it does limit it.

However two flies will still tangle, and inevitably they wait until they can cause the maximum disruption, such as during evening activity when fish are moving freely and confidently taking, with the light levels lower. This of course means that untangling becomes even more intensely frustrating as time is of the essence, and with failing light unpicking a bird's nest becomes even more difficult and infuriating. If you do not have another rod set up, my advice is to play safe. As soon as the light starts to fail, take the fly off the dropper – your sanity may depend upon it! Even then, the change of light levels has a disorienting effect and inexplicable knots can form like magic. It is as well to mention here that a simple wind knot – an overhand knot created in casting – can have a disastrous effect. When it is pulled tight in monofilament, the nylon is severely weakened and its breaking strain dramatically reduced. To demonstrate this effect, tie a knot in nylon and test it yourself. The nylon will always break at the knot, and with much less pressure than normal. It pays to check the tippets constantly for knots, and if they are not too tightly drawn, undo them. If they are drawn tightly the damage is already done and all you can do is replace that section, making sure that you test it for security once it is retied. Regular attention to this aspect will certainly pay off.

Fishing the wet fly
The actual fishing technique for small wet flies differs from that of lures in several ways. As the small flies are generally that – i.e. smaller than lures – any food items they represent will be more at the mercy of the currents, since they will not be as strong swimmers as larger creatures. It is therefore inappropriate for them to be moved too quickly through the water, especially against the current. Indeed, on some occasions the fish will not show any interest unless the flies are presented on a dead drift – i.e. cast out and allowed to drift round only at the pace the current moves them and with not even the slightest additional movement applied by the angler. If this allows slack line to develop, it should be retrieved but not past the point at which hand movements will affect the natural motion (or lack of it) of the flies. Dead drift is not usually necessary but it should not be overlooked as a possibility if takes are slow coming.

The normal method of fishing small wet flies, however, is to cast out, typically down and across the wind, with movement applied through wind/wave action and also by small, short retrieves giving small twitch-like movements which suggest the kicking of a struggling creature. The small, irregular movements will of course normally attract the attention of a predator more than an inert object being carried round by the current, and with a retrieve on a floating line, the flies will be given a sink-and-draw action whilst being maintained at or close to the surface and visible to fish for some distance below against the sky or reflected in the surface 'mirror'.

The time taken for a retrieve with small flies will obviously vary according to the distance cast, the angle and speed of the wind and the direction of current – which may be different – plus the retrieve rate of the angler, but more than a minute on retrieval for each cast will be normal, sometimes considerably longer. A take will normally be felt as a sharp, confident tug on the line, which will also be seen to straighten out and move away – sometimes before any resistance is felt. However this will not always be the case. Sometimes, perhaps when a slow-moving fish takes and travels towards you, the line may merely feel heavy or different in some way. It may be caused by floating weed, it may be your imagination (which should always be active when angling) or it may be a fish brushing against the line or leader, but whenever something seems unusual react by tightening up the line. However, try not to respond to disturbances you see in the vicinity of the flies which do not affect the line or leader. It may just be a fish splashing at the flies to 'drown' them or turning towards them for a better look and sudden tightening may merely snatch the flies away or spook an interested fish. React only to things that affect your line and leader, not to fish moving independently of your line.

With regard to the problem of maintaining position close to the surface for flies moved very slowly, the traditional method of overcoming this is to grease the leader, or part of the leader, with a floatant. In theory – and possibly sometimes in practice – this keeps the flies well up, supported by the floating leader. But there are some problems with this method. First, the greased leader will float above or in the surface film. This will make its presence very obvious indeed to the fish beneath and there will be little difference between it and a floating fly line when one is used. The leader is used to disguise the presence of the line; if it acts in the same way there is little advantage – the nylon will not be very visible *below* the surface but *on* it, its presence will be very noticeable to a fish. Secondly, although a greased short leader for short-lining would present no problem, a longer leader will travel in and out of the rod rings, coating them with floatant which will be a nuisance later when you may want your leader to sink.

A better method of maintaining proximity to the surface is to use a mixed-fly leader. This means using one fly with good floating properties to support another without them. Using a well-oiled dry fly with a wet fly used to be a popular method, but a very large dry fly was often needed. For reservoir fishing this is less of a problem and a large dry fly with bushy hackles fore and aft (and sometimes also in the middle on a long-shank hook) should float well enough to support a small wet fly close to the surface. Retrieving, however, especially to recast, will drown the dry fly and impair its floating properties. A more effective option is to use very small Muddlers, or deer-hair sedge flies which are tied like Muddlers from deer hair but clipped to a wedge shape, and dress them with a silicone floatant such as Gink. They will then float admirably, come what may, and create interesting surface disturbance which will draw fish in to investigate and hopefully become aware of the wet fly in the process. The Muddler, preferably fished on the dropper, will act as a float or bite indicator for shy takes, and should remain visible even in a good wave. It will also sometimes be taken itself by the fish. In fact this is an excellent combination generally for searching the water without putting fish down when they are expected to be at or near the surface searching for food. It is always worth a try during late spring or through summer and early autumn.

You may have gathered by now that I am very enthusiastic about the Muddler in its various forms because of the sheer excitement it can generate on suitable days. This enthusiasm may not be shared by other anglers, but I would, without hesitation, recommend you to add to your fly collection some 'mini-Muddlers', scaled right down to be tied on normal hook sizes (not long-shank) of size 8, 10 and 12. They should have short, fluorescent bodies of chenille, wool, seal's fur etc. in orange and lime green in addition to more natural colours and gold tinsel – which may be taken by the trout as fair representation of skittering sedges or, failing that, at least drawing them in for a close look with the option of taking. This combination in warmer weather conditions when fish are taking on the surface can be very productive and exceptionally stimulating, with the possibility of action throughout the day if you make intelligent changes to cover the likely options. It can be particularly deadly at or approaching dusk in summer, when the rays of the sun are low and obliquely golden, picking up the hot orange body of the mini-Muddler behaving like a skittering sedge with broadly similar coloration under the same lighting conditions. The orange palmered dressing of the Dunkeld or Grenadier flies can be similarly rewarding at such times, and for the same reason.

For instance, a greased-up mini-Muddler on the dropper of a two-fly leader will not only control the fishing depth of the tail fly (in conjunction with the speed of retrieve and distance between), but also advertise its presence by the furrow it will make in the surface film (mirrored beneath) and be attractive in its own right to fish so inclined during the day. More usually, however, during the hours of daylight, the mini-

Muddler will draw in fish to investigate the disturbance, and they will sometimes then debate whether to take the other fly on offer. If this is the case, stay with the configuration. But if the mini-Muddler is consistently preferred then it is worth trying dispensing with the small fly and experimenting with size and colour combinations on mini-Muddlers (or even trying larger sizes).

Another option to explore if success is slow in coming would be to swap the mini-Muddler and the small wet fly, thus changing the depth of presentation. With the mini-Muddler as a tail fly and retrieve rates not unduly slow, the small wet fly on the dropper will ride higher in the water; this element of depth (even to a minor degree) is often the key factor between success and failure.

With the advent of summer, the water becomes warmer and we see the start of sedge activity. These overwhelmingly hatch during the onset of dusk, as the sun drops below the horizon, and they can sometimes pour off the water in vast numbers in a very short period. The fish often react very positively during this activity and can cause anglers to become rather demented – when trout race through the surface, slashing after hatching sedges, one's reason and self control can evaporate! There can be so many natural insects rising like a cloud from the water that trying to attract a fish to a single artificial may seem futile. There are many standard hatching sedge patterns, all of which can be very useful, but on an excited retrieve they can have flotation problems. A suitable mini-Muddler, in a small hook size and with a body of a suitable colour in fluorescent material as I have already suggested, will have none of these problems and will display the correct size, profile and coloration. During much of the summer I would feel decidedly at a disadvantage if I was to be fishing without a selection of mini-Muddlers.

You may have a problem finding a source of these very versatile and useful flies tied in accordance with your wishes with regard to size, style and colour, but they are easier to come by than in the past. Moreover, they are by no means difficult to tie oneself and full instructions are given in chapter 12.

The normal area in which the wet fly is used is at the surface or just below; when the flies used represent adult aquatic or terrestrial insects, this is logical and near-surface fishing with a floating fly line is the normal technique. However, as I have said, small flies can also be tied and used to represent other aquatic food forms such as water beetles, small fish etc., which are obviously not necessarily found at the surface. However, small flies can be productively fished at all depths. It is possible under calm conditions to fish deep-sunk flies on a floating line (especially when they are tied onto heavy wire hooks or incorporate lead in the dressing) but on other occasions a sinking fly line of either slow-, fast- or very-fast-sink rate can be used according to the depth and retrieve speed you require.

Dry flies

Stillwater fly fishing is a matter of continual assessment of the most appropriate techniques to be used to achieve either maximum success or maximum enjoyment (although for many these are synonymous). Most of the fish's food forms spend either all or the overwhelming majority of their lives below the surface. Aquatic flies (those that spend their earlier stages under water) can spend up to two years of their life subsurface, a few moments at the surface as they emerge, and a day or so above it. The females then return to the water to lay their eggs before they die.

From this it can be seen that it is only during hatching or egg-laying (or as 'spent' flies which are dead or dying after mating or ovipositing and have collapsed on or in the surface) that most aquatic flies will be found at the surface. In this adult form, therefore, they will only present fish with relatively rare opportunities for a meal. The much longer time they spend beneath the surface makes it far more likely that it is at that stage that they will feature on the menu. It is therefore not surprising that a great deal of stillwater fly fishing is done in or below the surface.

Having said that, when they are at the surface, the flies are clearly visible and therefore vulnerable to the fish. This vulnerability is something to take advantage of and it does not make sense to ignore any avenue which might extend our opportunities for success and pleasure.

Trout do take flies from both on and in the surface, a fact which should be of interest. There are several possible reasons for this. Variety could well be one, although since trout often appear to act in concert, it is likely to be variety (or a variation) in the mass availability of a current food source. Another could be the instinctive awareness that flies at the surface are on the point of disappearing beyond reach, which may have the effect of stimulating increased interest. Then there is the fact that the environment of the fish is bound by two fixed parameters: the bottom of the available water, which will vary according to depth, the nature of the lake bed and the extent of effective penetration of daylight to sustain the conditions for growth; and the non-variable surface, with a mirror-like effect when calm but where surface indentations, movements and penetration of the surface film will stand out very clearly. Just as we will be very aware of items in the sky, so objects at the surface must be very clear to fish below – probably from some considerable depth. The fish will have a field of vision or window through the surface, generally described as an inverted cone – i.e. the closer to the surface the fish is, the smaller will be the area of the window of vision. Even within this window, with water movements and light refraction the fish will have an imperfect image of items out of the water, although it will certainly detect movement. In essence this will mean that for much of the time the fish's view of food objects in or above the surface will be confused. This is useful for the angler to know, as it means he need not be too concerned over precise replicas of food items but can take the view that effective representations in terms of position, size, shape and colour can be fished with a measure of confidence.

The occasions when small dry flies can be fished successfully are difficult to define precisely. In theory they may be fished at any time, and this style of fishing holds a particular appeal – many anglers are dedicating more time to fishing dry flies on stillwaters and finding success at what may previously have been considered to be the most unlikely times. Certainly more fish are currently being taken to dry flies than in the past. There are, however, still times which would seem to be inappropriate. Since it is extremely helpful, if not absolutely vital, to see the dry fly and the activity it generates, light conditions should be adequate to keep it under observation. For the same reason, fishing a dry fly in a large wave, which would again inhibit visibility, would also be a handicap. Apart from these circumstances, however, there is no reason not to try it at any time, although there will be conditions when the attempt may be very short-lived!

Of course there are also occasions when using a dry fly is positively indicated. For instance seeing fish taking flies regularly at the surface when it is relatively calm may lead one to try, especially if wet flies are regularly ignored. One point to bear in mind, however, is that the stream-fishing idea of dropping the fly in the ring of a rise will not necessarily apply on stillwater. It may be all right if there is no other clue to the path of a feeding fish but it is not really likely to be the most productive method. On streams and rivers the fish will often hold station in moving water, letting the water bring food to them. On stillwaters there will be surface movement but most fish, and especially rainbow trout, will be actively moving in search of food. Moreover, anglers will necessarily fish at much longer range, which means more time needed to recover line, aerialise and cast out. To do this into the ring of a rise some way out will mean dropping the fly into an area the fish left some seconds ago. This may not be a total disaster, as trout will often move in groups or shoals and you may cast just right to another fish – but then again you may not! Casting to a specific, noted fish on stillwaters is of necessity rather different, whatever technique or fly type is used.

Unless the water is particularly rough, a fish moving at or close to the surface and taking at the surface can be seen and the direction and speed of travel noted. Then, if the water disturbances were made by a single fish and not a moving group, you can arrange to cast the fly or flies so that they land some distance – 3 ft (1 metre) or so – ahead of the expected current position of the fish. This way the fly and line will not land unduly close to the fish and spook it, and the slack line can be taken up and the fly perhaps very lightly 'twitched' to advertise its presence just as the fish comes into awareness and taking range. If only one local movement is noted it is normally better to guess at the likely direction of travel (upwind for choice) and cast there rather than aiming for where the fish was.

If no movement has been noted it does not necessarily mean that there is no fish in the area. You can still cast out to a likely spot to 'ambush' any patrolling fish that might be close or might come along shortly. A high-floating fly can be seen for some distance in good light. It is this that lets you know when a take occurs, so it is essential it should float well and that it is well anointed with an effective floatant (Permaflote and Gink are particularly recommended). When the fly is taken it disappears, and the take is usually accompanied by a splashy water disturbance as the fish rises and turns down. The tendency is to react and tighten immediately to this disturbance, but natural as it may seem, it is wildly wrong. Until the fish has turned down completely, when tightening will draw the fly into the 'scissors' (the tougher corner of the mouth) for a secure hook hold, you are more likely to pull the fly out of the mouth. Worse still, sometimes a fish will splash at a floating fly with its tail to 'drown' it, and take it more leisurely, secured by the surface film. Striking at a disturbance will then pull the fly away from the fish, so disturbing and spooking it.

With a floating or dry fly you should never strike too early; you should display the patience for which the sport is popularly renowned (although why it should have that reputation has always been a puzzle to me). The advice of dry fly fishers on streams not to react to a take until you have finished saying 'God Save the Queen!' is good in principle. The idea of battalions of stillwater anglers constantly saluting the monarch in this fashion does however seem to be rather Monty Pythonesque, and I am sure the fish will not mind such expressions as 'Well I'll be damned!' being used instead.

For stillwaters a single dry fly or multiples may be used (as allowed by the regulations of the water in question), and droppers used in the construction of the leader. A dry fly can also be used in conjunction with a wet fly or nymph. The standard patterns and sizes of dry flies used on streams can be used, of course, but they are usually very small and not clearly visible at the ranges fished on stillwaters. Moreover, these smaller flies are very likely to be 'drowned' upon being retrieved for recasting and lose much of their floating quality. It is usual to fish larger and more bushily dressed examples on reservoirs particularly. The construction is normally simplified and, to create added interest and to assist with flota-tion, advantage is taken of the fact that fish can be greedy and cannot count. To create flies that float well, 'knotted' dry flies are tied – imitating paired, mating flies, which sometimes appear on the water. This is done very simply by tying simple hackles in a 'fore and aft' style – one at the usual hook eye and another at the bend (see figure 19). These float with better balance, and from the trout's point of view offer two for the price of one. Sometimes indeed this effect is taken a stage further with three hackles, one at each end and one in the middle. What the trout's opinion is of what is going on in this case is open to conjecture, but these flies float even better, are even more obvious and offer even better apparent value to the fish!

There is one dry fly pattern which is certainly not new to stillwater anglers and which is not always exclusively fished as a dry. This is a representation of a very obvious food form, which fish often find totally irresistible – the crane fly or daddy long legs. There are many patterns of the 'daddy', most of which are very effective. Fished as a dry fly, however, it is important that it should float. Unfortunately this is one fly which cannot realistically be dressed to float with the support of hackles, and many patterns rely on representing the prominent body in a material with good floating properties. Deer hair either rolled and tied in a thin bundle or spun on as for a Muddler head and tightly clipped to shape is good both for its floating properties when treated, and for its colour. Other options include closed-cell foam coloured with a spirit-based felt-tip pen, cork, or moulded hollow custom-made plastic detached bodies. The legs can be a problem – not tying them, which is simple with knotted pheasant-tail fibres, but keeping them splayed out and floating naturally in the water and not as a tangled mess following a vigorous casting action.

The efficacy of the floating 'daddy' on a suitable day can be a revelation. Naturally it works best when the actual flies are being blown around in profusion on the water. They are very easy to spot, as is the reaction of the fish, when one is fishing from the bank. However, at suitable times of the year it can also inexplicably work wonders when no natural flies are evident on the water. It does not always work, even when they are on the water, but when it does, stand by for a very special day! Do be sure to carry some examples with you ready for use. I can still remember the feeling when I was obliged to stand and watch as fish and coots took 'daddies' blown from my shore with complete abandon, within easy casting distance but being without a suitable pattern in my box!

Another very important family of flies which are normally very evident on most stillwaters in the summer months, and which are also most successfully fished in both wet and dry forms, are the sedges (Tricoptera). They are readily distinguishable from other aquatic flies by their wings which, when they are not flying, are carried folded over their backs in a

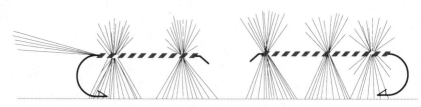

Figure 19   Examples of multi-hackled dry flies for reservoir fishing

wedge-shaped, roof-like triangular manner. Furthermore the wings are opaque rather than clear or translucent, and overall it resembles a moth. This similarity goes beyond the winging, as most sedges are nocturnal and will hatch and become active at dusk when the light begins to fade as the sun goes off the water.

They are typically flies of the hot summer months and a hatch of sedges in the gathering darkness can, on occasions, be like a blizzard in reverse. They rise up, and are dark in colour (certainly in the darkness), but like snow flakes they are everywhere! The fish go mad for them; when they are hatching, they attack them with total abandon. This is at no time more apparent than when they are at the point of eclosion (hatching) and then skittering across the surface in their attempt to get out of the surface film and airborne – quite possibly at the same time shaking out their wings after bursting out of their pupal case to enable them to fly. They can travel quite considerable distances across the water surface (about 10 to 15 ft or 3 to 5 metres) in their anxiety to become airborne, and in so doing they displace water in front of them to make a significant furrow, which is quite noticeable to the fish. Since this activity generally coincides with the light failing the angler only sees the earlier part of the performance in the main, and can only guess at the spectacular nature of the finale in full darkness! The obvious and more intense part of the action is fairly short-lived and, as soon as darkness proper falls, the intense activity on the part of the fish ceases – at least on the surface and for the period that most water companies allow anglers access to the water.

In imitating this frenzied effort, history and fly tying have done the angler proud in the range of options available. They are all worth trying, but they do tend to swell the range of patterns in your fly box if you are determined to be equipped for every possible eventuality. There is nothing wrong in being so equipped – so long as you can recognise the opportunity, and the fly to suit it, in time. It is extremely galling to be aware that you have the answer to a particular situation in your box – but to match the answer to the situation a minute, an hour or a day too late! However, as is so often the case, whilst history provides many patterns for us to use, it does not always give us clear, succinct guidance as to when to use them. I would therefore suggest that 'historical' patterns, which may well largely relate to running waters, be held in reserve to be tried when more modern, specific stillwater generic patterns fail to produce results.

Two modern dressings of dry hatching sedge patterns, which rely on totally different concepts of representation for their success, are worthy of automatic inclusion in every stillwater angler's fly box. Both are attributed to noted personalities in the stillwater fly fishing area.

The first is a brilliant and simple concept (how often these two essential characteristics go together), and was designed by the late Richard Walker, an engineer who was also an ardent and successful angler in various disciplines, who commanded respect from a vast number of followers and whose death a number of years ago deprived angling of one of a few elite enquiring and perceptive minds. The Walker's Skimming Sedge (see figure 20) pattern is a modern classic and a superb pattern to entice the sedge-chasing 'gourmet' trout on a summer's evening. Not only is it unquestionably effective when trout chase hatching sedges but it is simple to dress and is constructed from easily accessible materials at low cost.

The Walker's Skimming Sedge is designed to be pulled across the surface on its hackle tips, dressed with a floatant such as Permaflote (an outstandingly effective preparation, again associated with Richard Walker), to emulate the sedge struggling to become airborne. In this role it is very effective indeed. As many people find by accident, it is also good as a semi-submerged imitation caught in the surface film when insufficient floatant is applied or an earlier application is in need of renewal. It is, however, as a truly dry fly, rising on its well-oiled hackle tips to skim across the water in the evening rise that it is most effective, and most exciting.

It is simply constructed. The hackle is of wound cock hackle; the wing fibres are of larger hackles tied in and cut level with the end of the body in a triangular, fan shape; and the body is of wound and clipped dyed chestnut ostrich herl, tipped with fluorescent wool in yellow, orange or lime green.

The other noted dry sedge pattern is the G & H Sedge ('G & H' standing for Goddard and Henry, the developers of this pattern). This fly has a narrow clipped triangular wing silhouette shape made from clipped deer hair with a body tied in beneath of dubbed green-dyed seal's fur spun onto tying thread and tied in after the wing is completed. The fly is then finished off with a throat hackle (usually cut off above the body) and antennae of stripped cock hackle tied in to protrude forward beyond the hook eye and separated. When dressed with a floatant, it will float like a dream and create a very enticing wave when retrieved, even slowly. And when fished on a dead drift, with no movement applied by the angler, it is also very acceptable to fish taking migrating, floating snails.

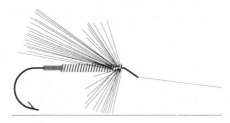

Figure 20   Walker's Skimming Sedge

Chapter 9

Fishing the nymph

Fishing the nymph is considered by many people to be the cream of stillwater fly fishing, especially when practised on the nutrient-rich waters of English reservoirs. It is also one of the more logical approaches in the representation of the aquatic insect food opportunities available to the trout. Aquatic flies start with an egg stage, which is of little use to any trout of a size of interest to an angler. The final stage is that of a winged insect, which is most certainly of interest, but is only available for brief moments. The stages between, those of larva and free-swimming pupa, present ample opportunity for featuring on the trout's menu. An examination of a trout's stomach contents will confirm that nymphs, together with daphnia (water fleas), will feature in quantity and range throughout the season. This stage of aquatic insects' life forms the mainstay of the trout's diet and is available to the fish on every feeding day of the year.

From the angler's point of view, fishing the nymph offers scope for detailed analysis or contemplation in an effort to maximise results. Because nymphs (in this context the term also encompasses free-swimming pupae) are small and relatively slow movers, this method of fishing uses considerable finesse and delicacy. Moreover, the representations offered are presented to the fish entirely in their own environment, giving them ample time to inspect them and make their mind up whether what they see is a food item or not. The trout which takes a nymph does so because it considers it to be a natural food item. In effect the angler deceives the fish rather than exciting it by curiosity or fear of loss or confusing it in the surface film. Because of this, takes to a nymph usually reflect confidence and are unhurried. A fish sipping in a nymph does so in a more leisurely way; it is aware that the nymph has limited swimming ability and there is no need to snatch at it – unless it is in a shoal with other hungry fish. Takes are therefore often deliberate but, once taken, the presence of the hook or attached nylon leader may soon be noted and quickly rejected.

The style of the take, as experienced by the angler, will depend largely upon the speed and direction at which the fish is travelling. If it is travelling away from the angler the take will obviously be a distinct tug as any slack in the line or leader is taken up. If it is travelling towards the angler, the sensation will be much less pronounced – if it is felt at all. The line may just become 'heavy' or feel different, without the angler really understanding why. When that happens, one should react by tightening the line on the assumption that a fish is responsible.

Whilst nymphs are weak swimmers, they do swim within water currents. In waters where up-winged flies (Ephemeroptera) occur their larvae are mobile and can swim reasonably well. The pupae of sedges (Tricoptera) and buzzers (chironomids) are also able to swim weakly. None of them is able to travel quickly in the water, however, and all rely to some extent on being carried by water currents. It follows therefore that if they are to be mistaken for natural food objects artificials should not move quickly – at least not as a matter of course – and should be subject to movement caused by water current and wave action.

Tackle for nymph fishing

This awareness of the nymphs' vulnerability to the actions of the water will influence the selection of terminal tackle. To allow freedom of movement, leaders will taper down to relatively low tippet breaking strains. How low you go will depend on the hazards in the water (weeds, rocks etc.) and the size of fish you anticipate finding. For the larger reservoirs, where fish can be big, 5 lb (2.25 kg) breaking strain is as low as I would wish to go in normal nylon, although in the stretched 'double-strength' nylons an 8 lb (3.6 kg) breaking strain will usually give similar suppleness and thickness with much more security. In addition, to give the appearance of uninhibited free movement, as well as the ability to explore a greater range of depths, the overall length of the leader is usually extended to between 15 and 20 ft (4.5 to 6 metres) or more. Since the fish has ample time to study the nymph, the fact that the thicker and very noticeable fly line is not within its sight is not a bad thing either!

The assumption here is of course that the nymph will be fished on a floating fly line, whose use for nymph fishing is very widespread; indeed, many will not normally fish the nymph on any other line. The fish may be found at any depth and, although many larvae will spend most of their time at or close to the bottom of the water, to hatch they and the pupae must migrate to the surface. It is more than likely that they will do this more than once, so the sight of larvae and pupae rising and falling in the water will not be uncommon, and the fish can be expected to avail themselves of the feeding opportunities they provide. A sinking line can certainly be used to fish the imitations below the surface, but it should be remembered that sinking lines come in a very wide range of densities, with differing sink rates. Once cast they will continue to sink through the water, pulling the leader and flies down in an arc, not in a level plane. The sink rate and the following arc of the leader will vary according to the line density. One other factor which will influence it will be the retrieve rate. The faster the retrieve the greater the water resistance on the line, which will support it higher in the water. This will not be a major problem on a slow-sinking line but a medium-, fast- or very-fast-sinking line will require a fast retrieve rate to maintain a level in the water or to keep clear of tangling with weeds on the bottom. This fast retrieve rate will be unnatural for a small, weak-swimming larva or pupa and you will not be in control of the presentation of the nymph to the fish.

There is one particular technique which does require a fast-sinking line and we will look more closely at it later. But in general, non-floating lines present problems in nymph presentation; even a very slow-sinking line does not enable us to know what is happening or to react quickly to small movements that may be seen in the straightening of a floating line or the leader 'disappearing through a hole in the water'. Except in the most severe wind conditions a floating line will enable you to maintain contact with the nymphs and control the depths at which they are fishing. It will at the same time signal any interference, whether by fish or anything else.

Techniques for nymph fishing

The degree of control you have will depend upon a combination of various factors and it will be up to you to determine the effect of these factors in a three-dimensional situation. It is a simple and largely intuitive process of watching and thinking about what is happening at the business end of the tackle. If the water were totally still with no wind, any line cast out would not move without assistance but, assuming that the nymphs do not incorporate any floating materials, they would sink, pulling the leader down very slowly because of their light weight and the fact that the specific gravity of nylon would be offset by the water resistance of the monofilament being dragged down in an arc through the water. The effect would be greater if heavier-gauge wire hooks were used, which would sink more quickly, and even more so if you used nymphs weighted with either copper or lead wire wound as an underbody. There would thus be considerable variation in sink rates.

This very rarely happens, however, since temperature changes and wind effects usually cause water movements. One major effect on water movement at the surface is caused by the wind. If the wind is blowing from behind you, your casting will be wind-assisted, and with the surface water movement almost certainly being away from you the sinking rate will be less than for a totally neutral situation. With the wind blowing towards you, it will be more difficult to achieve your casting distance and you will be obliged to retrieve line to remain in contact with the flies. This will result in a quicker sink rate – unless the faster retrieve compensates.

In fact nymphing into a strong headwind is a nightmare. It can often be productive because food is washed to your area by the upper water current, but casting into a headwind creates problems with the fly line meeting increased air resistance, thus reducing the distance cast. This problem is compounded by the leader turnover being adversely affected by the wind and being blown back to you to some extent. Then you have to retrieve faster than you want to, merely to stay in contact with the flies, thus losing the opportunity to explore deeper water. Fishing into a wind can be very hard work indeed and not many people choose to try it. As an option, especially for competent casters, it should never be disregarded, but for most of us pleasure comes from satisfactory results, not from frustration, so if you find that fighting against a wind is just not worth while, move to a more comfortable position, and keep thinking (and moving if necessary) until you get results.

The best conditions for nymphing – as indeed for most other forms of fly fishing – are those where you are casting onto water where there is a light wind blowing diagonally from behind you (from left to right is most suitable for a right-handed caster, or right to left for a left-hander). This will enable you to use the natural water movement to best advantage with a floating line.

If you cast in an arc upwind, the nymphs will quickly cut through the surface and start to sink in a natural manner. As they do so, the floating line will come under the influence of the top layer of water as it is pushed across by the wind in a wave action. This will create a large bow in the line – which is no problem, as contact with the flies is still maintained – and as this bow is carried round, with the rod tip as an axis, it will slow down the sinking rate of the nymphs until the line comes to the end of its arc. Then the water action will tend to straighten out the bow, bringing the nymphs closer to the surface. This means that the nymphs will be fished at a variety of depths according to the wind speed. If the wind is too strong to allow the nymphs to reach the required depth, the floating line cast can be 'mended' after it starts to drift. This is a brisk circular action with the rod top with the line on the water, which rolls it back upwind but does not unduly affect the sunken leader and nymphs. This mending action can be repeated several times to prevent the line drifting and starting to slow the sink rate of the flies until you feel that an appropriate depth has been reached; it can then be allowed to drift normally.

You will see that the use of a floating line (except under adverse wind conditions) in no way restricts the fishing depth of your flies, and at the same time is more pleasant to use, can easily be manipulated and is far easier to lift off the water to recast. And as I have said, it does not require rapid line retrieval in the same way as a sinking line. In fact, with the measured drift of a floating fly, there is often no need to retrieve line at all except possibly to stay in contact and avoid slack – although a slight quickening and subsequent lift at the end of each 'swing' before recasting can often prompt a more positive response from a fish that may have been in two minds!

Part of any retrieve is likely to involve taking up slack in the line, which is essential for a rapid response to takes. Beyond this, there is just the movement conveyed to the flies, and in the case of nymph fishing this will be very, very slow. The speed you convey to your nymphs should always relate to their natural speed, both in the water and in relation to it – they will often merely be carried along by current or wave action, in motion but not moving in relation to the water which carries them.

Any movement you apply will affect the position of the fly in the water. One style of retrieval uses this effect. It consists of a series of short, slow tugs (sink and draw), with the line running lightly through the fingertips of the hand holding the rod, with the flies rising on the pull and sinking on the rest. It can be very appealing to the fish but soft, fast takes may be missed on the rest. The other method is more continuous but also normally very slow, and is called 'figure-of-eight'. The hand twists to and fro at the wrist, slowly gathering and bunching up the fly line in the hand and dropping bunches of excess line as necessary. With a figure-of-eight retrieve, contact can be more fully maintained and you should be able to feel all contacts with the nymphs more reliably. In addition, recasting from a bunch of line held initially in the hand is much easier, with far less resistance from the water tension, and better distances can be obtained.

I mention feeling the contact because experience over very many years suggests that this is by far the most reliable way of detecting any interest in the nymph – or in any other fly for that matter. Sometimes, of course, it is possible to detect a take by seeing the line straighten out, or the leader disappear, before you feel anything through the line. This is more evident with some slack line, but that is not to be encouraged. Overwhelmingly, however, any take will be signalled via a tug or tightening, which will be felt by the fingertips over which the line is laid – often before any visual sign becomes evident, especially in water with a strongly rippled surface. In normal wave conditions this initial tactile awareness is inevitable anyway. However good your eyesight may be, there is a limit to the visual perception of takes under all wave and light conditions. If I had only reacted to takes I had seen rather than felt, then I believe my catch rate to nymphs (and probably all other patterns) would be less than 10% of what it actually is. There is nothing wrong at all in reacting to visual indications, but never wait for them. React to any suggestion that a fish is taking and always to a tactile indication of its presence, regardless of how slight it may be.

In fishing with nymphs, explore the depths thoroughly by allowing them progressively more time to sink after casting before you apply lateral movement by a retrieve or drifting fly line. In order to understand more clearly the relative depth at which the flies fish, count them down, perhaps in ten-second stages – i.e. ten seconds on the first cast, twenty on the next and so on according to the overall depth of water being fished. As a normal light nymph will have to pull the nylon leader down through the water in an arc after it, the sink rate is likely to be slower than you might expect. And if you are intending to fish deep, do not be too concerned if the leader does not straighten out on casting and lands in a heap on the water. It may not look pretty but the nymphs will in all probability be able to sink more quickly as a result, pulling the nylon leader vertically down more directly after them, instead of in a large arc. This reduction in water resistance on the leader will enable you to achieve more depth in any given time. In fact you might consider a deliberate harsher 'braking' of the line on casting so as to cause the leader to bounce back and create this effect.

There are other means of achieving faster sink rates of course. The usual one is by using flies weighted with lead or copper wire wound on the hook shank under the dressing. There are disadvantages in using weighted nymphs, however. Their entry into the water can be rather less discreet and may disturb any fish in the area, which might otherwise have been moved to investigate and take. Their sink rate may also be too fast to explore the descent and prospect for fish on the way down. Moreover, their movement through the water will not be as natural as that of unweighted nymphs, and they may have to be retrieved at an unnaturally fast rate to prevent them catching in weed on the bottom. Nevertheless there are occasions when they are the only way to achieve success at the required depths so it is always worth carrying a selection of examples.

Types of nymph

The term 'nymph' is difficult to define in terms of fly fishing. It is actually the larva stage of an aquatic fly but we use the term to cover not only free-swimming pupae but also many dressings without wings which are moved slowly in the water in deference to their size, including water boatmen (Corixa), various beetles etc. The range of artificial dressings available is therefore vast, and many have no obvious counterpart in nature. This diversity of patterns can be quite bewildering as various dressers try to enhance characteristics which they feel are important or just seek to develop experimental permutations of materials and colours in the hope of finding some untried but irresistible concoction. All of them may sometimes catch fish, but there are just a few standard patterns, based on logic and successful experience, which will each season take the overwhelming proportion of nymph-caught trout. It is worth while concentrating on those few proven patterns rather than experimenting with the vast number of often garish or unusually colourful patterns which take a very small percentage of fish. As with other types of artificial flies, size, form and colour can be critical to optimum results. The advice is to carry a selection of standard nymphs in various forms (mainly plain but a few weighted ones and some dressed to be floating) in a range of likely sizes. Inevitably some oddities will in time creep into your fly box and may even be used, perhaps successfully on occasions, but nevertheless a few patterns will catch the majority of fish.

The nymphs which should form your front-line attack are those which form the staple food of trout, and which can be practically copied. There are four widely distributed groups of aquatic flies which form this basic food resource and which are most often used by anglers.

The first group is the up-wing flies (ephemerids), the family to which the mayfly belongs. Although the mayfly nymph itself is successfully copied, for much of the time it will be buried in the mud and inaccessible to fish. The nymphs of lake and pond olives and similar flies, however, are more available to trout and therefore more reliable to use. An excellent general dressing for these is the straight Pheasant-tail Nymph, a wonderfully universal, flexible and successful pattern which in most of its variations is sublimely quick and simple to dress (see figure 21). Its colour and form make it one of the most versatile of all for wide-ranging representations, in a very wide variety of sizes. Of course the same construction can be used with different feather fibres in other colours for different nymphs, but the simple reddish centre tail fibres from the cock pheasant (especially an older bird taken at around the Christmas period) seems to be the most ideal for the purpose, as well as being freely available and very cheap. It is so versatile that, tied in various sizes and with suitable modifications in style, it would be perfectly possible to use it as a single pattern to represent all the various aquatic food items that nymphs in general are

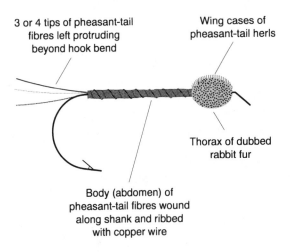

Figure 21   The Pheasant-tail Nymph

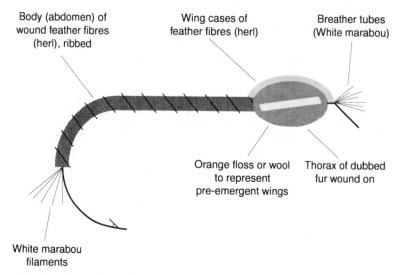

Figure 22   The Buzzer Nymph (pupa)

used to cover. This may be carrying simplification a little too far, but it does illustrate just how important this very basic and simple nymph pattern is.

The next group of aquatic flies which is important to the fly angler, probably overwhelmingly so on the larger English reservoirs, is the buzzer (chironomid), sometimes referred to as a duck fly. This fly is distinctive, with the appearance of a mosquito. In fact it is the similar whine of its small wings when in flight that gives it the angler's name of buzzer. There are two stages in its subsurface existence which are represented by nymphs. The first of these is the larva (known as bloodworm), which is normally confined to the bottom but can be washed up by underwater currents. It is called bloodworm because most of them are bright red, although pale green is another common colour. The next stage is the most important from an angling standpoint. It is the free-swimming pupa which can be found at all levels of the water and which features so frequently and reliably in autopsies or 'spoonings'. The pupae move by threshing the lower part of their body (the abdomen) vigorously to and fro. This is followed by periods of rest, when the body shape is usually carried in a curve – for the fisherman most conveniently very similar in profile to the bend of the hook.

Sedges (Tricoptera) form the third group. They are small, moth-like flies which also have two subsurface stages, both of great interest to hungry trout. The larva form is the caddis, a whitish grub which lives in a protective and camouflaged tube made of mud, grit particles or small fragments of vegetation cemented together – just the head and legs emerge

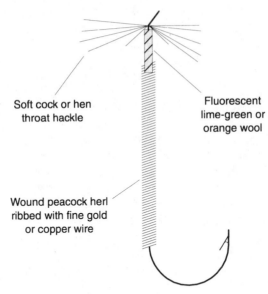

Soft cock or hen
throat hackle

Fluorescent
lime-green or
orange wool

Wound peacock herl
ribbed with fine gold
or copper wire

Figure 23   The Stick Fly – a caddis representation

from the tube for movement and feeding. This stage is definitely a bottom existence but some water currents can wash out and carry the cased caddis through mid-water, where it will be gratefully received. Just as there is considerable variety in the genuine form, so there are many representational patterns to select from. A simple and effective version, however, is one of the various group of patterns which are collectively termed Stick Fly (see figure 23).

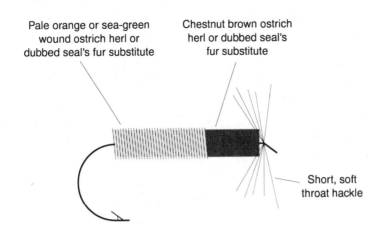

Pale orange or sea-green
wound ostrich herl or
dubbed seal's fur substitute

Chestnut brown ostrich
herl or dubbed seal's
fur substitute

Short, soft
throat hackle

Figure 24   A typical sedge pupa imitation

The other stage in the sedge's subsurface life is the free-swimming pupa, which can be found at all depths. Again, with the diversity of species within this group, all with significant differences, there are many individual patterns to represent them but non-specific, general patterns work well when fished at the correct time and place in appropriate sizes and colours.

The fourth group is rather more seasonal, and possibly not quite as significant as the other groups, but it is nevertheless very important for that part of the season when many anglers are most active. This group is the small dragonflies – damselflies (Odonata). The most rewarding time to fish these considerably larger nymphs is in the summer months (late May through to August). They are normally fished towards the bottom of the water fairly close to the margins, but can also be successful at the surface, moving somewhat more quickly than would be appropriate for other, smaller nymphs. Takes to these more interestingly sized food items can often be somewhat less than subtle.

As I have said, all these general classes of nymph can be made faster-sinking by the use of lead or copper wire wound on the hook shank under the dressings. In the case of the Buzzer, which will normally adopt a vertical posture in the water – often at the surface – it is difficult to get a normal dressing to remain there. Greasing the leader heavily will slow its sink rate but a greased leader leaves a very obvious furrow in the surface mirror. However, you can present a floating Buzzer Nymph in a very natural posture by modifying the dressing slightly. Enclose a small piece (larger than one would originally be inclined to use) of closed-cell foam (such as Ethafoam) or a suitable small polystyrene bead in a

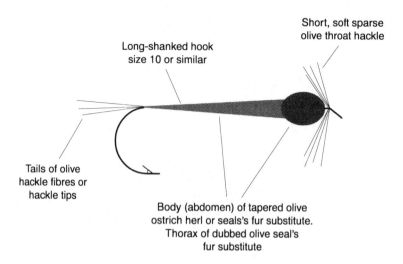

Short, soft sparse olive throat hackle

Long-shanked hook size 10 or similar

Tails of olive hackle fibres or hackle tips

Body (abdomen) of tapered olive ostrich herl or seals's fur substitute. Thorax of dubbed olive seal's fur substitute

Figure 25   The Damselfly Nymph

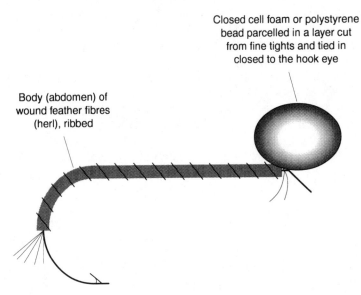

Closed cell foam or polystyrene
bead parcelled in a layer cut
from fine tights and tied in
closed to the hook eye

Body (abdomen) of
wound feather fibres
(herl), ribbed

Figure 26   The Suspender Buzzer Nymph (pupa)

small piece of material cut from a pair of ladies' fine tights and tie it in at
the head of the nymph (see figure 26). This will usually not be enough to
keep the nymph floating so a touch of floatant (Mucilin or Gink) rubbed
into this 'flotation chamber' is often necessary. However, once dressed,
the Suspender Nymph, as it is called, will be suspended in the surface film
in exactly the correct position and will maintain this position beautifully
as the line drifts round in a side wind until it straightens out downwind
and the flies are 'drowned'.

There is another nymph pattern which is designed to be fished only at
the surface and which has deservedly become very popular in recent years:
the Shipman's Buzzer (see figure 27). This is an excellent representation
of a hatching nymph, either in the normal process of eclosion or possibly
trapped in the surface film. It is difficult to say whether this pattern is
actually a nymph or a dry fly, a quandary which will not bother the trout
one iota, but it might concern a few tidy-minded anglers. Like most excellent patterns it is beautifully simple to dress and has no doubt been the
subject of a great number of variations. In the case of the Shipman's
Buzzer, the entire dressing is treated with an effective floatant to ensure
that it sits well up in the surface film, creating an enticingly confused
impression for the trout beneath. It is fished in the same manner as the
Suspender Nymph and works well when bank fishing, if it is allowed to
drift round in a gentle breeze when fish are seen rising to surface flies –
and very often when they are not!

The Suspender Nymph and the Shipman's Buzzer are both designed to float at the surface, and are usually most effective during the warmer months or perhaps in the slightly less warm months at dusk when there is an evening rise. There is also another floating nymph pattern devised in recent years called the Booby (see figure 28). It differs from the other patterns in that it is designed to float up from the bottom of the lake on a short leader tied to a fast-sinking line – the short leader is to keep the floating nymph clear of bottom weed and other obstructions. On retrieve, the nymph is pulled down, simulating a small creature diving to the bottom weed for cover. This nymph can be used successfully at any time of the year when fish are feeding on or close to the bottom. It makes sense, of course, to dress this nymph with its two polystyrene flotation beads 'back to front', with the 'head' of the nymph at the hook bend and the eye of the hook at the tail.

The 'reversed' style of fishing the Booby Nymph (floating pattern with sinking line) can of course be used in any depth of water. This basic method, normally with a longer leader, can also be used for the water boatmen (Corixa) representation, providing of course it is dressed to float. The water boatman is a water beetle which has a flattish body, brown on top and normally with white and silver underneath, with a pair of 'paddles' or swimming legs. It has a habit of rising to the surface, gathering a bubble of air (seen as a small silver bubble) and swimming back down. It is not normally a major food item, but it can be in late summer in relatively shallow water. This makes it well worth a try during difficult spells at these periods, especially from the bank where you can get at the depths it favours. The normal approach would be with a weighted pattern on a floating line with intermittent faster retrieves to cause the nymph to rise up in the water. In the long days of late summer, when activity often slows down, there will be plenty of time to experiment!

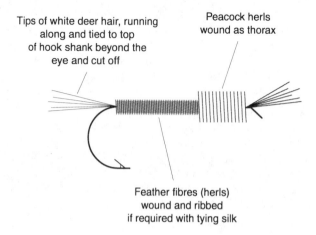

Figure 27   The Shipman's Buzzer

As I have said, because the fish will have much more opportunities to inspect your nymph, the pattern should conform as closely as possible to their expectations. Key recognition features can usefully be slightly exaggerated, but I feel that essential characteristics such as size and profile should be given critical thought – the tendency in tying is to produce over-bulky patterns. In addition, I am convinced that, where possible, the selection of material and tying style should aim to achieve some semblance of life in a slowly presented pattern. Try to bear these points in mind when tying or purchasing these flies – the extra care can only add to your confidence in the equipment you use and will result in greater enjoyment.

There is of course a transition which takes place at the surface from the sub-aquatic nymph (or pupa) to the air-breathing adult fly stage. This transformation usually happens quite quickly and, being at the surface and in the surface film, will present something of a muddled image to the fish, with the elements beneath the surface being reflected in the mirror-like surface when seen from below. At a stage in this hatching process the emerging fly will show key recognition features of both the subsurface nymph/pupa and the adult fly. The nymph body casing or shuck will still be attached to the emerging fly until it finally struggles clear and is free to fly off. This specific stage has recently prompted some successful experimenting with 'emerger' patterns, which display elements of both life stages, emulating what the fish will be accustomed to seeing during this process. The Hopper patterns, with distinct short knotted fibres for legs is one such pattern. Looking at some of our historical wet-fly patterns, however, leads one to think that this is possibly not quite such a new line of imitation. Many of the traditional wet flies are tied with a 'tail' of yellow topping feather – fibres from the crest of a golden pheasant. This can ideally represent the larval integument of the shuck.

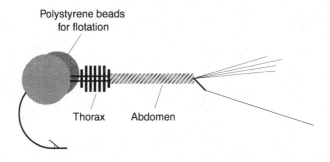

Figure 28   A Booby-style Nymph

111

Chapter 10

Boat fishing

Partners

For safety reasons, fishing regulations frequently require that boats are occupied by a minimum of two and a maximum of three anglers. Economic considerations also encourage the cost-sharing involved.

Boat fishing liberates the angler from the constraints of the shore and at least in theory allows access to all the water. But it also imprisons one in a confined area for a whole day with one or two individuals! Since we fish for pleasure, it is as well to remember this and choose partners who are compatible and reassuringly free from any annoying habits. Every angler will have his own likes and dislikes. If your idea of enjoyment is tranquillity whilst fishing, for example, then a partner who cannot resist chattering away continuously about trivialities may well drive you to distraction. It is therefore prudent, where possible, to try to select partners you know are going to be good company – whatever your definition of that may be! Try also to ensure that their angling technique and limitations are not likely to cause difficulties in the confined space of a boat and that their preferred styles and methods of fishing in a boat are not incompatible with your own.

If these criteria are successfully met, a boat gives you a double advantage: the freedom to cover 100% of the water and an opportunity to try various methods of approach to determine the 'where, what and how' of the moment. In deciding the most appropriate style, patterns, depth, retrieve rate and technique, two or three people in a boat allow you to try several methods at once, shortening the time it takes to reach the optimum one (in theory at least!).

In addition to compatibility as companions, there are some very practical considerations to take into account when choosing partners – if you can. It can be very helpful for a right-handed angler to share a boat with a left-handed partner, as this will enable the rod and accompanying line movements to be as widely separated as possible, leading to fewer mutual tangles and less lost time if your casting rhythms deteriorate. Even if this does not actually happen, there is always the worry that it might, and there is an important safety factor involved when you are fishing with very sharp hooks travelling at considerable speed close to you. I am sure that we all fish better and derive more pleasure when we are fishing in comfort and a sense of physical safety. Ducking at your partner's casting, or seeing him duck at yours, suggests tensions building up with regard to safety which are not really conducive to enjoyment.

It is often as well not to change partners too often – if you are obliged to, it may well be a promising area for self-analysis. Knowing a partner's style adds to your confidence in fishing – and in knowing what to expect. Some partners expect to fish through 360° as and when it suits them, others recognise that there are territorial divisions of air and water and restrain themselves to a reliable and safe 90° angle of forward attack. It helps to know which, as an unexpected action can lead to problems when space is at a premium.

A boat can generally be used to cover all the available water and is extremely helpful in this role of mobile, floating casting platform. It also enables you to keep all your gear and clutter with you and instantly available at all times without inconvenience. Since most people are right-handed and boats have individual quirks of movement in drifting, one particular position is often obviously advantageous under the prevailing conditions. Because of this it is generally accepted that positions are changed at fixed intervals in the interests of fairness – although if both partners are content to remain in positions that suit them, of course, that is fine.

Fishing on the drift

Boat fishing is subtly different from other forms of fly fishing. When fishing to the front from a drifting boat, broadside to the wind, the line and flies are subject to the effects of water movement caused by wind and current, as is the angler in the boat. However, since the angler and the boat are higher, and subject to greater wind resistance, these influences are not uniform, and the boat will tend to drift faster and overrun the line. Some form of retrieve is therefore necessary to avoid excess slackness in the line and maintain contact with the flies, even without moving them in relation to the water. So to make the flies move in the water, a faster retrieve rate is required. One sometimes has to work harder in a boat, and often with fewer opportunities of rest.

However, although most boats exhibit a unique, and frequently irritating, tendency in drifting, to the best of my knowledge, none will drift into and against the wind. Casting from a drifting boat is therefore normally to a greater or lesser extent wind-assisted. This is helpful in achieving extra distance and straighter lines, with a better turnover of flies and leader.

Since a drifting boat sometimes moves quite quickly through the water and drifts onto 'new' fish, it is important that the flies start to fish from the moment they touch the water. So it is a good idea to present a straight line and leader in front of you by gently checking the passage of the line or backing through the rod rings right at the end of each cast.

A great deal of boat fishing is conducted on the drift – with the boat allowed to drift through the water, normally broadside on, propelled by the wind. In this way, new water is constantly covered, which helps one find where the fish are – or more importantly where the feeding fish are. And having found a drift where fish can be taken, it makes sense to drift the same stretch again for as long as there is activity there, and then immediately adjacent to that area if sport ceases or slows down markedly, on the assumption that the fish have moved along. If this does not bring any results then remember that the situation is very much more three-dimensional when you are in a boat and try the original drift at varying depths – the fish may merely have changed depth in the same area of water. This is not always good news, as changing depth can often mean a change of 'mood' and a revision of the earlier approach may be called for.

On most days, however, the boat will be continually covering and searching new water, often on a systematic basis. Drifting onto a shore from deeper water is often productive, as varying depths of water are usually covered as one approaches the shore. It pays to keep an eye on the land on the shore where it approaches the water, as there may be strong clues to the local subsurface contours and features. For instance try to drift in where drop-offs are indicated by the shore contours, and also across shore points and into the small bays behind. On man-made

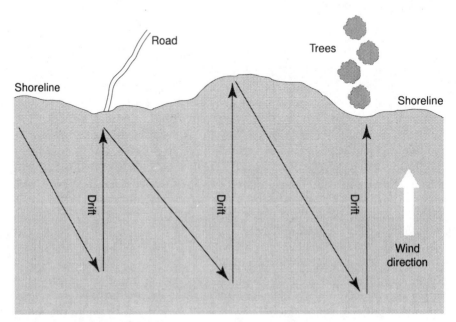

Figure 29   A typical search pattern when fishing from a boat on the drift.

reservoirs look out for lines of trees and hedges which would have run down to where the water now is before the area was flooded. These features can continue for many years after the reservoir is formed and offer cover for food and special interest for fish. Other very obvious features to try to drift into would be roads and tracks which appear to run into the water and drainage ditches, all of which will offer sudden changes of levels under the surface, which are likely to be of interest to fish.

The person directing the boat should mentally map a positive search pattern so as to cover the water in a methodical manner. This will usually take the form of a zigzag pattern, adjusted to allow for wind direction.

Clearly if this is done in a controlled fashion, this is very helpful in covering water. But sometimes uncontrolled drifting can present problems. Nowadays most boats will be of fibreglass and will therefore be lighter and tend to float higher in the water than wooden boats. This exposes more surface to the wind and less to water resistance, so they usually drift faster. The anglers in the boat present yet more surface area for the wind, effectively acting like a sail. If they stand up this area is increased. If only one stands up the speed of drift is increased at that end of the boat. By using this knowledge, you can regulate the movement of the boat – only to a limited extent, admittedly, but it can be useful just the same.

There is of course a safety aspect to standing in a boat. It will not only provide more wind resistance but will also involve a greater risk for the angler, especially in lively weather conditions. On the other hand, standing does allow greater freedom of movement in casting and retrieve and most anglers, especially those of normal build, find the unnecessarily low thwarts found in most boats unbelievably uncomfortable and cramped. However, standing in a boat also makes you more visible to the fish. To what extent the sight of an angler suddenly appearing disturbs the fish is uncertain, but there is bound to be at least some disturbance and if one angler is sitting and fishing perhaps small flies on a short line he may not be happy about his partner standing up in full view and creating a greater disturbance by false casting over the fish he is delicately trying to cover. Some common sense and consensus in approach is therefore necessary if relations are to remain cordial at the end of the day.

An additional control is a drogue (effectively an underwater 'parachute' which is allowed to drag behind the boat). This will have the effect of slowing down the drift rate and, if it is adjustable along the gunwale, it can also be used to regulate any tendency the boat may have to yaw (rotate in the water). In windy conditions a drogue is really essential for comfort and to some extent safety. Some waters provide forms of drogue with the boats but generally these are not large enough to be fully effective. For those who intend to fish from a boat on a regular basis the acquisition of a large drogue is very highly recommended. They are not unduly expensive and fold up so that they are light and easy to carry, fitting into most fishing bags very comfortably. Made of nylon they dry quickly but they will obviously be wet immediately after use so it is advisable to have a waterproof bag to put it in, to stop other tackle getting wet.

There are other methods of reducing the rate of drift. The conventional method of drifting is with the boat broadside to the wind, exposing the maximum area to wind and waves, with the anglers fishing the water area to the front. However, if the drogue is attached to the prow (sharp end) and the boat fishes down the wind stern (blunt end) first, with the anglers fishing either side of the boat, the minimum area is exposed and the drift rate will be markedly slowed accordingly. Whilst this is a practical method of fishing, and is sometimes used, many people find it somewhat uncomfortable and most will persevere broadside on regardless – and I have to confess that I am one of them. With a good drogue it is unusual, in safe, sensible conditions, not to be able to fish with the boat drifting in the conventional manner. What comprises safe, sensible conditions depends on the water. Man-made reservoirs will rarely, if ever, contain such hazards as submerged or semi-submerged rocks, but the same cannot always be said for such waters as Highland lochs. So always be vigilant and consider the dangers of fishing unknown waters in turbulent conditions.

A drifting boat is ideal for lure fishing and also for small wet flies. The angles of systematic coverage in windy conditions will be limited by the relatively rapid movement of the boat but when conditions allow, the water in front of the boat should be covered as fully as possible – without encroaching upon your partner's territory (see figure 31).

In addition it is often as well, when casting out towards the side of the boat, to allow the line to swing round to the side and sometimes even to the rear of the boat. This will inevitably put a bow in the line itself, but the water pressure on this bow will maintain adequate contact with the flies in the event of a take. The water action on this bow on flies which may have been allowed to sink, caused by the forward motion of the boat, will eventually cause them to rise up in the water – a particularly irre-

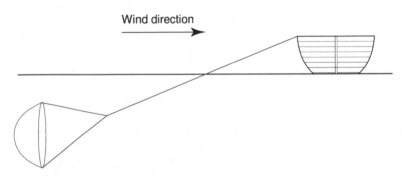

Figure 30   Operation of a drogue to slow down the rate of drift of a boat

sistible action on occasion. This technique is particularly suited to flies which offer greater appeal when fished relatively slowly such as nymphs and small wet flies. Dry flies may also be fished in the same manner providing the drift rate is not too fast. Small lures fished with a slow retrieve also lend themselves to 'fishing round the bend'. In addition, apart from very calm conditions this is one of the few methods in which a nymph can be fished with the requisite degree of control and contact from a drifting boat.

In drifting, you will become aware of wind lanes running along the water surface. These are strips of flattened water, where the wave effect is absent or markedly less pronounced than in the water to each side. It is likely that aquatic flies trying to hatch in these areas will find the surface tension a particular problem and that they are more likely to become delayed by or trapped in the surface film. The fish show a marked tendency to travel along these wind lanes – especially along the edges – and it is very often well worth while to manoeuvre the boat so that it drifts along in or adjacent to them so that you can cast down them, paying particular attention to the edges where they border normal wave action. And fish moving through, close to the surface, are easier to spot and cast to. This applies particularly when fishing from a boat, which gives greater access to the enhanced opportunities but can also be tried from the bank as circumstances allow.

Sometimes, of course, the boat will drift over deep water, often deeper than is practical to fish in the normal front-of-the boat manner, even with long casting using ultra-fast-sinking lines. To get to these depths, which can on some occasions be very productive, you can cast out (with due

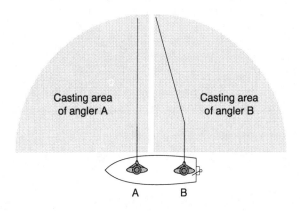

Figure 31   Casting territories of boat anglers

regard to the safety of your partner) with a fast-sinking line obliquely towards the side of the boat and allow the line to sink as the boat overtakes it to its side and drifts past it. Then, when the line is at an angle to the rear of the boat and has been given ample time to sink, it can be retrieved in the normal manner. To achieve even greater depth after having cast out, more line or backing can be stripped off from the reel and allowed to be pulled through the rings by the submerged and sinking line and the action of the drifting boat, before starting the retrieve. Takes can come at any time but be particularly alert to this possibility when the deep-sunk line starts to be pulled up almost vertically from deeper water on the latter part of the retrieve.

All the techniques used from the shore can also be used in a boat. There is one phenomenon however that you are not likely to encounter from the bank but which you may occasionally experience from a boat, and which could well require the above-mentioned technique, but this time with a floating line. Sometimes in summer, fish may be seen to be very active in great numbers at the surface, taking in a very distinctive 'bobbing' form of rise. The action can be fast and furious but totally frustrating for the angler who, try as he may, cannot make contact when fishing normal flies in the usual manner. It would appear that water snails sometimes migrate in the water and travel upside down with their 'foot' to the surface film. When this happens, fish are generally not slow to capitalise on the opportunity it presents but experience shows that they are likely to ignore any retrieved fly pattern, since the snail is incapable of swimming as such and totally dependent upon the movement of the water at the surface to transport it. A specially dressed 'snail' pattern in coloured and shaped spun deer hair, complete with a shaped black polythene sheet 'foot' can then make its rare appearance – although I have been successful with a small G & H Deer-hair Sedge (virtually a flattened delta-shaped Muddler head with seal's fur substitute dubbed on a strand of tying silk tied in

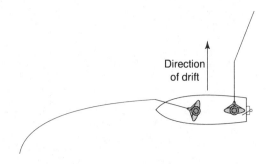

Figure 32   Fishing round the boat

below the hook shank). It can be effective if allowed to drift without any additional imparted movement. Remember, keep alert to a frequent bobbing action by the fish and then try this method when others fail. And remember that it is vital to fish these floating patterns on an absolutely dead drift, i.e. with no imparted movement whatsoever, only what is provided by wind and wave action. Also, do not allow the boat to drag the fly – although you must maintain contact with the flies. The fish taken at this time are likely to be stuffed with snails and if one is taken then there is no doubt about it; they can be clearly felt grating against each other in the stomach when holding the fish to unhook.

Fishing at anchor

As I have said, much of your time in fishing from a drifting boat, as from the bank, will be spent in the search for concentrations of feeding fish. Having found them, you can of course drift over them again – although if there are other boats in the immediate vicinity and drifting the same area you may need to keep drifting down in rotation. However, if the fish are tightly localised and there are no other boats around, then you can anchor in a position from which, with due allowance for the anchor rope, the water can be cast into on every cast. And successively lengthening the anchor rope will allow slightly different water to be covered again. But be warned: a boat with a good anchor hold in a stiff breeze is subject to battering by the waves, so you should put on waterproof trousers – preferably before you become soaked!

You should remember, however, that with a stiff breeze the anchor will hold more reliably with the rope on a more oblique line to the surface (i.e.

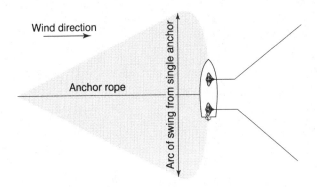

Figure 33   The boat's swing when anchored

with more rope out) than with a nearly vertical or short rope. It will also hold better with a short length of heavy chain attached by shackle to the anchor than with the rope attached directly. An anchored boat on a good length of rope (and as I have said, short lengths are useless in a good wave) will not be static in the water but will swing in an arc like a pendulum. The longer the rope and the stiffer the breeze, the larger the arc of movement.

As figure 33 shows, this means that on the swing the 'legitimate' area of water into which you cast can a few moments later become your partner's territory. This calls for some discipline and regulation but the swing rhythm is soon absorbed and it is not difficult to modify your casting angles to allow for it. If you are both fishing the same type of lines there will be few problems anyway; a floating line can usually be retrieved over another floater without snagging and two sinking lines will be fishing at different depths, but a sinking line cast out over a floating line may well test your sense of humour.

The swing on the anchor rope does not present any difficulty when fishing small flies or lures either on the surface or sunk, and it allows systematic sunk-line fishing in deep water, which would otherwise be virtually impossible except in a practically flat calm situation. Deep-sunk fishing in deep water always holds the promise of better (i.e. bigger) fish and can therefore be particularly appealing. Indeed, one will occasionally be treated to the sight of an alarmingly large dark shape following the lure up from the depths – all too often to turn round and casually return!

In fact swinging on the anchor rope in breezy conditions can be quite helpful as it can offer slightly different water for successive casts. The change of lateral retrieve angle can present problems, however, when one is intent on delicate nymphing. There is a way to overcome this; you can

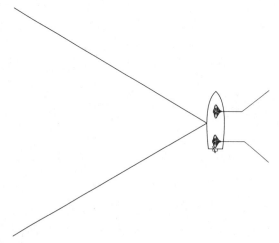

Figure 34   Using two anchors to prevent the boat from swinging

provide additional stability with a secondary anchor, dropped separately to form a triangle with the boat (see figure 34). This will overcome the tendency to swing in an arc. However, you will be lucky to find a boat with one decent anchor which will hold and with sufficient rope to be practical under all conditions – to find one with two is expecting too much! Having said that, the second anchor only needs to fulfil a stabilising role – the main anchor takes the full brunt. The second can therefore be a simple, light, cheap one and it is a good idea to be equipped with an independent anchor anyway. A good length of rope is still essential, however.

A boat will certainly add extra dimensions to a day's fishing, providing additional possibilities, and it has a slightly different character from fishing from the shore. Each approach is appropriate on occasions, and I feel they complement each other in offering a range of enjoyable and absorbing experiences. I have virtually always felt that the type of fishing I was doing at the time was the best for the occasion and I am very pleased that it has been so – the alternative would have been a clear indication that my enjoyment was waning.

Although extra water can be covered in a boat – and often the catch rate is better – it does not always follow by any means that taking to a boat will help you avoid frustration or provide an assured route to greater success. Sometimes it merely provides a good view of bank anglers enjoying rewarding sport and at other times a clear view of nothing much at all happening! I have a clear memory (I wish that I didn't!) of a hot, sunny, still summer's day, when both bank and boat anglers clearly exhibited the lethargic body postures and movements which reflected not only the heat but the clear conviction that nothing was going to happen. Yet one boat – always the same one – appeared always to have bent rods, despite the seemingly impossible conditions, whenever I looked up from my fruitless labours. It transpired later in that forum of all fishing knowledge and experience, the local pub, that the anglers were practising for an international team event, and had fished in the unrippled calm conditions with small wet flies smothered with grease and with greased-up leaders dragged quickly across the surface – just what any self-respecting textbook would advise you not to do at any cost! Sometimes 'knowledge' can be a very heavy burden!

In boat fishing it is easy to make assumptions that are not shared by the fish. For instance because one cannot distinguish fly, line or fish movements in a very big wave, it is all too easy to assume that the fish will have problems and to fish large lures for the sake of visibility. This is by no means the case; the fish are more than capable of seeing and taking the smallest of flies in the biggest of waves, ignoring larger and seemingly more visible items – when it suits them of course. Also, in an attractive ripple when fish movements could be spotted easily but none are seen, it is almost impossible not to conclude that the fish are deeper, but this may not necessarily be the case. Fish feeding close to but not at the surface do not always betray their presence and many anglers have had memorable and productive days' sport fishing just below the surface without ever seeing a fish move until it is hooked. It is necessary to have a starting point in one's approach to the problem of where the fish are, what they are taking and how they want it presented, but this should be only the first step in a systematic search for the truth. It can be fatal to make unwarranted assumptions – and it is not necessary when one can easily check out the full range of available options, particularly from a boat.

A further point to remember is that when you are fishing deep, the vertical action in the water, either rising or falling, is a particularly attractive one. So be alert to any indication of a take 'on the drop' by watching the line (and leader if it is visible) for any sign of unexpected movement, however slight. Also be prepared for takes 'on the lift', when the sunk line having been drawn in to the boat starts its upward, more vertical movement.

Chapter 11

Seasonal patterns

Although stillwater fly fishing is agreeably full of surprises, there are patterns of activity within the sport which are more or less recurring themes. The seasonal availability and behaviour of the food items of interest to the fish will of course also be of major concern. This is a vast and very complex subject, covering many diverse species and, if dealt with in detail, calculated to daunt all but the most fanatical of fly fishermen. But the range of aquatic and terrestrial food forms which may conceivably be used in the course of angling for trout can, for the purposes of practical angling, be condensed into groups. I will only deal with the groups which are of principal interest, on the basis of what anglers need to know.

The coverage is intended to be practical. You may at some stage develop a specific interest in a particular food form, which may lead you to study it in more depth, unrelated to your needs as an angler, but here I will restrict the discussion to immediate angling applications, and possibly briefly stray into a bit of background information when this may help you understand the what, where, when and how of the presentation of appropriate representations. But always remember that there are food items which are available throughout the year and others with only seasonal availability, at least in the form or stage of development used by anglers.

Upwinged flies (Ephemeroptera)

These are the 'traditional' fishing flies and the genera to which the celebrated but elusive mayfly (*Ephemera danica*) belongs. By any standard, they are beautiful creatures, and their early and longer life stages are spent in the water with only the final but brief stages out of it. The adult flies can be recognised by their two large upright wings (which may be crystal clear or opaque), much smaller back wings (except in the pond olive, *Clöeon dipterum*, the lake olive, *Clöeon simile*, and the angler's curse, *Caenis* spp.), segmented smooth long, thin tapering body and two (sometimes three) long tails. Hatches will be variable according to location, species and weather conditions but in general occur from May through to September. The nymphs of course are present for most or all of the year.

The initial stage of the Ephemeroptera is the ova (eggs). These are deposited on the surface by the adult female and sink down towards the bottom, becoming attached to plants, rocks, stones etc. as they do so. Clearly this stage is of no practical interest to the angler.

The eggs then hatch out into nymphs (larvae) and depending on species burrow into the mud, cling to or crawl among stones or rocks or seek shelter as crawling and free-swimming nymphs in the foliage of sub-aquatic plants. In this stage many of them are of interest to the angler and can effectively be represented by artificial nymph patterns, principally of olive green to brown coloration. The time spent as nymphs will vary according to species and possibly other, environmental, factors, but will generally be between a couple of months and two years. As the nymph grows it will, like a caterpillar, shed its skin to allow for further physical development.

When it is ready for the next stage in its life-cycle the fully mature nymph swims to the surface for its transition to the first of its non-aquatic stages. Once there it will rapidly go through the process of hatching (eclosion) to become a flying insect. It will generally be rather dull in colour, with opaque wings. In anglers' terminology this appearance is described as a 'dun', but to an entomologist it is a 'sub-imago'. During this transition it is in danger during the hatching process of entrapment in the surface film. Against the sky on the surface, it is very visible and vulnerable, and the fish are generally not reluctant to take advantage of this. This knowledge is also used by that other predator, the angler, who will employ nymph patterns at or rising to the surface, emerger patterns used to portray the point of transition and dun patterns to suggest the first stage of a mature fly either trapped in the surface film, drowned by wave action or waiting for its wings to unfold and dry prior to taking flight.

The dun will generally fly off to the shore where it will rest in the foliage of trees, bushes etc. prior to undergoing its final transition. Within a few hours, or two days at the most, it will move to the final stage, that of mature adult fly, by again shedding its skin to become much brighter, cleaner coloured, now generally totally hairless and with clear wings. This is the angler's spinner stage ('imago' to the entomologist). This mature fly can mate, often in flight, and the female will return to the water to lay her eggs and set the process going all over again. After egg-laying the female will usually collapse and die on or in the surface film, with wings collapsed and outspread, offering a final opportunity to the waiting fish. A proportion of spent males will also of course become similarly available.

There is one group in which the hatching to dun and transition to spinner is very much accelerated. This group is the broadwings (*Caenis* spp.), also known as the angler's curse. They normally hatch prolifically, often encasing the angler in a cloud, and can cause great excitement amongst the fish and immense frustration for the angler as these tiny flies are not only prolific but also too small to be effectively portrayed with an artificial pattern. To add insult to injury they delight in using one as a staging post in their development, and their transition to spinner will often leave one's clothing and equipment covered in their delicate cast-off shucks, still retaining their shape in a translucent, ghostlike form.

There are a number of upwing species with widespread or sporadic distribution in British stillwaters. These will be largely olive-green to olive-brown as nymphs and as hatched duns, varying in size from the mayfly to the pond olive. Imitations dressed on hooks in the size range 8 to 16 should cover the variations adequately. Nymphs with short tails in shades of olive or brown (such as the ubiquitous Pheasant-tail Nymph) will be found to be most popular, dressed in the smaller sizes on slightly longer-shanked hooks. There are many useful patterns to choose from for dun patterns but the standard Greenwell's Glory (or a variation) will be practical in appropriate sizes for the wet (or dry) dun stage of this group. This saves space in the fly box, although there can be some benefit in carrying species-specific patterns – possibly only a psychological benefit, but remember this is a pleasure activity and if it gives us more pleasure and is ethical and legal, why not do it?

Buzzers (chironomids)

The buzzers, or midges or duck flies as they are sometimes called, are very widely distributed throughout the U.K. They are part of the order Diptera which can be recognised by their wings (two in number) carried flat, sometimes overlapping, against their bodies. They are mosquito-like aquatic flies which are of principal interest to anglers on most of the larger reservoir fisheries. In their aquatic stages they must form the major food item for much, if not all, of the season for many fish, and therefore are of significant interest for stillwater anglers. Many anglers carry a form of marrow spoon to scoop out the stomach contents of fish caught and killed to determine what they have been feeding on and, more importantly, what has been their most recent meal. It is rare indeed for buzzers not to be found in English reservoir trout, in either the larval or the pupa form and in different colours and sizes denoting different species. There are a great many species and it is quite possible that some examples of adults may be seen at the water for most of the year, but the period mid-April to the end of September will see the greatest intensity of activity.

The female deposits eggs on the surface. On hatching the larvae are bottom-dwelling, feeding on dead plant material. Their size and colour will vary according to species and stage of development. However, some are red, due to their haemoglobin content, and for this reason are called bloodworms by anglers. Not all larvae are red, however; some are green, dull apricot or brown. Much of their time is spent at the bottom, buried in detritus or mud but emerging to feed. Their swimming movements involve an attention-grabbing lashing around of the lower part of their body. This very distinctive movement is a limiting factor for the angler in fishing a pattern as an artificial representation, as it is virtually impossible to emulate. A small and very thin Tadpole type of dressing, often in bright blood red can sometimes be used to good effect and is worth a try fished deep in very small, jerky movements. 'Deep' in this context is difficult to define accurately – some reservoirs, lochs and lakes have very deep areas in which it may be considered eccentric to fish in this manner – but where buzzers are known to exist and form an important part of the food supply, it is worth while fishing the areas of between 4 and 15 ft (about 1 to 5 metres).

It is the next stage in development, however, that will present the greatest opportunities for exciting sport, especially on the large Midland reservoirs. From the larval stage the chironomid transforms into a free-swimming pupa. Movement through the water again involves the thrashing to and fro of the lower part of the abdomen, but with frequent periods of rest. They may rest with the body straight, or more commonly curved – in fact by a remarkably helpful coincidence hook-shaped! Prior to hatching at the surface these pupae must ascend from the bottom, and during their ascent they will be evident to and taken by trout. It is likely that this ascent will not be a smooth movement but will take place in stages, with some periods of descent before they reach the surface film. They also sometimes have difficulty freeing themselves from the pupal shuck and also the surface film. In this predicament they are easy and very welcome pickings for strategically placed patrolling trout.

Hatches may take place at any time when the angler will be at the water – i.e. from dawn to dusk – but may be most prolific when the sun goes off the water and the light starts to fade at night. This is the time of the celebrated evening rise. It has probably developed as a survival tactic for aquatic flies as at that time insect-feeding birds (swifts, swallows, martins etc.) will have left the water and the night-shift of bats will not yet have appeared. It does not always occur but when it does it can be most disconcerting to an angler who has fished through the day, possibly nurturing a growing conviction that the water is devoid of fish life, to find the area alive with fish in a determined feeding mood. He will probably be tired, suddenly stimulated with excitement, disoriented by changing light conditions and concerned that in this plethora of opportunity time is very limited. This state of mind, of course, all too frequently leads to lack of control, mistiming in casting and horrendous tangles of the leader, resulting in a frenzy of frustration. This is hardly the fitting end to a perfect day and prior to this period of frenzied activity it is advisable to take measures to protect your sanity. Remove excess flies from the leader

Above: Tightening into a fish from a boat.

Below: An olive nymph pattern. In larger longshank size this pattern would double for damsel nymph.

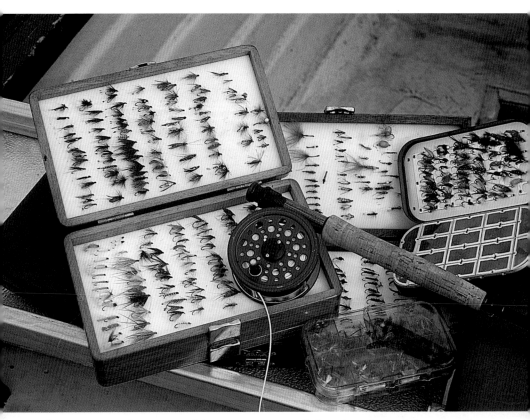

Above: It pays to be prepared for many fly changes during the day. *(Peter Gathercole)*

Below: Another rainbow confirms the attraction of the stick fly. *(Peter Gathercole)*

Above: A good rainbow succumbs to a well-presented small fly. *(Peter Gathercole)*

Below: The object of our dreams – a double-figure rainbow in superb condition. *(Peter Gathercole)*

Above: Loch style wet fly fishing for wild brownies. *(Peter Gathercole)*

Below: Fishing the drift in an ideal rippl... good for business.

Above: 100% wild and natural – beautifully marked brownies from an acid loch.

Above: Last stages of a good battle.
(Peter Gathercole)

Below: Almost there! *(Peter Gathercole)*

bove: A satisfying result to a delicately fished nymph. *(Peter Gathercole)*

Above: Success by tea-break. *(Peter Gathercole)*

leaving just one (or at the most two, with the second on a short dropper) to reduce the chance of tangles. In addition, since it is very difficult to unpick tangles or replace leaders in the failing light, it is preferable to have a second identical rod set up, again with simple terminal tackle which is unlikely to invite tangles. If a dropper is used, have scissors or clippers ready at hand so as to be able to remove it quickly should there be any indication of a problem developing. The light fails quickly and the fish can stop moving without notice. The evening rise is a golden opportunity of excellent sport but every second is precious, and this is not the time to be fiddling about with recalcitrant nylon!

The final stage, following on the hatch is that of the adult chironomid. It is the mosquito-like whine of the adult insects' wings that gives rise to the angler's name of buzzer. The value of the adult as an effective pattern is open to question. There are specific patterns which give a good representation and these are taken by fish, but they do not generate the same excited response as the pupa or emerging midge. Certainly I have only encountered a few adult midges in autopsies, compared with a myriad pupae. On the other hand general patterns are sometimes freely taken when the most likely natural fly for which they may have been mistaken would seem to be adult chironomids. It is most unsettling how facts sometimes challenge strongly-held opinions and theories, without necessarily contradicting them – particularly in fishing.

Sedges (Tricoptera)

Sedge flies (or caddis flies as they are sometimes called) are easy to distinguish. They have the general appearance of small moths, with opaque wings which, at rest, are folded over the body in a triangular shape. A further characteristic they have in common with moths is that many (but not all) of them are nocturnal and will be a very positive feature of the evening rise of the summer months as the light fades and beyond. The size range in adult sedges is quite broad, as very many different species are represented in the British Isles. However in general, from the angler's point of view, the adults are very much flies of the warmer summer months – i.e. late May through September.

As with all aquatic flies, the first stage – the eggs (ova) – is of no interest whatsoever to the angler. The next stage however, that of the larvae, is of great interest. Most anglers will be aware of the sedge larva or caddis grub. It is similar in appearance to a creamy white grub or maggot but the head and eyes are more pronounced and it has six long, thin legs. The sedge larva is an intriguing creature which builds a protective, camouflaged tube in which it lives (and which it enlarges by extending from the front as necessary), made from small fragments of stones, grit, small pieces of vegetation etc., all carefully cemented together. They search for food on the bottom by extending the head and legs out of the case and move around with the case on their back, rather like a snail, prepared to make a rapid strategic re-entry when danger threatens. In the wild the larval stage can probably last approximately twelve months, which means that this food form is available throughout the year, and fish are certainly not averse to caddis grubs.

The cased caddis fly representation is a fairly simple one. The case (the genuine article, that is) can be made of virtually anything small enough and accessible to the larva. As a consequence a 'patchwork' body of various dubbed furs in drab colours over a long-shank hook, weighted with lead wire, will be suitable. The larva is resourceful in this respect, so the fly tier can be as well. The front part of the dressing, which will represent the partly emerged 'head and shoulders' of the larva, can be made of creamy-coloured fur or chenille (occasionally a little licence is taken with fluorescent yellow or lime green chenille) with a 'head' of black tying silk, after tying in a sparse collar hackle of dark red/brown cock or hen fibres to represent the legs. Since the larva is a bottom feeder, it is of course usual to fish this dressing slow and deep, on or close to the bottom. However, it is quite likely that subsurface currents may occasionally lift larvae from the bottom and transport them through the water, particularly in view of the frequent success of the Stick Fly (see figure 23), which I have always held to be a representation of a cased caddis. I am aware that this is not a universally held view, but if it represents some other food form, then I am at a loss to know which. The Stick Fly can take fish at a variety of depths, not only at or close to the bottom, although it is without doubt more successful when fished there. It is often fished as a lightly weighted pattern, but unweighted patterns can sometimes also be very effective.

The next stage is that of the pupa, which swims to the surface to hatch. In its ascent it is of course at the mercy of underwater currents which may carry it along, as well as being at the mercy of the trout! The pupa is generally shorter and stouter than the caddis grub and will normally be similar in colour to the adult. Two colours that are particularly successful for pupa imitations are orange/amber and pale (sea) green, although pale fawn and deep chestnut are also useful patterns to carry. Dubbed seal's fur substitute can be used but I have had more consistent results with wound ostrich herl suitably dyed. This dressing material is also used in another very effective pattern when sedge pupae are about, the Tom Ivens 'Brown and Green Nymph'. In fact Tom Ivens, in his classic *Still Water Fly Fishing*, also describes another excellent sedge pupa dressing called simply the Green Nymph. This pattern is admittedly rather fiddly to tie but it is a very durable pattern once dressed, and most effective when the occasion is right. Many anglers fish sedge pupae by allowing them to sink to a reasonable depth and retrieving quickly to the surface. From my own experience, however, I would suggest that a rather slow retrieve, as with other types of nymph, brings more takes. Nevertheless, when takes are slow coming an occasional attention-grabbing short, faster movement may give added encouragement to fish to investigate and take.

Sedge pupa fishing, from either bank or boat, is usually associated with long, languid summer afternoons when surface activity slows down and any sense of urgency becomes dormant until the sun slips down towards the horizon, heralding possible brisk action during the evening rise. This is often caused by the appearance of the final stage in the life-cycle – the adult sedge or caddis fly. The hatch of sedge is not often a discreet occasion. When the pupa hatches and the adult sedge emerges, this fly often seems to have trouble taking off from the surface. It flutters across the surface, often for several metres, creating a small wave of water to be pushed in front of it. This creates a very noticeable disturbance in the surface which, at that stage of the evening, is often flat calm. This highly visible progress is frequently emphasised by a trout skimming along just below the surface in hot pursuit. The fish seem very excited by this movement and good fish are taken with patterns fished to create this type of disturbance (small Muddlers and Richard Walker's Skimming Sedge patterns for instance). However, I am still puzzled why, since the fish apparently take these sedges with relish, I have yet to discover any adult sedge flies in an autopsy. Other anglers I have mentioned this to have also admitted that they do not recall seeing an adult sedge when examining a fish's stomach contents, although pupae are by no means uncommon during the warmer months. Clearly when fish are taken in this magic period, with time limited and the light poor, one does not usually stop to scoop out their stomach contents, so it is possible that when such fish are left overnight and examined later the adult sedges may have been digested.

Dragonflies and damselflies (Odonata)

There are very few problems in recognising this group of aquatic flies because of their impressive size, distinctive coloration and large, crystal clear wings. The larvae are likewise large enough not to be mistaken by the angler – or the fish. Whilst a few anglers gifted with exceptional perseverance may claim otherwise, most would subscribe to the view that only one of the life stages of this order is of any consequence to the fly fisher, that of the underwater, larval stage. The larvae of both dragonflies and the smaller damsels will be attractive to trout, but since damsels are more prolific in many larger stillwaters this size will probably be more familiar to and more readily taken by the fish.

The patterns which match these flies can be tried with confidence virtually from the beginning of the fly fishing season, particularly in the southern part of the country. However, since the nymphs will, in their developing stage, be bottom dwellers, concealed in the vegetation, rocks or mud in search of their prey (they are carnivorous), they will not be very noticeable to the trout.

However, later in the year – from late May, depending on weather conditions, until about the end of July – the nymphs will become more active and migrate to the shore, often in the upper part of the water, where the trout can find them irresistible. On a good day excellent bags can be taken, sometimes at all levels in the water. The nymph pattern (see figure 25) is not a difficult one to tie on long-shank hooks from size 12 to 8. However, in swimming the damsel nymph does display a waggling action which is difficult to create with a firm hook shank. Some patterns suggest an articulated body, but there is no certainty that a similar action will be achieved on retrieve – it is possible that the pressure of the water will keep the articulated body in line unless some imbalance is incorporated in the dressing. If you do not have a specific dressing on an occasion when the damsel nymph is indicated, an olive-coloured small Tadpole-type dressing fished slowly may do the trick, as the flowing marabou tail on a slow retrieve can often give an enticing throbbing movement, not too dissimilar to the swimming action of the nymph. I have also had similar success with a simple dressing of a small natural deer-hair Muddler head followed by a 'wing' of dyed olive/brown marabou feather, fished slowly subsurface on a slow-sinking line. It may also explain why a Matuka-style dressing from the body feathers of a hen pheasant and body dubbed from blended seal's fur with a decidedly olive/brown overall hue produced the goods against all the odds on a difficult bright summer's day when nothing else would work. This shows again how lures can be effective, deliberately or not, as representations of natural food items.

Terrestrial flies

Terrestrial flies do not normally appear on the water *en masse* as hatching aquatic flies can do. However at varying times and under suitable conditions they can be present in sufficient numbers to merit patterns to cover them.

Most notable among this group are crane flies (daddy long legs). They can appear on the water, blown from the shore, for much of the season, but are more prevalent in or following damp spells in mid- to late summer. The artificial pattern, although generally impressive in appearance, is not at all difficult to tie, and can be fished as a floating dry pattern or as a wet one, just below the water surface. I find that it can be a wholly unpredictable pattern. In late August or early September it can produce truly memorable and very exciting sport. It can also on isolated occasions be devastating fished dry when neither natural crane flies nor fish are evident. Often very good fish come from nowhere to take it. Yet, on the other hand, there are occasions when conditions seem ideal for the 'daddy' but despite this fish seem to be totally oblivious to it. Most anglers will carry a dressing in their fly box, and I am sure that many would do better with it if only they brought it out and used it more – not just on those occasions when its use seems blatantly obvious or in moments of desperation, but at any time when the natural could be expected to be blown onto the water, even if none have been noted.

The hawthorn fly (*Bibio marci*) is noticeable around bankside vegetation during a short period towards the end of April and into May. Very similar to and larger than the black gnat (*Bibio johannis* etc.), it is a rather weak flyer. It is small, with a dark black, hairy body and legs, and a pair of longer legs that dangle awkwardly in flight. It is generally locally prolific and can be blown onto the water in gusts in fair numbers, where they are readily taken by fish alert to this opportunity. Any suitably sized black dressing will be acceptable, although there are specific dressings, some of which emulate the long trailing legs with short lengths of black ostrich herl or similar feather fibre. They can be fished to good effect either as submerged wet or floating dry patterns.

There is a very similar fly which is associated with heather and is called, reasonably enough, the heather fly (*Bibio pomonae*). It is found throughout Scotland and I should think also in Wales and Ireland. Where heather surrounds stillwater its use is indicated in its season, which will usually be August onwards, unlike the hawthorn fly and black gnat, which are essentially spring phenomena. The heather fly is also black but with the top part of each leg bright red. The Bibio pattern, which is a black palmered fly with a red central body section, obviously owes something to this fly but a simple representation is created by adapting the simple Black Gnat dressing and replacing the back hackle with a Coch-y-bondhu hackle, a game red hackle with a black list (centre) and black tips.

There are also a number of black-bodied flies (house flies etc.) which can find their way onto the water and which can be reasonably represented by a suitably sized black gnat type dressing.

Snails (*Limnaea* sp., *Planorbis* sp.) and leeches (*Hirundinae*)

These are aquatic invertebrates which are not in any sense associated with fly life but, by virtue of the fact that they can feature in the diet of the fish and can be imitated by using fur, feather etc., they are worthy of mention. Both are present in the water and available to the fish throughout the year, and both are relatively slow-moving. The sinuous movements and long, slim, worm-like shape of the leech presents a case for using slim marabou-dressed black or dark lures in an 'imitative' form. Fished slowly they could be taken as a fair representation and certainly do take fish, reliably and in numbers – possibly greater numbers than an examination of fishes' stomachs would suggest.

Snails are slightly different. A deliberate snail imitation is just that – nothing else. Representational patterns are simply dressed from spun deer hair (either dyed in suitable sombre colours and clipped to shape or in natural deer hair, clipped and then coloured with spirit-based, waterproof felt-tip pens). They will usually be fished subsurface, so some lead wire should be incorporated to enable the pattern to sink. I have to confess, however, that whilst I do generally carry a snail pattern or two with me, it is very rarely used. Subsurface fishing of snail imitations can be productive on some occasions but to me it is by no means one of the most exciting or riveting means of fishing. However, as I said in the previous chapter, there are occasions where snail can be fished at the surface to good effect. Here floating ability and a profile which is suggestive of the snail's 'foot' are important. Heavy-gauge black polythene sheeting as used by builders, cut to shape, can be used in such a dressing but a triangular floating pattern (such as the G & H Floating Sedge) will also give an acceptable profile. Whatever is used, it should only be fished on a dead drift – that is with no movement applied but with line retrieved where necessary to eliminate slack line and to maintain contact with the fly in the event of a take. The typical 'bobbing' rise and a refusal by the fish to show any interest in other, more normal patterns will give strong clues as to when to try this method – and when it is indicated, the sport can be very exciting indeed.

Water fleas (*Daphnia pulex*)

Daphnia are very small crustacea which are an important food form to the fish all year round. They feed on algae and are usually found in large concentrations, rising and falling in the water as they follow their food, whose position is governed by light levels, in conjunction with other factors. The stratification of algae leads to a similar stratification of the daphnia and also, as a consequence, of the fish that feed on them, which explains why trout are sometimes sensitive to the precise depth at which they feed. Daphnia are without doubt an important food supply, and varying numbers are invariably found in the stomachs of captured trout – on occasion they are the only food item found, and sometimes fish will be gorged on them. It is very probable that the high populations of daphnia on the larger reservoirs are responsible for the extremely rapid growth rate of trout (and rainbows in particular) in those nutrient-rich waters. The high nitrogen levels, with high light levels and rising temperatures, create an algae bloom which supports a population explosion in the short life-cycle of daphnia, which in turn provides excellent feeding for trout coming out of winter and looking for a rapid increase in body weight in preparation for their impending seasonal breeding activities. This breeding cycle is of course frustrated in many waters because of a lack of suitable breeding streams, but nature nevertheless takes its course regardless.

Daphnia is in a sense bad news for the angler – more so for those who seek to fish close copy imitations – for this food form is very small – at about 3 mm not much larger than a pin head – and far too small to sensibly consider copying. Although it is available as a food item throughout the year, the population, with a very short life-cycle, can grow very rapidly when conditions are particularly suitable and a 'bloom' usually occurs in the warmer summer months when conditions are appropriate for algae growth. It is at this time that fish become attuned to daphnia in particular. With this in mind, how then do we tackle the problem of daphnia-feeding fish? The answer is, in all honesty, with difficulty. We can only try to present alternative offerings in patterns large enough to represent other available food forms, in the hope that they will be recognised as providing more food for less effort. However, daphnia-feeding fish can be most perversely locked on to their chosen food and seemingly oblivious of our alternative offerings. So although other flies and nymphs may be taken occasionally, the success rate is frequently disturbingly low. As a result of this, what may be described as shock tactics are usually adopted – on good days with at least a fair measure of success. The 'shock' is to distract the fish with something so unusual and wholly unexpected that they cannot fail to notice it and to be knocked off balance by it. Probably the first 'unusual something' to show success came in the shape of Albert Whillock's Whisky Fly. This is a lure in gold, hot orange and red designed to be difficult to overlook, and it is often very effective in diverting the attention of trout away from daphnia. There has been some speculation about its success, it has been suggested, possibly in mitigation of its use by those who are reluctant to admit using lures that cannot be construed as known representations, that in breeding mode daphnia show an orange coloration. This suggestion is said to be based on autopsies, but there is some question as to whether it is true; it is thought that the initial digestive processes may cause a colour change. Whatever the reason there is no question that the Whisky Fly and various similar hot orange/gold/red lures can catch daphnia-feeding fish. It has subsequently also been found that other less than discreet lures, such as the Leprechaun, in fluorescent yellow, lime green etc. – all highly obtrusive colours which have fairly recently become available through modern dye technology – can also be successful under these otherwise rather trying circumstances.

Freshwater shrimps (*Gammarus* spp.)

Although imitations of shrimps are often very useful in rivers, they do not often feature regularly in autopsies, although on occasions individual fish do favour them. It is considered most likely that they may feature strongly on the menu during the winter period when other food is more scarce – and when any interest they generate will be of no consequence to anglers. Shrimps would seem to be well distributed especially in the central and southern part of the country, probably because of the alkaline nature of the water in these areas. However, Highland lochs, which are not noted for their alkalinity as a rule, can often support populations, and I have been struck in the past, when unhooking brown trout, to see how similar the wet Teal and Black pattern is to the shrimp – examples of which I have found in the mouth at the same time. This similarity I must confess is entirely incidental and the Teal and Black, although apparently effective, is scarcely a standard pattern to represent the shrimp. There are a number of specific patterns which will emulate this food form, but in tying and using them, remember that the natural species will swim on their sides. Where they are present, shrimps will be generally freely available throughout the year.

Water louse or water slater (*Asellus* spp.)

In appearance this creature is very much like the familiar wood louse and it also has many similarities to the freshwater shrimp, although it is

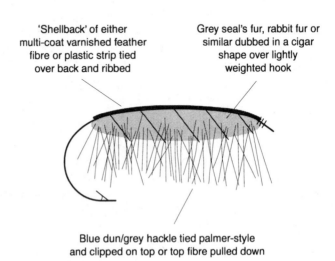

'Shellback' of either multi-coat varnished feather fibre or plastic strip tied over back and ribbed

Grey seal's fur, rabbit fur or similar dubbed in a cigar shape over lightly weighted hook

Blue dun/grey hackle tied palmer-style and clipped on top or top fibre pulled down

Figure 35   A typical freshwater shrimp pattern

perhaps less fastidious over specific water qualities. Like the shrimp, the water louse is more commonly encountered on or near the bottom in fairly shallow water and is again freely available throughout the year to feeding fish. Any effective shrimp pattern could be used confidently to represent it as the size, colour and shape will be generally similar. Another representational option which can be effective would be a well teased out Gold Ribbed Hare's Ear pattern lightly weighted or fished on a long leader, which is allowed to sink and fished slowly, keeping the pattern at or close to the bottom.

Fish fry

Trout are of course carnivorous and small fish represent a considerable supply of vital protein. Whether or not they are available to trout all year round does to some extent depend upon the size of the trout! Certainly those given to fishing dead bait for pike during winter months can find themselves returning trout of some size.

In fry feeding, however, there is a strong seasonal element which closely follows the progress of the new season's coarse fish fry. Late spring and early summer will find large numbers of very small pin fry (very small fry) in waters where there is a mixed fish population. The standard range of silver-ribbed or silver-bodied flies (Teal, Blue and Silver, Silver Invicta, Sinfoil's Pin Fry etc.) are likely to cover this option well enough. As the season progresses, however, and rich feeding becomes available, the survivors of this annual bounty become larger and tend to shoal up – although the shoals can appear to become broken up and dispersed in very rough weather. At this stage in late summer/early autumn, with fry at or in excess of 2 in (5 cm) the representational role is taken over by patterns such as Floating Fry, white lures, white Muddlers etc.

This element of the available food form is a very significant one indeed. All trout are likely to succumb to a fry representation pattern towards the end of the season. Many heavy fish can be observed surging in amongst the fry in the shallows, where the shoals have been pushed in search of cover among marginal weed growth, and the fry skitter in panic across the surface.

The fish may be observed time and time again, but they are often very difficult to catch. One method which is likely to bring success is to cast out a Floating Fry pattern into the middle of this disturbance and just leave it there to await the return of the trout to mop up any fry which were stunned or injured in the violent onslaught which has just taken place.

It is believed that, acting together, groups of fish will herd fry into a concentrated shoal to make it easier to feed on them. Features which offer fry some measure of protection may well harbour them – and interested trout – so the edges of weed beds, moored boats, submerged tree stumps,

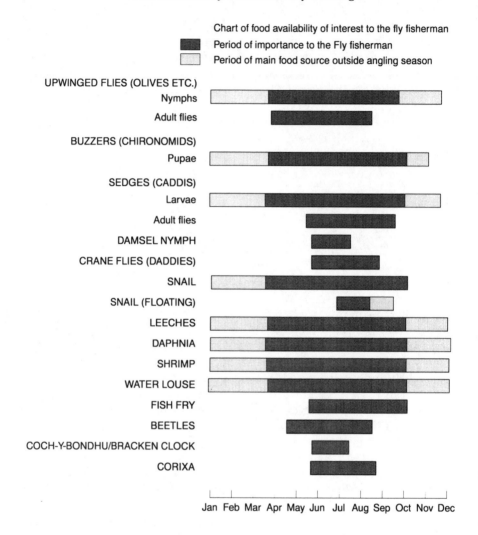

Chart of food availability of interest to the fly fisherman

- ■ Period of importance to the Fly fisherman
- □ Period of main food source outside angling season

quays, jetties and buoys are all worth a cast or two when it may be reasonably expected that fry feeding is afoot. During September the tendency is often for the fry to be in the shallows so that the bank fisherman is often at no disadvantage during the height of this activity, which can bring the bigger fish onto the scene, feeding with less caution than normal.

Beetles (Coleoptera)

There is of course a very large number of terrestrial beetles which may find themselves blown or falling onto the water. Some of them are in fact quite celebrated and have given rise to specific dressings. Probably the most notable of these is the beetle rejoicing under the Latin name of *Phyllopertha horticola*, although its much more familiar name from Wales is not much easier to deal with. The Coch-y-bondhu (which, I am informed, translates as 'red with black trunk') is also known, particularly in Scotland, as the bracken clock. It is found principally in some districts of Wales and Scotland and is active, sometimes in very large numbers, in June. The artificial pattern is a very simple one which can be used as a representation of many other similar beetles and is in fact used much more widely than just in the areas in which the original beetle may be found. The artificial pattern is dressed on hook sizes 12 to 14, and has a flat gold tinsel tag, with a body of bronze peacock herl (gold wire ribbing is advisable to protect this), with a Coch-y-bondhu throat hackle (a red game hackle with a black centre and black tips to the fibres, see figure 36).

Probably of greater significance (though much less well known) are the various species of aquatic beetles, since these will present more assured feeding opportunities to the fish. Some species are interesting in that their larval stage is fully aquatic but the mature beetles, although they still live in the water, breathe air which they obtain at the surface. When I was first introduced to fly fishing on the Scottish Highland lochs, I initially had considerable difficulty understanding the relationship of some of the flies I used to what the fish may take them for. In particular, the effectiveness of what is a scaled-down version of a dapping fly, the Baby Loch Ordie (see figure 36) gave me cause to wonder. It is a very heavily hackled fly made from a number of dark red/brown hackles in very close Palmer style, finished at the front with a pure white throat hackle. For a long time I found it difficult to relate it to any living object. Then, whilst eating a sandwich on the bank of a Sutherland loch, I noticed some activity very close to the shore in the sunshine. A number of water beetles were rising from the shallow bottom to the surface, capturing air in a bubble, which then appeared to be silvery white, and swimming back to the bottom with it. Until then I had been unaware that water beetles obtained their air supply in this way. Clearly the fish were much better informed and the mystery of what the pattern could represent was finally solved. It did not, however, explain why it should also be effective in deep water, where water beetles could not be expected – but then fishing is like that!

It may also be that the general outline and 'busy confusion' of this pattern is suggestive of terrestrial beetles blown onto the water. This may be borne out by an experience recorded in my fishing diary for a July day on Loch Torr (Isle of Mull). I was fishing with a minimal selection of flies from a bracken-covered shore from which small beetles were clearly being blown onto the water. Making the best of the few flies I had with me at the time, I see that the diary notes a mixed bag of five browns and rainbows, two to Soldier Palmer, one to Dunkeld, and the two biggest to the Baby Loch Ordie.

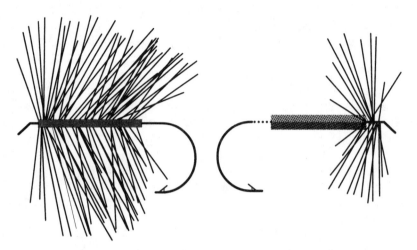

Figure 36   Patterns suggesting beetles. Right: Coch-y-bondhu. Left: Baby Loch Ordie

Alder fly (*Sialis* spp.)

The alder fly seems to receive a disproportionate amount of coverage in angling literature. It is an early season aquatic fly, very similar to a dark-bodied sedge but with shiny wings. The adult fly rarely seems to be of interest but the carnivorous larva can be put to good use as a portly, segmented pale/mid-brown nymph pattern fished slowly on or near the bottom in the first two months of the season.

Chapter 12

Fly tying

I f you have no experience of fly dressing and feel that this is an optional area which creates difficulties which you can do without, you may feel inclined to flick quickly past this section. If so, it would be a major error. I am convinced that in fishing for pleasure – as opposed merely to catching fish – the tying of flies is an integral and important part of the overall activity, and virtually essential for the fullest sense of achievement.

In the first place, there is an undeniable pleasure in being able to land a fish with a fly which has been fashioned by one's own hands. It represents an additional level of accomplishment which contributes to the overall satisfaction and pleasure of the event. Fly tying also knows no seasonal limitations; sculpting in fur, silk, feather etc. keeps one fully in touch with the sport during the dark winter months and is an intrinsically rewarding and relaxing occupation in its own right. Whilst the fingers are creating the fly in the vice, the mind is projecting itself to its use. Thinking ahead about how the fly will be fished will be most helpful in the construction, to ensure that any movement one wants in the materials is allowed for and can be built in. This custom-building of a fly to match one's angling techniques and style can only imbue one with greater confidence when it is time to bring it into use. Confidence is a vital feature for our enjoyment and success.

By doing the job yourself, you have total and absolute control over all aspects of the construction of the fly, the style, the durability, the profile and relative proportions, the range of hook sizes and the precise colour tones created. This means that when tied on at the waterside, you will be quite confident about them, which is not always the case with flies which may be imported from an area of cheap labour, tied by someone who has never fished, are overdressed with poorly selected materials and whose ability to hold together for more than a few casts is suspect.

This raises the question, of course, of why since the benefits of self-tied flies are so obvious, more anglers do not become involved in this aspect of the sport. Probably the main reason is the perceived difficulty in fiddling about with clumsy fingers with small hooks and delicate materials. In reality, although very tiny flies (which are rarely fished on stillwaters) can be difficult, the main run of flies in the sizes actually used do not present problems except to those who are particularly handicapped in their hand and finger movements or have poor vision.

Despite the apparent complexity of most finished flies the actual construction is really quite simple and can be comfortably done by most people with a little guided practice. Most non-tiers are unaware that much of the work in tying a fly (possibly 90%) is quite simply winding onto the hook shank. It is used to tie in tails and wings, create bodies and rib them, and add hackles; there is nothing difficult in that. It is more difficult to assess the overall proportions and achieve those you want, but this comes more easily with practice and a good notion of what proportions or style you require.

Lack of time is another reason given for not tying flies, yet a simple and effective fly can be tied, with the materials to hand, literally within a few minutes. Quite often setting up the vice, sorting the tools and combing through the materials box for the required hooks and feathers, fur, silk, ribbing etc. takes longer than the actual tying. With a vice set up in readiness and materials to hand, a fly should take less than five minutes. Most of us would not miss five minutes a day – and of course that would add up to 365 flies a year, many more than most of us could ever contemplate needing in a season. Cost seems to be another consideration but a quick count of your accumulated flies multiplied by the rough average cost will soon put this argument into perspective.

Tools and materials

Although most fly tiers put all potentially useful oddments together and store all types of clutter, the basic requirements are quite simple. The most useful items are as follows.

Fly-tying vice
This simply anchors the hook whilst it is being dressed, leaving both hands free. There are various types of jaws, some with rotating options. The essential requirement is that the jaws should securely hold the range of hook sizes you are likely to use and be capable of simple and sure tightening without damaging the hooks. Most vices clamp onto tables and it helps to ensure that the model you choose has jaws of a size that will fit the table being used (allowing for suitable table surface protection in the form of beer mats etc.).

Bobbin holder
This holds the bobbin (reel) on which the tying thread is wound. The spigot type is useful in directing the thread more accurately in winding – providing the spigot has an internal diameter large enough to facilitate easy threading and cleaning as necessary. The reason for the bobbin

holder is to allow only thread which is required to be released and to keep pressure on the thread when it is released from your hand and left to hang.

Scissors
These are important and should be of the fine pointed blade type used in eye operations etc. They are essential for clean cutting and trimming of threads and soft feather fibres such as ostrich herl etc. The best pair should never be used to cut quills, hackle stems, tinsel wires etc.; a second pair of lower quality should be kept for this purpose.

Hackle pliers
These are simple sprung clips with small jaws to hold the ends of hackle feathers when winding on. They also have a large ring to accommodate a finger so that you can wind on round the hook shank more easily and accurately.

A dubbing needle
This is a simple but useful tool which can be made by embedding the eye end of a large darning needle into a handle. It will be helpful if the handle is triangular or modified so that it does not roll about on the table. It is used to pick out longer fibres of dubbed wool or fur to make shaggy bodies with more translucency when viewed against the light. It is also handy for separating the feather fibres to size for winging flies, and for the final part of the whip finish. Unfortunately it is also very handy for applying a drop of varnish to the finished fly head for security and durability, but this will not assist in its original role and I would suggest keeping a separate needle handy for head varnishing.

Fly-tying wax
A simple and cheap piece of the solid type of wax is best. This can dry out and become brittle with time but a little Vaseline rubbed into its surface will soften it. The idea is to draw about 10 in (25 cm) of tying thread rapidly across the wax under your thumb so that the friction melts the wax and coats the thread with a fine layer. It is possible to buy ready-waxed thread, which is fine, but it should still be rewaxed to make it slightly tacky. Waxing the thread will make it grip to the hook shank better and also to feather fibres, hackles, ribbing etc., holding them more securely when tying in. Waxing the thread also helps in dubbing wool or fur onto the silk when creating bodies.

In addition you will need a selection of suitable hooks plus feathers, various coloured tying threads, wools, fur, silk floss and gold and silver flat, oval and round tinsels – and of course a box or some sort of storage to contain it all. Beginners are also advised to use a varnish for finishing off fly heads to ensure that the thread does not come undone and to give a glossy finish. The varnish should be applied very carefully, as a single drop on a needle point, whilst holding the hackle fibres well out of the way. It should be of a rapid drying type diluted sufficiently to run into the turns of thread. Fly-tying material shops will stock suitable varnishes specially packed into small bottles but I find that clear or black cellulose dope (kept at a runny consistency with a little dope thinner) obtainable from model-making shops in very small tins is ideal. Clear nail varnish can be used at a pinch!

Techniques

The techniques used in fly tying are quite simple and remarkably few.

Dubbing

This merely involves rolling fibres onto the tying thread to create a light, translucent body. Some people manage to make heavy going of this but it is a simple process, although it will be found that some fibres lend themselves much more readily to it than others. To practise I would suggest a dubbing material that is totally co-operative: rabbit fur.

A tacky thread is required for dubbing. It is usually done when the fly is partly completed so that the thread cannot conveniently be drawn quickly against the wax to recoat it. The thread, which will invariably at this stage be anchored to the hook shank, having been wound round it to take it to the hook bend, should therefore be held taut whilst the wax is rubbed briskly back and forth along it several times to coat it. Keeping it taut, take a small pinch of teased-out wool or fur, mixed as required, between the forefinger and thumb to the end of the silk closest to the hook and dub it on – i.e. roll it on with the finger and thumb in one direction only. If the rolling action is done both ways, the fur would be dubbed on in one direction and unrolled in the other. Repeat the process until the dubbed fur is of the required length, thickness and shape (which only trial and error will tell you). Then to make the dubbed fur even more secure take one turn round the hook where the dubbed body is to start and, still keeping the thread taut, twist it several times in the same direction the dubbing was applied and continue winding on, keeping the twist in the thread. Generally the coarser, springier fibres are more unruly and give most trouble, coarser genuine seal's fur often being very challenging. However, since genuine seal's fur has been universally supplanted by less intractable materials, this problem is not likely to be encountered and most dubbing materials now are far more user-friendly.

Whip finish

This is often used to finish the fly off neatly at the head. A couple of half hitches, fixed in place with some carefully positioned varnish, a single drop at a time, will do the same job but the whip finish is neater and more secure. Like most knots, it is easier to tie than describe. On completing the fly (leaving sufficient but not too much space for the head), make an open loop of silk round the open fingers of your right hand (if you are right handed). Put a full twist into the open loop and, still keeping it open, wrap the inside of the loop against the shank with the outside round it. Repeat this procedure with the same side of the loop three or four times. With the loop held open draw the free end of the thread tight, closing the loop over the hook shank and drawing it tight. In the restricted space, to prevent the loop tightening and trapping hackle fibres, it is easier to control the tightening if instead of using your fingers to hold the loop open, you use the dubbing needle, which can then guide the tightening loop right down to the hook shank. It can then easily be slipped out before you finally tighten it and trim it with sharp pointed scissors. Be certain to ensure that once it is formed the loop stays positioned over the hook shank all the time, otherwise nothing will be secured.

Winging

This can cause some problems for beginners, but again is not difficult if the correct technique is used. Two things can also help greatly in producing wings which are not lopsided. First, try to use fresh feathers, as older ones can dry out and lose their flexibility and fibre adhesion. Secondly, tying wings onto an even base of wound waxed silk will be much easier and more successful than on an uneven base.

Matching slips, pulled carefully off quills from left and right wings should be laid carefully together and, if necessary, fibres removed from one to ensure they are of equal size. Any excess lengths of quill fragments can be snipped off with scissors but I find it easier to manage the slips if they are kept together with the tiny slip of quill which results from tearing off the quill rather than cutting it off. Sometimes, however, these are longer than required and should be trimmed. In laying out and matching the wing slips, decide whether the outside (matt) or inside (glossy) surface

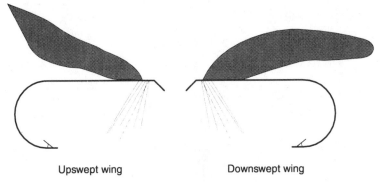

Upswept wing   Downswept wing

Figure 37   Different wing settings

should show. Also, the shape (up-curved or down-curved) of the wing is determined by which section forms the base.

Tying a wet fly

As with most unfamiliar operations it is best to start with the simplest, most basic procedure and once familiar and confident move on to the next step. You should carry out each step precisely and correctly, otherwise problems will escalate. If one stage is not absolutely correct, do not move on to the next but backtrack, unwind and redo it so that you move to the next step fully satisfied with the last. Strive to achieve the exact proportions you need for balance and also do not over- or underuse the hook shank for your particular pattern. Making allowances for 'style', do not go too far round the hook bend and too close or too far from the hook eye for a balanced fly. I cannot give you the exact distances, since these are proportional to the hook size and type and also depend on the fly pattern, but you will quickly get a feeling for correct balance.

The simplest fly, a Spider pattern such as William's Favourite, is a good starting point. Being a good basic black pattern it will be useful in many situations.

Set up the vice and securely fasten a suitable hook in the jaws (a size 12 normal shank would be appropriate), giving it a light tug to ensure that it is held securely. Draw off about 10 in (25 cm) of black tying silk (which today is more likely to be a synthetic fibre than actual silk) from the

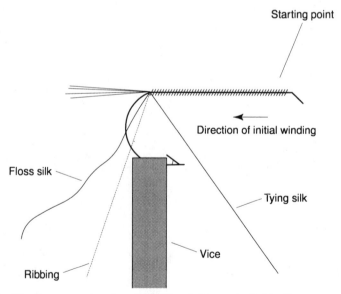

Figure 38   The first stages in tying the William's Favourite Spider fly

144

bobbin, hold the top end against the fly-tying wax with your thumb and draw it briskly through. Repeat a couple of times to wax it thoroughly, then wind it back onto the bobbin until all but 4 in (10 cm) are free. Hold the end of the silk against the hook shank about ⅛ in (3 mm) from the eye and wind it round over itself in touching or near touching turns, moving towards the bend of the hook. After five or six turns allow the bobbin to hang and cut off the free end of the silk. Then continue winding as before until about ⅛ in (3 mm) short of a point above the barb of the hook. Tie in a short length (2 in or 5 cm) of silver ribbing (wire, fine flat or fine oval tinsel/Mylar), followed by a similar length of black floss silk. The floss normally comes as two or three twisted strands on a bobbin. Taking only one set of untwisted strands, continue winding until a point directly above the hook barb or just before the bend of the hook starts to curve down. Then take four or five black hackle fibres, preferably from a larger hackle than required for the collar hackle and, ensuring that the fine tips are aligned level, tie them in by winding forward (towards the eye), allowing a free length to the tips from the point of tying in of about two-thirds of the hook shank length. The fly should now look like figure 38.

Now spiral the tying silk to a point near where you started and allow the bobbin holder to hang, securing the silk by its weight. Wind the black floss silk forward under moderate pressure so that each turn slightly over-laps the previous one and makes a smooth flat body. Just short of the original starting point catch it under the tying silk with a couple of turns and again let the bobbin holder hang. Cut off the surplus floss. Next take the ribbing and, moving forward at an even speed in open turns, wind it

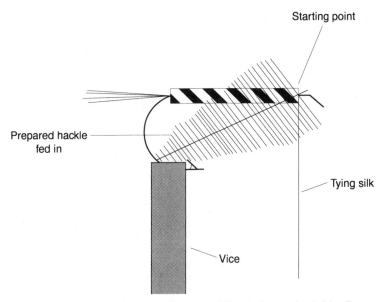

Figure 39   The intermediate stage in tying the William's Favourite Spider fly

145

on in the opposite direction to the floss and tie it in the same way, at the same point. Then wind on a couple of turns of silk towards the eye if necessary to ensure that the hackle stem is not tied onto the bare hook shank.

Select a hackle with the side fibres towards the base of a similar length to the distance from the hook eye to the point and strip off the fluffy flue at the base with your fingers. Hold the hackle stem so that the point at which the fibres now begin at the base meets the tying silk at the hook shank (see figure 39) and tie it in firmly in a figure-of-eight movement, with the silk ending behind the hackle (nearest the bend side). Give it a couple of firm turns. Cut off the stem. Grasp the hackle at the tip with your hackle pliers and, keeping the tying silk behind it, wind the hackle on in touching turns, moving towards the hook bend. Give three to five turns and then tie in the hackle by winding the tying silk forward to trap the end with a couple of firm turns. Continue to wind the tying silk forward, moving it to the left and right so as not to trap down any hackle fibres.

When the tying silk is to the front (eye side) of the hackle, gently stroke the hackles back slightly towards the bend out of the way with the fingers of your left hand (for right-handed tiers) and give a few turns of silk up to the base of the wound hackles. All that now remains is to finish off the head with a whip finish, or two or three half hitches and a very carefully applied small drop of varnish on a needle point, making quite sure there is no danger of the varnish flowing onto the hackle fibres or into the hook eye. Allow the varnish to dry and you have tied your first Spider pattern, which should look like figure 40.

Having finished, look at the fly critically. Does it look right? Do the proportions look natural, like those in the tackle shops? Is the body smooth and the ribbing tight and even? Does the hackle sit evenly and is the collar of fibres even and circular? Is it too thick or too thin? Having

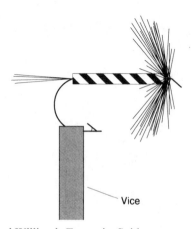

Figure 40   The completed William's Favourite Spider pattern

answered these questions critically, you will also have gained the knowledge to tie the next fly, until each comes from the vice as a perfect replica, scaled up or down or adjusted in style as required.

It is important for your sense of satisfaction to have a clear concept of the perfect fly in the pattern being tied, and for each fly leaving the vice to be very close to that standard. It is pointless to tie flies in an uncontrolled fashion, so that although they are of the same pattern they each look wildly different. Every turn of the ribbing or silk should be made in the confidence that it is absolutely correct; if it is not, undo it and start again from the point when it was. You cannot fish happily and confidently with untidy irregular flies, particularly when with just a little extra effort and care in tying, every fly can be virtually perfect – allowing of course for natural variations in the materials we use. It is far better to tie five flies you are pleased with than twenty you are not.

It annoyed me intensely some time ago to read some advice to people tying flies for competition purposes, from somebody I would have thought knew better. He said they should practise tying up to fifty flies of one pattern over the winter period and entering the best three that looked most similar. This suggests a very random approach to tying, in which case tying up to fifty flies is not practising anything but bad methods and is a total waste of time. I entered that competition for four consecutive years. Three flies of three types were specified. I never tied more than three flies of three types, and none left the vice before I was happy with it. In two of those years I won and in the other two I was runner up. The flies were tied in precisely the same manner and spirit as I tie for my own use – in fact the flies I fish with are more important to me, as it is the fish that is the ultimate judge. To suggest that anyone should tie a lot of flies in the hope that some will be good does not help any tier, let alone a beginner. It is far better to recognise when any action or proportion is not right and put it right immediately.

Although the Spider pattern I have just described is very simple, it embodies most of the basic techniques of fly dressing. Tied with hen or soft young cock hackles it is ideal as a wet fly, being softer and therefore more mobile as it is drawn through the water. Tied with stiffer cock hackles it is a dry fly with better floating ability, especially when treated with a modern floatant. For an effective reservoir floating pattern, with good visibility for both the angler and the fish, it can be dressed on a longer-shank hook, with or without the whisks (tail fibres), but with a cock hackle tied at each end of the shank (see figure 19). Reservoir trout are nothing like as fastidious in their dry-fly requirements as the privileged chalk-stream brigade!

Of course the body materials, rib, hackle colours etc. can all be varied to meet the requirements of other patterns of similar construction. One stumbling block encountered by novice tiers, however, is winging. Two key points should always be remembered in tying wings in. First, as with

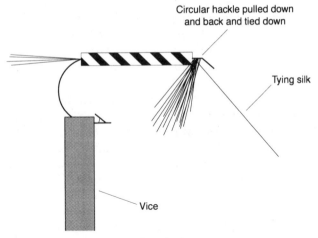

Figure 41   'Beard' hackle tied in ready for winging

any other operation, it is always easier and more satisfactory to tie them in on a smooth, even surface, so try to ensure that the previous stages of dressing leave such a surface. The second point is that the winding and tightening action will tend to roll the wing slips, which are composed of interlocking fibres, over. You need to compress these fibres vertically down to the hook shank with the silk. To achieve this, let the silk travel loosely up one side of the slips and down the other. Then, with the slips supported between finger and thumb, pull the tying silk so that the feather slips are compressed by the silk from both sides (see figure 43).

The traditional method of tying a winged fly is to follow the procedure outlined above for the Spider pattern (allowing for pattern variations as required) to the point where the hackle is wound. Then pull the hackle

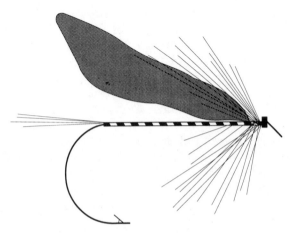

Figure 42   An alternative to the 'beard' hackle on wet fly

fibres down below the hook shank and to the rear (towards the bend) with the moistened fingers of your left hand (assuming you are right-handed) and wind the tying silk carefully diagonally behind the hackle over the top of the hook shank and to the front of the hackle below the shank. A couple of turns will secure the hackle in a beard shape (see figure 41). An alternative method is to offer up a bunch or small bunches of hackle fibres torn from the feather and tied in below the hook shank, also to form a beard. To my mind this is not as simple as the first method, and is liable to develop baldness in use.

Two slips of wing feather from the left and right wings are paired, either turned so that the shiny underside is showing or not, depending on the dressing being followed. They are then offered up to the hook shank in the desired position and the silk is loosely passed up over and down the other side of the slip and then drawn tight carefully, either pulling down on the silk or up from under the bottom of the hook shank (see figure 43). The finger and thumb should meantime support the wing slips but allow the fibres to move and compress vertically in relation to each other. Then, moving forward to the eye in touching turns, tie the wing in securely with five or so turns before releasing, trimming off the surplus and finishing off with a whip finish or half hitches and varnish. With luck your wing will be tied in evenly and upright. I say with luck because this procedure is not without risk as there are a number of factors involved which can cause a wing to pull to one side. If the wing is not quite right, sometimes a manual adjustment and fresh tightening with the tying silk will work – if not, try again.

One problem is the unevenness caused by tying down the hackle. This can be overcome by a non-traditional approach which I believe results not only in less troublesome winging but also in a better wet fly. This method calls for the wing to be tied in before the hackle, which is then

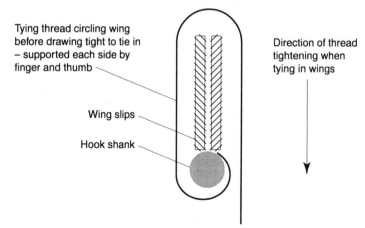

Tying thread circling wing before drawing tight to tie in – supported each side by finger and thumb

Direction of thread tightening when tying in wings

Wing slips

Hook shank

Figure 43   The procedure for tying in wings

wound on in front and pulled back over the wing before finishing off. This will not result in the traditional 'beard' hackle but will produce a less disciplined and more mobile one which lightly veils the wing. I first came across this method demonstrated by that big (in every sense) and enthusiastic fly dresser and fisherman Ray Sugg many years ago and have used this variation extensively and with immense confidence very frequently since.

Tying a lure

In the fashioning of a lure, there is generally more hook space to work with, which usually makes it easier to see what precisely is going on during the tying process. This should not be construed as meaning that your procedures should be relaxed. A sloppily-tied lure is not going to impress you when you come to tie it on. On the other hand a neat, well-tied, well-proportioned and balanced lure with scope for good movement and 'life' on retrieve, which does not wrap round the hook bend or tend to rotate, can be fished with the expectation of something positively happening.

A useful lure, and a simple starting point for the beginner, is the Tadpole type. This offers an excellent fluttering effect in the water under slow retrieve rates, is much less likely to lodge under the hook bend in use than standard lures and, tied on short-shank hooks, offers less leverage than a long-shank hook during a long tussle with a strong fish and accordingly less danger of tearing free. It is very simple to tie, using the same techniques as the Spider wet fly mentioned earlier. It is suggested that heavy-gauge, wide-gape, short- or normal-shank hooks be used in size 10 or 8.

For a black Tadpole, start by securely fixing the hook in the vice and testing it for firm hold. Wax a 10 in (25 cm) length of black tying silk and wind it back over the free end towards the bend, starting about ⅛ in (3 mm) from the eye. Cut off the surplus free end after six or seven turns and continue winding back to a point above the hook barb. Take a dyed black turkey marabou plume feather, tear off a bunch of the fluffy side herls and match up the tips. If these are not fluffy to the end but thread-like at the tip, pinch the thin end pieces off with your fingers. These pieces of marabou have a life of their own and writhe around in the merest air current. To control them for easier handling, run lightly moistened fingers down them.

A good bunch is needed for the tail, so it will likely be necessary to tear off and match up a second bunch, and possibly even a third. Remember that when wet the bunch will appear much smaller than it actually is. Then measure the bunch up to the hook, leaving a tail equivalent to the overall length of the hook protruding past the bend of the hook and tie in on top of the hook by winding the silk firmly back towards the hook eye, starting from the point at which the hook bend starts to curve down from the horizontal. After between $1/8$ and $1/4$ in (3 to 6 mm) cut off the surplus marabou feather and immediately tie in a length of fine lead wire. Wind this carefully in touching turns to a point just short of the initial starting point. Then spiral the tying silk up to tie in the end of the wire, cut off any surplus and spiral back to the point where the marabou was initially tied in. Take a length of black chenille pinch and pull off to expose $1/8$ to $1/6$ in (3 to 4 mm) of the cotton core and tie in with the silk. Spiral the silk back to the original starting point and allow it to hang under the weight of the bobbin. The lead wire can sometimes twist round the hook, even with the double spiralling of silk, so if you wish you can apply a coat of varnish to the wire at this stage to prevent this and allow it to dry, or become partly dry, before proceeding further.

Then wind on the chenille in touching or very slightly overlapping turns to form a smooth, continuous body back to the original starting point, covering the lead wire. Finish off the head with a whip finish (or half hitches and varnish) and that is simply it.

There are variations to this of course. For instance, although it is not strictly necessary, a throat hackle can be tied in before finishing off the head, which could give extra movement. Alternatively it can be made in a contrasting colour – red, yellow or orange for instance – and either left as a full collar or brought down to two horizontal tufts with figure-of-eight lashing with the tying silk and slightly tied backwards by butting turns of the silk. This will form fin-like appendages, again giving extra movements as well as contrasting colour 'aiming points'. The colour of the chenille and marabou can of course be varied (both white or orange for example, or indeed different from each other), or the marabou tail can be of mixed colours. Whatever the combination, the lure has an enticing action, can be easily cast and is simple and quick to tie.

Of course, a more traditional lure can be tied in a similar way on a long-shank hook, with the marabou tied in at the head as a longer, flowing wing, although this is more inclined to wrap under the hook bend in casting and use. For a fuller wing, the chenille can be stopped halfway along the hook shank, a shorter marabou wing tied in, then the chenille continued to the point before the eye and another, longer wing tied in (see 'Blond' style winging in figure 13). For a fuller profile, cock or hen hackles can be tied in each side of the marabou, although this will restrict the enticing rippling motion of the marabou feather. The hackle feathers can also be tied in, back to back, without the marabou, or a bunch of hair (such as dyed squirrel tail) tied in instead for a hair-wing lure. Hair wings can easily work loose so they need to be tied in securely, and a drop of strategically placed varnish helps to anchor things. Body materials can be varied: ribbed tinsel bodies add flash as does ribbing over chenille.

Dubbed seal's fur or substitute, ribbed or unribbed, also makes an attractive body and when teased out with a dubbing needle or small patch of Velcro, has a very attractive translucent effect when viewed against the light.

The Tadpole Muddler

Of the many variations of the Muddler lure to be encountered on still-waters I favour the very simple and very light Tadpole-style dressing. It is a very easy fly to tie, despite its somewhat formidable appearance. Take a short-shank heavy, wide-gape hook and start working back towards the hook bend, this time starting at least halfway and preferably three-quarters of the way back from the eye. Tie in the marabou in the same way as previously at a point above the hook barb and continue winding forward for about ¹/₅ in (5 mm). Cut off the surplus marabou feather. Then cut off a bunch of deer hair from the skin and hold it up against the hook shank, free of wound silk, and loosely wrap the silk twice round the bunch of deer hair in about the middle and at the same time round the hook shank (see figure 44).

Pull the silk tight, whereupon the deer hair will splay round the hook. Do not use too big a bunch of hair at a time – little and often is much better. Keeping the tying silk under pressure, force the splayed bunch back along the hook shank towards the bend, offer up another bunch of deer hair and repeat the process until just short of the hook, each bunch being compressed towards the hook bend. The result of this will be something like an unruly miniature hedgehog (see figure 45). To convert this unprepossessing object to a Muddler, finish off the head with whip finish (or half hitches and varnish) and cut off the tying silk. Take a pair of

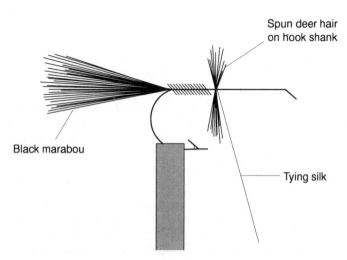

Figure 44   The partly completed Tadpole Muddler lure

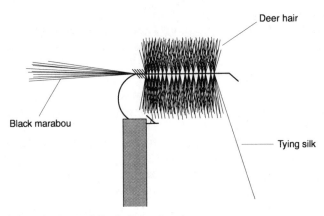

Deer hair

Black marabou

Tying silk

Figure 45   The Tadpole Muddler before trimming

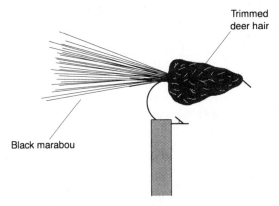

Trimmed
deer hair

Black marabou

Figure 46   The Tadpole Muddler after trimming

sharp, pointed scissors and carefully trim to the size and shape of a rough cone, leaving a few longer fibres at the back of the head if desired.

Tying a nymph

With no wings or hackles to worry about, the nymph should present few problems. It is a no-nonsense straightforward imitation, but it is the one style of artificial fly of which the fish is able to make a leisurely and detailed examination with little or no sense of urgency in the take. You therefore need to feel confident that the pattern is appropriate in every detail and neatly tied and presented. For this reason you should make a special effort to get it right. The basis of your confidence in fishing it starts the moment the hook is placed into the fly tying vice, and every action from that point on should be considered as an integral part of your fishing of the pattern.

The Pheasant-tail Nymph

The simple Pheasant-tail is a convenient and passable representation of the nymph of the lake or pond olives. It can also pass for a chironomid pupa – or at least it is frequently taken when fish are feeding on that food item. A lightweight hook in a relatively small size and with a slightly longer shank than normal is especially suitable. Depending on the manufacturers' inconsistency in hook sizes, a 12 or 14 long-shank or 'half-long-shank' is ideal. Place it in the vice and check that it is secure. Wax the tying silk as normal, start winding on ⅛ in (3 mm) from the eye as normal and wind down the hook shank to a point just short of opposite the barb. At this point catch in a short length of fine copper wire for ribbing and continue for three or four turns.

Then take four or five herls from the ruddy centre tail feather of a cock pheasant. Tie these in above the hook shank by winding forward, leaving ¼ in (6 mm) protruding from the rear. Spiral the tying silk forward towards the eye. Wind on the herls in touching turns, moving forward quickly and trying to keep them flat so as to wind on as a tape rather than a rope. This will give a body with more 'pile'. About ⅕ in (5 mm) short of the hook eye tie the herls in with a couple of turns of the tying silk. Then rib the body by winding on the copper wire in even, open turns in the opposite direction to that used to wind on the herls, finishing at the same point as the herls. Tie in another, larger bunch of pheasant-tail herls on top of the hook to serve as wing cases and then rewax a few centimetres of the silk and dub on some mixed rabbit fur (see page 142).

Wind on the dubbed rabbit fur to form a ball-like thorax and draw the fibres over the top to form the wing cases. Tie down in front of the eye on the top of the hook shank and complete with a whip finish or half hitches and varnish. The Pheasant-tail Nymph is now complete (see

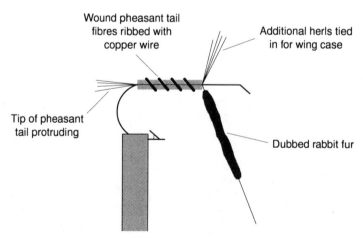

Figure 47   The partially completed Pheasant-tail Nymph

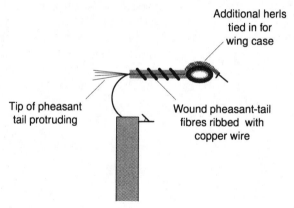

Figure 48   The completed Pheasant-tail Nymph

figure 48), and a very versatile and successful pattern it is. It is one of the few universal patterns which can be used on any water on any day of the season with confidence. It may not always take fish, but it is always likely to. If I were restricted to one pattern only, then this would be the one I would choose.

The Buzzer

For the larger, rich, Midland reservoirs my next choice would be the chironomid pupa, the black Buzzer pattern. The hook sizes can range from 8 to 16, 12 and 14 being most useful sizes. With the hook in the vice and the silk waxed, winding on commences as usual ⅛ in (3 mm) from the hook eye for a few turns towards the hook bend. Then spiral back to the starting point and tie in a small bunch of white turkey marabou feathers making sure they remain on top of the hook shank with the end protruding up to ½ in (12 mm) beyond the eye. Wind back towards the hook bend for ⅕ in (5 mm) and cut off the surplus (on the hook bend side). Continue winding to a point just beyond where the hook bend slopes down. Then catch in the ribbing. This is either a narrow 1/12 in (2 mm) strip of stretched polythene (heavy-gauge polythene has a 'grain' and a narrow strip will stretch out and narrow down to a crystal clear strip) or a single strand of pearl Lureflash. Then tie in a flat tape of black feather herls from natural or dyed wing feathers so that when wound the matt surface will be on the outside. Continue winding on, if necessary until approximately one-third of the way round the hook bend. Then spiral back the silk to the point ⅕ to ¼ in (5 to 6 mm) from the hook eye where the thorax will begin.

Carefully wind on the black feather herls in touching turns, as a tape, moving quickly forwards, and tie in. In the opposite direction wind on the ribbing and tie in at the same point. Cut off both surpluses. Tie in a bunch of black feather herls for the wing cases and at the same point but under the hook shank a short length of single strand hot orange wool or floss in the middle. Then dub on some mixed rabbit fur (guard hairs and under fur) and wind on to form a roughly spherical thorax. Draw up the orange wool or floss strand diagonally each side of the thorax to the top and the front and tie in. Draw the herls over the top of the thorax and tie them down in front of the eye. Lift the white marabou and finish off just behind the eye with a whip finish or half hitches. Trim off the white marabou with a clean, square vertical cut $1/12$ to $1/8$ in (2 to 3 mm) in front of the hook eye. The Buzzer is now ready for fishing and should look something like figure 22, which also features an optional white marabou tuft at the tail.

Sedge pupa nymphs

The final type of nymph I would like to describe, which will complete the range of representations usually used, is the sedge pupa. Like many representational patterns, a great array of colour and material combinations will be used and there will be many refinements which may – or may not – make the difference between success and failure on a particular day. Because I have had more success with very simple representations than more laboriously constructed, closer imitations, the pattern I describe here is very straightforward. Needless to say, as your confidence and experience develops, you may try more challenging patterns but I would suggest that the more complex patterns do not supplant your earlier and simpler ones, at least until their superiority under virtually all conditions has been incontrovertibly and conclusively established.

There are special sedge-shaped hooks, with a curved shank, available. These are designed to produce a more realistic body shape and they do give an interesting pattern to the nymph – at least to the eyes of the angler. The fish do not seem averse to them either but I have found that their hooking ability is not on a par with conventional hooks – although I must confess that this was on a very short trial. Fly dressers do tend to be very experimental, and there is no harm in this – otherwise where would innovation come from? However, I would suggest that, at least to start with, you use conventional hooks, preferably wide-gape and heavy-wire (better a heavier, stronger hook for a sunk nymph than a weaker lightweight one with lead wire added, which will cause the body to increase in size as a result). A size 12 would be a reasonable size to begin with in most patterns.

For the very simplest form of sedge pupa representation the tying silk is waxed and wound back to the point at which the hook bend starts to curve down or very slightly beyond. Tie in a short length (about 4 in or 10 cm) of fine tinsel wire. Whether it is gold or silver is immaterial, as it is only to protect the herl body from damage from the fish's teeth and is unlikely to be seen. Then tie in a length of single ostrich herl dyed either a dull orange or washed-out sea green. A word of advice should be given here. A close examination of the ostrich herl will show that the centre quill

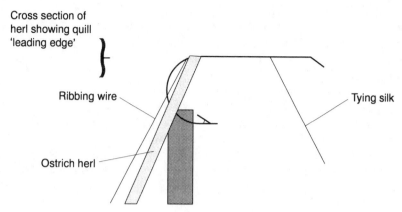

Cross section of
herl showing quill
'leading edge'

Ribbing wire

Tying silk

Ostrich herl

Figure 49   Tying a simple sedge pupa pattern

is flat and is extended as a leading edge on one side. This should be tied in to face forward (towards the hook eye) and when wound on this edge should lead clear of the flue (soft, fluffy fibres on the herl), otherwise it will flatten the rounded body shape you are trying to achieve (see figure 49).Wind the herl up the hook shank until it is ¹/₆ to ¹/₅ in (4 to 5 mm) from the eye and tie it in. Then wind on the reinforcing ribbing wire in open turns and again tie it in. Immediately in front tie in a single ostrich herl dyed a rich chestnut brown and wind it on to just short of the hook eye. Tie it in and finish off with a whip finish or half hitches and varnish. That is all there is to a perfectly serviceable and effective sedge pupa pattern.

In a small, sheltered bay at Grafham Water a few years ago on a warm summer's afternoon, I felt both elated and cheated by taking a very fast eight-fish limit in about half an hour on this pattern. An experience like this tends to suggest that this pattern needs no elaboration but confidence is a very personal thing and an 'optional extra' you might want to try is a very sparse soft throat hackle of brown (preferably) or grey

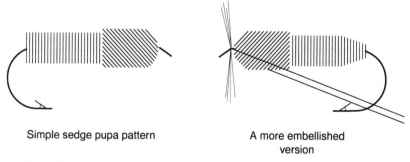

Simple sedge pupa pattern

A more embellished
version

Figure 50   Sedge pupa variations

partridge-feather hackle. Another option would be to add emergent antennae. These are usually represented by two long (150% of body length) centre tail fibres from a cock or hen centre tail feather tied each side of the body, sloping down and back from the eye (see figure 50).

These simple procedures cover all the techniques you need to produce excellent flies from scratch – indeed most of those used in fly dressing generally, although as new materials and ideas are applied these sometimes bring new methods. Familiarity in handling the materials is of course important, but it is acquired easily and naturally, and in a surprisingly short time. Some patterns require different combinations of the techniques, but where this is the case, it will be clear from an examination of a completed fly or from a written dressing. Other situations require a little common sense. For instance I described a simple Spider pattern; the only difference between this and a palmered dressing is that the hackle (or sometimes a second hackle, tied in first) is taken down the body in an open spiral towards the hook bend and there tied in with the ribbing wire or oval tinsel, which is then wound up to the eye (using the same to and fro motion as in tying in a throat hackle) and then tied in normally. Of course, in the event that no ribbing tinsel is used then the tying silk should be returned or a further length tied in earlier for the purpose of tying in and tying down – eventually to be tied in at the head with the main tying silk.

Similarly a Damselfly Nymph is a simple adjustment to the Pheasant-tail Nymph. The hook is scaled up and olive feather and fur used in place of the natural pheasant tail – although you can use dyed olive swan, goose or anything similar.

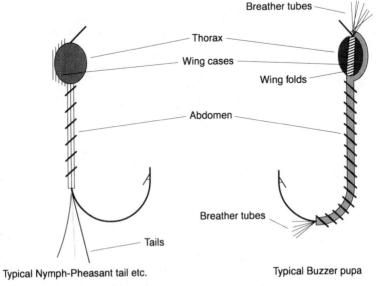

Typical Nymph-Pheasant tail etc.   Typical Buzzer pupa

Figure 51   Parts of the nymph artificial patterns

Useful dressings

Nymphs
Pheasant-tail Nymph 1
HOOK: 8–14 long-shank or regular

TAIL: tips of cock pheasant centre tail fibres

RIB: fine copper wire

ABDOMEN: herls (fibres) from centre tail feathers of cock pheasant tied flat as a 'tape'

WING CASES: as for abdomen

THORAX: dubbed natural rabbit fur (mixed blue dun under-fur with khaki guard hairs).

Pheasant-tail Nymph 2 (as Buzzer Nymph)
HOOK: 8–14 regular-shank

RIB: fine copper wire

ABDOMEN: flat cock pheasant centre tail herls dressed from part-way around the bend

WING CASES: as for abdomen

THORAX: dubbed natural mixed wild rabbit fur.

Olive Nymph
HOOK: 14 long-shank or 10–14 regular-shank

TAIL: tips of olive herl fibres or olive hackle fibres

RIB: thin (1–1.5 mm) strip of stretched polythene

ABDOMEN: dyed olive feather herls (swan, goose etc.)

WING CASES: as for abdomen

THORAX: dyed olive fur (rabbit, seal's fur substitute etc.).

Black Buzzer
HOOK: 10–14 regular-shank

BREATHER TUBES: small bunch white turkey marabou clipped short when fly is finished. This can optionally be run through the body with the tips as 'tails'.

RIB: thin strip of stretched polythene or strip of pearl Lureflash

ABDOMEN: flat 'tape' of black feather herls (3–5) – rook, crow, dyed swan or goose etc.

WING CASES: as for abdomen

THORAX: dubbed wild rabbit blue/grey under-fur. Optional diagonal hot orange wool or floss 'wing folds'.

Claret Buzzer
HOOK: 10–14 regular-shank

BREATHER TUBES: small bunch white turkey marabou clipped short when fly is finished

RIB: thin strip of stretched polythene or strip of pearl Lureflash
ABDOMEN: flat 'tape' of dyed claret feather herls (3–5), dyed swan or goose etc.
WING CASES: as for abdomen
THORAX: dubbed rabbit under-fur or seal's fur dyed claret. Optional diagonal
hot orange wool or floss 'wing folds'.

Ivens Brown and Green Nymph
HOOK: 10–14 regular-shank
TAIL: tips of 4 strands bronze peacock herl (¼ in or 5 mm) (The remainder of
the herls are left to form the 'back' and the 'head' later)
RIB: fine oval gold tinsel
ABDOMEN: dyed green and dyed brown ostrich herl tied in and wound together
along shank to form banded colours (i.e. not twisted together); when the
ostrich herls are tied in and ribbed the bronze peacock herls are brought over
the top (on top of hook shank only, tied in then twisted together to wind as a
thorax).
THORAX: twisted bronze peacock-herl fibres.

Red Buzzer
HOOK: 10–14 regular-shank
BREATHER TUBES: small bunch white turkey marabou clipped short when fly
is finished – these can also be run along top of hook shank to form short tubes
at tail
RIB: thin strip of stretched polythene or strip of pearl Lureflash
ABDOMEN: flat 'tape' of dyed bright red feather herls (3–5), dyed swan or goose
etc. starting a short distance round the bend of the hook
THORAX: twisted 'rope' of bronze peacock-herl fibres.

Stick Fly
HOOK: 10–14 long-shank
RIB: fine copper wire
ABDOMEN: bronze peacock herl (2 fibres twisted together) or cock pheasant
centre tail fibres for the smaller sizes; front ¼ in (5 mm) of fluorescent yellow
or lime green wool
THROAT HACKLE: 2 or 3 turns at most of light red game hackle of small size
for hook

John Poole Deadly
HOOK: 12 or 14 long- or half-long-shank
RIB: fine copper wire
TAIL: short, thin tuft of fluorescent lime green wool
ABDOMEN: cock pheasant centre tail fibres
THROAT HACKLE: one or two turns of a short 'dirty white' cock hackle.

Green Sedge Pupa

HOOK: 10–14 regular-shank
RIB: fine wire (any colour)
ABDOMEN: rear two-thirds pale (washed out) wound green dyed ostrich herl; front third chestnut/brown wound ostrich herl
HACKLE (OPTIONAL):   sparsely wound brown partridge.

Orange Sedge Pupa

HOOK: 10–14 regular-shank
RIB: fine wire (any colour)
ABDOMEN: rear two-thirds dull orange dyed ostrich herl; front third of chestnut/brown wound ostrich herl
HACKLE (OPTIONAL):   sparsely wound brown partridge.

Wet flies
Black Pennell

HOOK: 10–14 regular-shank
WHISKS: three tippets (fibres from golden pheasant neck hackle) with (normally optional) shorter golden pheasant topping over approximately half the length of the tippets
RIB: oval silver tinsel
BODY: black floss silk (or similar)
HACKLE: black hen or soft black cock.

William's Favourite

HOOK: 10–14 regular-shank
WHISKS: small bunch black hackle fibres
RIB: oval silver tinsel
BODY: black floss silk (or similar)
HACKLE: black hen or soft black cock.

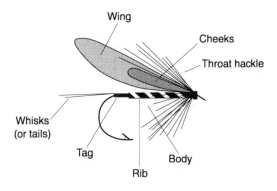

Figure 52   Parts of a wet fly

General Representative
HOOK: 10–14 regular-shank
WHISKS: small bunch natural red game hackle fibres
RIB: oval (or wire) gold tinsel
BODY: dubbed mixed fur from hare's ears and mask
HACKLE: natural red game soft cock.

Mallard and Claret
HOOK: 10–14 regular-shank
WHISKS: 3 or 4 golden pheasant tippet fibres (from neck hackles)
RIB: gold oval tinsel
BODY: seal's fur (or substitute) dyed claret
WING: bronze mallard shoulder feathers (mallard shoulder feathers often give problems in tying in; to overcome take the two slips of fairly generous size and instead of matching them up back to back, lay the 'best' slip on top of the other then fold the slips in half, tying in in the usual fashion)
HACKLE: black hen or soft cock, normally tied beard style.

Greenwell's Glory
HOOK: 10–16 regular-shank
RIB: fine gold wire
BODY: well-waxed primrose tying silk
WING: slips from hen blackbird-wing quill substitute (starling-wing quills – inside or outside – will do)
HACKLE: hen (or soft cock) Greenwell hackle (basically a ginger hackle with a dark, almost black, central stripe running the length of the hackle).

Soldier Palmer
HOOK: 8–14 regular-shank
TAIL: short length of red wool
RIB: gold oval tinsel
BODY: dubbed red wool or seal's fur (or substitute)
HACKLE: natural red cock tapered down the body to the tail.

Walker's Skimming Sedge
HOOK: 10–14 regular-shank
TAG: fluorescent orange wool or floss
BODY: dyed green or chestnut brown ostrich herl wound over a nearly dry varnished shank and then trimmed with very sharp scissors
WING: natural red hackle fibres tied in as a delta shape and cut off square level with the hook bend
HACKLE: natural red cock throat hackle (same colour as wing), tied full.

Baby Loch Ordie
Hook: 8–12 regular-shank
Body: tying silk ½ to ⅔ length of hook shank
Hackles: a series of red/brown soft cock hackles tied close together the entire length of the body with the final hackle at the hook eye being white.

Coch-y-bondhu
Hook: 10–14 regular-shank
Tail: very short orange floss silk
Rib: fine copper wire
Body: two twisted strands of bronze peacock herl
Hackle: a Coch-y-bondhu hackle (a natural game red hackle with a black central stripe running the length of the hackle and black tips to the hackle fibres); Coch-y-bondhu hackles are likely to present a problem and the furnace hackle, which is natural game red with the black central stripe but without the black at the hackle fibre tips, is usually used instead.

Dunkeld
Hook: 10–14 regular-shank
Tail: golden pheasant topping (from the crest)
Rib: gold wire
Body: flat gold tinsel
Wing: bronze mallard shoulder feather
Cheeks: jungle cock
Hackle: orange cock, tied Palmer-style (in the smallest sizes the hackle is often tied at the throat only – also since few people have access to jungle-cock cheeks, these are frequently omitted).

Teal Blue and Silver
Hook: 10–14 regular-shank
Tail: 3–4 golden pheasant tippet fibres
Rib: silver wire
Body: flat silver tinsel
Wing: barred teal feathers tied in thin and low over the hook shank
Hackle: turquoise blue tied in as a beard.

Silver Invicta
Hook: 8–14 regular-shank
Tail: golden pheasant topping (or red cock hackle whisks)
Rib: silver wire
Body: flat silver tinsel
Wing: hen pheasant centre tail-feather fibres
Hackle: natural red game cock tied Palmer-style with blue jay wing-feather fibres tied in as a beard.

Wickham's Fancy
HOOK: 10–14 regular-shank
RIB: fine gold wire
BODY: flat gold tinsel
WING: medium starling with the shiny underside tied to show to the outside
HACKLE: natural red game cock hackle.

Invicta
HOOK: 10–16 regular-shank
TAIL: golden pheasant topping
RIB: gold oval or wire
BODY: yellow seal's fur (or substitute) lightly dubbed
WING: Hen pheasant centre tail-feather fibres
HACKLE: natural red game cock (Palmer-style) with blue jay wing fibres tied in as beard at throat.

Butcher
HOOK: 8–14 regular-shank
TAIL: red ibis substitute (or short scarlet dyed swan)
RIB: silver wire
BODY: flat silver tinsel
WING: blue mallard wing feathers (tied with blue to outside)
HACKLE: black soft cock or hen (or dyed bright red for the Bloody Butcher version).

Kingfisher Butcher
HOOK: 8–14 regular-shank
TAIL: small bunch kingfisher blue feather fibres
RIB: gold wire or oval tinsel
BODY: flat gold tinsel
WING: blue mallard wing feathers (tied either way round)
HACKLE: orange soft cock or hen.

Lures
Black Tadpole
HOOK: 8–10 regular-shank
TAIL: bunch of black dyed turkey marabou feather as long as or very slightly longer than the hook shank
RIB (OPTIONAL): flat or oval silver tinsel
BODY: black chenille over wound lead wire.

Orange Tadpole
HOOK: 8–10 regular-shank
TAIL: bunch of hot orange dyed turkey marabou feather as long as or very

slightly longer than the hook shank
RIB (OPTIONAL):   flat or oval gold tinsel
BODY: orange chenille over wound lead wire.

White Tadpole
HOOK: 8–10 regular-shank
TAIL: bunch of natural white turkey marabou feather as long as or very slightly longer than the hook shank
RIB (OPTIONAL):   flat or oval silver tinsel
BODY: white chenille over wound lead wire.

Olive Tadpole
HOOK: 8–10 regular-shank
TAIL: bunch of hot orange dyed turkey marabou feather as long as or very slightly longer than the hook shank
RIB (OPTIONAL):   flat or oval gold tinsel
BODY: orange chenille over wound lead wire.

Yellowbelly Tadpole
HOOK: 8–10 regular-shank
TAIL: bunch of black dyed turkey marabou feather as long as or very slightly longer than the hook shank
RIB (OPTIONAL):   flat or oval silver tinsel
BODY: black chenille over wound lead wire with a strip of yellow chenille tied in under the hook shank only and ribbed together with the main body
HACKLE: two or three turns only of yellow dyed soft cock or hen hackle.

The Ferret
HOOK: 8–10 regular-shank
TAIL: bunch of natural white turkey marabou feather as long as or very slightly longer than the hook shank
RIB (OPTIONAL):   flat or oval silver tinsel
BODY: dubbed blood red seal's fur (or substitute) over wound lead wire and teased out with dubbing needle or combed with Velcro (the stiff part).

Jezebel
HOOK: 8–12 long-shank
RIB: silver oval tinsel
BODY: white chenille
WING: two long white cock hackles tied back to back and tied in Matuka-style (i.e. with the underside of the hackle stripped of fibres for the length of the hook shank and the rest of the hackle left; the hackles are then tied in firmly at the hook bend with the oval tinsel and this is used to rib and tie in the hackles as a wing, in the manner of a crest, running along the top of the hook shank to the hook eye to finish off).

White Blond Lure (for fry feeders)
HOOK: 6–10 long-shank
RIB: flat or oval silver tinsel
BODY: white chenille
WING: three good bunches of white turkey marabou tied in on top of the hook shank, of different lengths, to end at the same point; bunches to be tied in at the tail, midway along the hook shank and immediately behind the hook eye.

Black Blond Lure (for deep fishing)
HOOK: 6–10 long-shank
RIB (OPTIONAL):   flat or oval silver tinsel
BODY: black chenille
WING: three good bunches of dyed black turkey marabou tied in on top of the hook shank, of different lengths, to end at the same point; bunches to be tied in at the tail, midway along the hook shank and immediately behind the hook eye.

Black Tadpole Muddler
HOOK: 6–10 wide-gape, regular-shank
TAIL: a good bunch of dyed black turkey marabou feather fibres tied as long as the hook shank or very slightly longer
HEAD: spun deer hair clipped to shape and dyed with black waterproof, spirit-based felt-tip pen.

White Tadpole Muddler
HOOK: 6–10 wide-gape, regular-shank
TAIL: a good bunch of natural white turkey marabou feather fibres tied as long as the hook shank or very slightly longer
HEAD: spun white deer hair clipped to shape.

Mini-Muddler 1
HOOK: 10 wide-gape, regular-shank
TAIL: a small bunch of natural red game hackle fibres
RIB: gold wire
BODY: flat gold tinsel
WING: paired slips from hen pheasant centre tail feather
HEAD: spun natural deer hair clipped to shape.

Mini-Muddler 2
HOOK: 10 wide-gape, regular-shank
BODY: fluorescent orange chenille
WING: paired slips from hen pheasant centre tail feather
HEAD: spun natural deer hair clipped to shape.

Chapter 13

Tail piece

Knots and fixings

Very few people will view the prospect of learning knots from paper with unrestrained enthusiasm, and I sympathise with this view. However, angling of all sorts does require attachments of various kinds – nylon to nylon, nylon to hooks etc. Nylon is a very durable and often trouble-free material, but in monofilament form it is not the easiest material with which to tie simple and secure knots. We often find ourselves tying knots in poor light and with cold, wet fingers, yet they must be reliably slip-free. For this reason anglers require simple, foolproof knots, and fortunately these do exist. Ingenuity has in fact devised a wide variety of suitable knots but since we only need one reliable knot for each type of use, and since knots are to my mind not the most fascinating subject, I do not intend to dwell on the whole range.

Leader to flies
The leader is invariably attached to the flies with a simple half-blood knot, either tucked or untucked. The tucked version gives much greater security and is recommended, but I confess that I am frequently lazy in this respect – and pay the occasional penalty as a result! The knot is appealingly simple. Thread the nylon monofilament through the hook eye. Take the end over the nylon leading to the eye, keeping an open loop immediately above the eye, and wrap the free end round four or five times, working up the nylon (i.e. away from the hook). Then by simply passing the end through the open loop you left and tightening (after moistening the nylon to lubricate the knot) you have a secure untucked half-blood knot (see figure 53). This should be tested by carefully tugging on it,

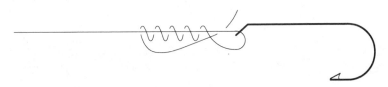

Figure 53   An untucked half-blood knot

Figure 54   A tucked half-blood knot

making quite sure there is no danger of impaling your fingers on the hook in the process!

To make this a tucked version (and in the process create an even more secure knot), instead of tightening after passing the free end through the open loop pass it through the loop which was formed when the free end went back down to the hook eye and the open loop above it (see figure 54).

Nylon to nylon
In addition to tying flies to the leader, you will need to tie knots in the leader to create a tapered leader and to create droppers to which you can attach other flies. My suggestion for this would be not the traditional blood knot, which can slip and is not as reliable under all circumstances as one would wish, but the water knot (also known as the grinner knot and the surgeon's knot). It scores on three points: it is slightly more reliable in practice, it allows a wider differential of diameters to be tied together and it is less fiddly and easier to tie with stiff cold fingers, in a pitching boat under poor light conditions.

Tying a water knot is really simple, in fact I think most anglers could literally tie it behind their backs. Take the two lengths of nylon to be joined and lay them end to end, with an overlap of about 8 in (20 cm) – slightly more if one end is to become a dropper. With the two overlapping lengths form a circle of about 2 in (5 cm) diameter, with the shorter length as the uppermost point at which the two double sections overlap. Take this shorter end round to the back of the circle and bring both ends through the circle. Take the ends back round and through three more times and then draw the moistened nylon tight (see figure 55). Test the

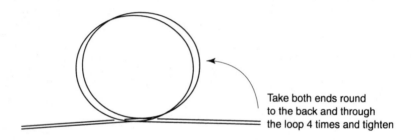

Take both ends round
to the back and through
the loop 4 times and tighten

Figure 55   A water knot

knot with a careful tug and trim the free end down to $1/12$ in (2 mm) unless a dropper is wanted, in which case trim to the desired dropper length.

Leader to fly line

Now the only joint not dealt with is that between the leader and the fly line. If the leader is of the tapered nylon monofilament type, the butt end to be joined will be of a reasonably substantial diameter. Take a sharp razor blade, scalpel or modelling knife and against a very safe surface (a thick magazine, for example, on a table or bench), carefully cut diagonally at the end of the thickest section of nylon to create a tapered end. Then take a pin or sharp needle and make a short tunnel through the end of the fly line, emerging after about $1/6$ in (4 mm). Thread the pointed end of the monofilament through. Take a large darning needle and lay it parallel to the fly line with the eye lined up with the end. Then take the end of the monofilament which has been drawn through the tip of the fly line and wind it round both the fly line and the needle four times (working up the fly line). Take the end of the monofilament back to the eye of the needle and pass it through. Draw the needle through the loops made by the monofilament and allow the moistened monofilament to be tightened so that it bites into the fly line, starting immediately above the point at which it emerges from the side of the line. Cut the free end off – and varnish the ensuing knot if you are nervous about it holding. This should give a secure link between leader and fly line, with uninhibited movement through the rod rings.

In recent years there has been a tendency to use braided monofilament leaders, and the method I have just described is not appropriate for joining this type of leader. Do not despair, however, as a more flexible and simpler option is available for braided leaders – you can either make or buy a braided loop attachment. To make one, you need a short length of braided monofilament (as used for the braided leaders). Thread one end through a large-eyed needle and make a loop of approximately ½ in (12 mm) diameter. Insert the needle point into the hollow braid and carefully run it down the hollow centre (away from the loop) for $3/5$ in (15 mm) or so and take the needle out of the braid. Gently pull the loop to tighten it up and, with sharp scissors, trim the free end as close as possible to the main braid. A drop of superglue can be carefully applied to the braid at this point for increased peace of mind. Then cut off a ½ in (12 mm) length of the plastic tube supplied with the braided loop kit and slide it up the non-looped end. Slide a blunt needle up the hollow end of the braid and slide the braid together on it. Carefully withdraw the needle and, holding the end so that it remains open, slide the end of the fly line into the hollow section. Carefully work the line into the braid until about 1¼ in (3 cm) are inside. Then slide the length of plastic tube up over the fly line end to the end of the braid – no further. Give the loop a pull to ensure that all is secure. There is now a secure loop fixed to the end of the fly line.

Make a similar loop at the end of the braided leader, using the same technique. This gives you a loop-to-loop system which will allow quick, simple and secure attachments. Remember, when joining on a loop-to-loop system, that the free end never goes through its own loop. To make the joint, take the leader loop and pass it over the line loop and up the fly line. Then take the free end of the leader and pass it through the fly line loop. Draw tight. (See figure 56.) This joining system allows rapid and simple changes and very free movement through the rod rings.

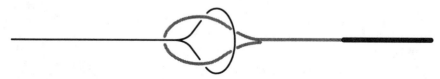

Figure 56   A loop-to-loop joining system

Landing the catch

Some extraordinarily casual means of landing fish can be seen on the water – for instance swinging in on heavy tackle, or lifting in by hand, by grabbing the leader. And if you are intent on offering your fish another opportunity to make a dash for freedom these methods are calculated to do that. However, most of us prefer a secure capture, and I would recommend a suitably sized deep net, strong enough for really large fish (there is no harm in being prepared), kept conveniently close to hand. Nets that fold are convenient to carry but most seem to develop problems in unfolding whenever a fish is attached. If you have one of these, play safe and unfold the net in readiness for immediate, anxiety-free use. When selecting a net pay particular attention to the length of the handle. A short handle is a frustrating abomination. I would suggest that a length of 4 ft (1.25 metres) is the absolute minimum. If the handle is of the telescopic type ensure that the mechanism is entirely reliable but even so take no chances: extend it before you start to fish – this is more easily managed with two hands.

When netting a fish a floating net is a frustrating nuisance and a dry net is most likely to float. So start the day by dipping the net into the water and continue to do so occasionally throughout the day to keep it wet so that it will sink as soon as it is brought into use.

If you are fishing with droppers, be aware of the effect of a free fly catching in the mesh of the net on your chances of safely landing a hooked fish. Establish which fly your fish has taken and handle the net in such a way as to avoid the risk of snagging the net with any of the others. In addition, do not try to net a fish too early. It will not like the look of the net and the sight will give it a fresh lease of life and energy. Be prepared for a sudden dart away once it sees it. Above all, except in the most dire emergency, do not chase the fish with the net. Always, but always, bring the fish in over the submerged net with pressure on to keep the head up wherever this is possible.

Keeping and preparing the catch

If we are realistic, we will admit that trout do not queue up for the privilege of taking flies – not in our waking moments, anyway. In fact at times they can demonstrate a totally unreasonable resistance to our invitations. Out of courtesy and respect to such an unobliging but wholly fascinating quarry it is only right to ensure that when they do take we keep them in a good and wholesome condition until we are ready to cook them.

Fish which have lain in the bottom of a boat for a full day in midsummer are not going to leave the water in a pristine condition. They will be in an even worse state if they have been kept in a plastic carrier bag, exposed to the sun all day. Although the skin colour may change, a bass or fabric bag suspended over the side of the boat from the rowlocks will keep fish reasonably fresh, even in the height of summer. If you are fishing from the shore a bag lying at the water's edge, held down and closed by heavy stones to prevent loss through wave action will have the same effect. A stringer – a cord passed through the gills and out of the mouth of the fish – with the end suitably secured by clip or knot will serve the same purpose. Alternatively, whether you are fishing from either bank or a boat, you can keep a fabric or bass bag moist by regularly dipping it in the water. This will keep fish in good condition even in a heat wave, but it is very important to remember to keep the bag moist at all times.

Having caught and kept the fish in good condition and having arrived home, what then? If you intend to eat it the next day, it will be good enough to transfer it to a food-grade polythene bag and put it in the fridge. If not, and they are destined for the freezer, they can be cleaned before being frozen. However, after a long day on the water, and possibly with a good bag to deal with, cleaning them late at night is not always an appealing prospect. I tend to consign them straight to the freezer packed in polythene bags, either one or two fish per bag, according to size – if they are in a big lump, they can be impossible to prise apart once frozen. They come to no harm when frozen intact; in fact if they are allowed to thaw partially when they are removed, they can be cleaned quite easily. Some cooks may well regard this as heresy but my view is that there is no point in cooking what is not going to be eaten. I have never had any interest in eating fish heads, and I see no merit in having an inedible head looking at me from the plate. Accordingly I remove it, which also assists in preparation generally. The method is the same, whether the fish has been frozen or not, but if the fish is partially thawed, with the guts still frozen so that they come out as a single lump, it does make the task a little easier.

Lay the fish on a cutting board in an upright position. With a sharp knife, cut down behind the head for approximately two-thirds of the depth of the fish. Then insert your thumb into the cut and pull the head off. You will find that the stomach, together with its contents will pull out with the head. Then take the sharp knife and slit down the central belly area to the vent and pull out any remaining 'attachments'. Take the point of the knife and slide it under the remaining transparent membrane along the backbone. Hold the fish under a tap of running water and, with the point of the knife, scrape and wash out all the congealed blood. That is it – your fish is now cleaned and ready to cook.

Cooking the catch

Very few anglers aspire to culinary achievements, and where trout are concerned, many are not even interested in personally consuming their catch. However there are circumstances when the food value of our quarry becomes something of more than casual concern. Friends may be interested in the difference between farmed, flavour-free, mini-trout and 'real' fish, but sometimes our concern may be even more personal. Whilst I am very partial to freshly caught fresh-run sea trout, I normally eat very few trout. However, for some years I spent a week or so a year with a friend on a very well-known salmon river in Scotland. We lived in a log cabin for our time at the riverside, a mile or so from the nearest village – and 'real' food. We were there to fish for salmon, although to be honest I derived as much pleasure from fishing the slacker water with small flies and light tackle for sea trout. The days, and the time of day, meant nothing to us. We slept little, rising from our bunks at any time which suited us, whether it was day or night. This total freedom was fine but meal arrangements were a nuisance. If our pangs of hunger came at times when the village was sleeping and we had no provisions left there was one simple remedy. Small brown trout lurked in the tails of the salmon pools. A short time with a small fly invariably produced a brace, which were quickly cleaned and slipped into the frying pan to give a simple, and under the circumstances, very enjoyable meal.

Most anglers will wish to do no more than hastily convert their catch into an acceptable meal, with the minimum of fuss. Frying is fine, but other methods are simpler, whilst also conserving the full, natural flavour. Talking about flavour, it should be noted that normally the deeper the colour the better the flavour and that mid- to late-season fish offer by far the best flavour. I would in fact go so far to add that pale-fleshed, early-season fish are best donated to others – but not to close friends!

For prime-condition fish there are a number of simple but often highly appreciated cooking options. Grilling is very simple and produces excellent results. It is quite trouble-free; just clean a fish of 1 to 2 lb (500 g to 1 kg), sprinkle a little salt in the body cavity and pop it under the grill until the skin starts to crisp and lift. Turn it until both sides are done and the flesh turns pinker and firmer, then serve with salad or whatever takes your fancy. For large fish over 2 lb, filleting with a sharp knife along the backbone after pulling off the skin and grilling with a pat of butter produces excellent results.

Another very simple method is to drop the cleaned fish into salted water and boil it until cooked. The change in the texture and colour of the flesh, which is difficult to describe, makes it obvious when cooked. Allow it to cool, skin it and remove it from bones and again serve with salad and perhaps mayonnaise or coleslaw.

The third option, which is suitable for fish of 1 to 1.5 lb (500 to 700 g) particularly, intrigues diners and is wonderfully simple for assured results, an absence of any smell and no pans to wash up. Clean the fish and salt the cavity; also enclose fresh herbs if desired. Take two complete pages from a tabloid newspaper and place the fish in one corner diagonally. Then wrap it up in the paper, rolling and folding in until it is fully parcelled up. Hold the parcel under a cold water tap until it is fully wet, and allow the excess water to drain. These parcels can be prepared some hours in advance and refrigerated, then when you are ready to cook, place the wet parcels directly on the shelf of a preheated oven. After twenty to thirty minutes the paper will be totally dry on the outside, with a tendency to become scorched brown. Provided the parcels are actually dry (which can be tested by prodding with a suitable utensil), remove them from the oven. Handling carefully (they are very hot) take sharp-pointed kitchen scissors and slit open one side of the paper down to the level of the fish along its entire length. By pulling back and removing the now dry (or virtually dry) newspaper, the perfectly cooked fish can be turned out onto a plate. It will be found that during this operation the skin will adhere to the newspaper and very neatly peel off and away from the flesh. The newspaper can then simply be rolled up and dropped into the bin. Serve the fish with salad and possibly new potatoes and wedges of lemon, and you may be in real danger of being regarded in a totally new light.

There are many other recipes which involve sauces to enhance and overcome shortcomings in commercially available farmed fish. The angler, however, has the overwhelming advantage of better-quality fish reared in a natural and virtually wild environment – and of wonderful freshness. These qualities are best enhanced by simple preparation and presentation to emphasise their advantages.

The value of fishing records

In every aspect of life we learn by experience; it is a natural and inescapable process. However, it is also an imperfect one – or rather it relies on our recall of earlier experiences in context, which sometimes fails because of poor memory or the fact that, at the time, we are only partially aware of some of the salient points to be learned.

Fishing is no different. We learn from our own experiences, and through books, magazines, videos etc. from the experiences of others. However, with the plethora of new experience which overwhelms our awareness every day, it is all too easy to miss things. Whilst one's mind quietly computes the complex environmental factors, together with one's actions and their effects, whilst at the water, the lessons learned there are dimmed with time and the influx of new data under new circumstances.

For some years now I have kept a fishing diary for my personal interest. Initially this was to keep alive in my mind the memories of sharply felt triumphs and pleasures which would otherwise have been dimmed with the passage of time. It is not a literary encapsulation of my feelings but merely a record of the place, date, weather conditions, companions, fish caught, flies used and other notable factors. My original requirements of instant recall of past pleasures is very adequately fulfilled by these simple details.

However, more and more the diary has become used as a reference source. What happened this time last year? Were the conditions similar to those I expect to meet tomorrow? Where were the fish? What did they take? How did they want the flies offered? There are a host of questions to which some answers are found in a fishing diary, which not only keeps past pleasures alive but serves to create confidence by recording experiences which may relate to one's forthcoming trip. The situations encountered subsequently may vary, as may one's response, but nevertheless one's confidence is high to begin with because of a memory of earlier experiences and a feeling that even before starting this time one may have some answers from the past. It takes only a few minutes to record the vital details of each trip but in the future these will prove not only fascinating but invaluable for further success and browsing can bring back to life some very acute and personal pleasures. I thoroughly recommend you to keep such a record – which may be anything from brief notes in a note pad to a formal, bound and illustrated record and scrapbook, including triumphant but redundant flies.

Variety in fishing

Since the environment and mood of the fish are subject to perpetual and cyclical changes, within each day, from season to season and from year to year, there is always an opportunity to enjoy variety in our fishing. Much of our angling day is spent fathoming the latest situation of the fish, with changes in location, variations in depth, alterations to their feeding pattern etc. There is rarely a chance to become bored – and thankfully so.

However, variety is always welcome as it broadens the appeal of our fishing generally and gives us a new perspective. Sometimes this variety can take an unexpected form. On the English Midland reservoirs, for instance, it is not only trout that inhabit the water, and large pike, bream and perch can offer some excellent – if unexpected – sport. All of these have enlivened my fishing days at Grafham Water on occasions and I still have very clear and happy memories of fishing at (and slightly beyond) dusk in the area of Savages Creek on a warm summer's night, when the fish being taken were unusually roach of about ½ lb (275g), all to very small nymphs at very long range and with very shy takes. They were not the fish I was there for but roach on the fly are extremely unusual (for me anyway) and I found the charm of this, the location and the overall atmosphere of a warm, still evening irresistible. I suppose that I was technically fishing illegally (after hours) at the time and should have packed up before I did, but the spot was isolated and I doubt whether even the most zealous bailiff would have begrudged me the simple and harmless pleasure I was enjoying. I am sure that I subsequently returned to 'proper' fly fishing after that with my overall appreciation sharpened and enhanced.

That was an accidental situation, but variation by deliberate choice is also to be recommended. It never hurts to broaden one's horizon, and if you habitually fish reservoirs for stocked fish you might try your hand at smaller waters, or truly wild fish from remote lochs or loughs – and of course vice versa. It is surprising how a diet of rainbow trout with the occasional 'brownie' can be enlivened by successful contact with an arctic charr, sea trout or even salmon, and the wholly different environment of unfamiliar territory can stimulate the thought processes and remind us that however experienced we are there is always something different waiting to challenge us. Running water also makes a very welcome extension to stillwater fishing, making further demands on our reasoning processes and setting our chosen sport against a broader background of experience which I feel sure encourages us to constantly challenge and evaluate what we are doing, how we are doing it and how we can improve. This creates a sense of alertness and brings added life and zest to our fishing which should not only help us to achieve better results in the tangible context (i.e. an agreeably heavier bag at the end of the day) but also that more lasting and fulfilling experience, the sheer pleasure of being there, doing what we want to do and having this enjoyment punctuated with the occasional moment of excitement which cannot be described or conveyed to those who have not experienced it.

Close season activities

The traditional fly fishing season is a relatively short one but this is in what most of us would regard as the best time of the year – even in Britain usually in the warmest and most agreeable weather conditions. Most still-water fishing is also governed by the hours of daylight, and during the summer months these are very long – in fact nearly twenty hours can separate first and last light, so that although our stamina may not stand up to the test too often, at least we have the opportunity of extremely good value in a day ticket where full-access daylight fishing is allowed.

Outside the season, although fishing is denied us, there are other agreeable pursuits. Tackle may need to be overhauled or replaced, flies can be tied at our own pace, and of course there is a rich storehouse of angling literature.

The fascination of the sport generally ·is certainly reflected in the volume of literature available. Thankfully many anglers have the ability to communicate well, letting us all share their knowledge, their experiences and their enjoyment. The printed page can bring to life situations which transcend time, distance, expense and discomfort and open up opportunities that might never otherwise come our way. With our shared interest we can learn to fish better and more intelligently during the close season without touching a rod. We can also 'fish' in every corner of the globe where a literate angler has cast a fly as well as experiencing the chances and flavours of fishing in a bygone area.

Whether old or new, whether an instructional book or an account of personal experiences with which we can all identify, one common factor links the myriad pages that have rolled off and are still rolling off the presses – enthusiasm! It is indelibly stamped on every page and is vibrantly and irresistibly infectious. Through the awareness of a host of experienced guides we can 'fish' through the close season to our hearts' content. Each writer has something new for us and a unique flavour. Part of the enjoyment is the personal discovery of an author with whom we, as readers, can develop a close rapport. Perhaps I can make a few recommendations to those who are casting their eyes along library or bookshop shelves. Broadly speaking, angling books will fall into two categories, the advisory and the recollective, although many will combine both and fall between the two.

For the group which have useful and valid advice to impart the title of 'the reservoir fisher's bible' must go to the extremely deeply considered and detailed *Still Water Fly Fishing* by Tom Ivens. I cannot remember how many times over the years I have delved into this, often just to check up on some point, and have become so absorbed that I have not put the book down until several hours later. The copy I have is now literally falling to bits but is a very valued volume and I can still pick it up and be wholly absorbed by it – anywhere I may open it. Fashions in angling may change, but apart from the fact that some of the tackle is now obsolete this book is as fascinating and valid now as when it was first published in 1952.

An author who was largely a contemporary of Tom Ivens, and another pioneer thinker in terms of new trout fishing opportunities, who is still very much worth reading is Richard Walker – an all-round fisherman of very high repute until his death. More up to date and with a new slant on the subject, *The Pursuit of Stillwater Trout* by Brian Clarke is highly recommended as a very pragmatic and down-to-earth view on the subject.

In the area of evocative experience we are truly spoilt for choice on a world-wide basis. In this area I can highly recommend *Going Fishing* by Negley Farson, a 'real' writer well able to communicate both his experience of and his passion for fishing of all types. Celebrated and highly articulate people who have contributed to writings on fishing vary from the ancient Claudius Aelianus, who described fly fishing in the third century A.D., through Dame Juliana Berners and Isaak Walton to Henry Thoreau, Ernest Hemingway, Anton Chekhov, Zane Grey, Sir Walter Scott, Robert Louis Stevenson, Arthur Ransom and Rudyard Kipling and the current crop of contemporary 'gurus'. There is one person left out of this list, but whom I can recommend only on the basis of a couple of excerpts which have whetted my appetite to a very high degree indeed. For the power to convey vividly the essence of truly international fly fishing I would suggest, if you are able to find it, that you snap up a copy of *Trout Magic* by Robert Traver.

Moral issues

There is one fact that sooner or later we all have to face. The 'gentle art' as it is described, is a form of field or 'blood' sport, and a growing number of people who see the need to impose their views on others as too pressing for the normally accepted civilised and democratic procedures are only too eager to ensure we are made fully aware of this. At times probably all anglers have to take stock of the situation and review their personal position in this regard. Certainly the angler is normally a predator as far as trout are concerned, and like many predators he makes it his business to learn as much as possible about his quarry. But in thirty years of fly fishing virtually everyone with whom I have fished has demonstrated a very high regard and respect for fish, have handled them with great care and either returned them lovingly after a brief appreciation or, where the rules of the water demanded it, despatched them quickly and cleanly without any delay. Only on very, very rare occasions indeed have I witnessed any sign of careless or disrespectful handling.

People who fish care for fish. They may kill them but in so doing they are taking a food resource and are harvesting creatures that have lived in a wild, or virtually wild, environment as nature intended. That environment knows other predators with less regard for humane treatment and it must be unusual for fish to die of natural causes. Falling prey to the hunger of another species is the natural order of things. The fish themselves are not vegetarians. Given a choice, a quick despatch by an angler must be better than to suffer at the mercy of otters, pike, herons or that recent scourge, the cormorant. The fact that our waters contain fish at all must be directly attributable to the lobbying power of the angler.

We cannot know how much pain or alarm is felt by a hooked fish, although one always hopes that a hook in the hard area of the 'scissors' causes no distress. No doubt fish do experience pain – but it is likely to be greater when eaten and digested alive by other fish. Hopefully, however, levels of distress are low; I have caught fish with savage pike gashes, and one which took my fly was literally articulated, having been virtually bitten through into two and being held together by little more than its backbone. Several have been stabbed at by a heron, which could not possibly have handled a fish of that size but which had made a hole right through the body with its beak. The distress of being played with a hook through the bony part of the mouth must, by comparison, have been nothing to these fish. Anglers should feel that they are aware of what they are doing, but they do not have to struggle with their consciences. Seeing fish taken commercially with nets at sea makes one realise that the fish taken with rod and line by a concerned angler can certainly be viewed as the lucky ones.

There is a natural order of things and hunting and fishing for food items seems to fit comfortably even into modern attitudes. It should be recognised, however, that more experienced anglers, especially perhaps those who are more mature, do have a tendency towards carefully returning their catch to the water, and the philosophy of 'catch and release' appears to be quietly and progressively gaining ground. Regrettably the rules on many reservoirs prohibit this practice and many owners of other waters with naturally maintained stocks request that all fish be killed in the interests of improving the fishing on overstocked waters. Doubtless in time these matters will be satisfactorily resolved but on the basic issue, upon considered reflection I continue to come down in favour of ethical and considerate angling for the enormous and growing body of fly fishermen.

Memorable fish

Memorable fish are legion and live on and on, as authors throughout history have testified. In the main these are fish which are significant because of their size or the problems involved in their capture. Inevitably the ones that got away emerge as particularly memorable – perhaps even growing in the telling, as sceptics amongst the non-fishing fraternity suspect. I have had memorable fish of all types which stay alive for me in my fishing diary. There is one fish, however, that predates the diary but still lives on in my memory, not for its size or reluctance to take my fly, but because of its misfortune in being caught despite the odds.

Many years ago I lived for fishing, particularly loch fishing in the wilds of the Highlands but, except for a week or so in the summer, I had to be satisfied in the main with reading and tying flies. In preparation for a trip to the west coast of Sutherland I had not only tied a vast array of flies but equipped myself with yet another new rod, specially built in split cane by a well-known maker then in the Redditch area. To complement this, of course, a new reel and floating plastic line were obligatory (dressed silk lines were still partly in vogue at the time).

Arriving for our week's non-stop fishing, briefly interspersed with appreciative malt tasting, out of the Drumbeg Hotel, my companion Don and I set out for our first day's fishing; naturally I took my new outfit on its maiden trip. The day was one of broken cloud and high wind, which was going to make handling the boat a bit tricky. Our first drift was very exposed and we were pushed along by the wind too quickly for comfort. Deciding that a more sheltered drift would be more comfortable we flicked the lines over the stern and I started rowing round into a more sheltered bay. On the approach, my reel started to scream as a fish took. My new rod shuddered through its length and as it did so, the reel slipped out from the thwart and the whole outfit slid over the back of the boat into the water. I could not believe it – my new and unused tackle was gone! As luck would have it, in choosing my landing net I had taken the advice concerning long handles for boat use seriously. The handle was of tele-scopic aluminium 4 ft (1.25 metres) long when collapsed and nearly 7½ ft (2.2 metres) fully extended. Added to this the net head was 2 ft (0.6 metres) in diameter and with arm fully outstretched over the boat I had at least 9½ ft (3 metres) reach. Trying desperately to scoop down into the dark brown peat-stained water was unproductive and very difficult in the high wind. When the sun broke through the cloud for a moment there was just a hint of a metallic flash from the depths, possibly the reel fittings, but nevertheless I could not reach down far enough. Looking round the shoreline produced no inspiration. That area of 'deer forest' naturally had no trees! It would seem that I had no alternative but to accept the loss.

Briefly taking lines on landmarks to fix our position in our minds we decided to make to the shore and take an early lunch whilst we consid-ered the matter. I was probably too disconcerted to appreciate the sandwiches but whilst eating them I became intrigued as to why the floating line on my rod was not floating. Pursuing possible expla-nations I looked at the mooring rope on the boat – it was a very long one. Tree branches may have been impossible but rocks of all sizes were all round us. Selecting a few suitably sized ones I unscrewed the net head, tied it to the mooring rope and weighted it with a few small rocks.

We then set off to row over the area where the rod had disappeared, in the hope of snagging the line with the weighted net head lowered on the rope. The first pass was unproductive. Trying again and peering intently into the shadowy brown depths with a surge of excitement, I thought that I saw something white glint on the second pass. Slowly and very carefully drawing in the rope as we gently made our way into sheltered and shallower water, I could see with relief that it was my white fly line. When we were safely in a shallow bay I pulled up the rope and was thankful to grab hold of the line and carefully eased up the rod which I had expected never to see again. Then I became aware of something I had not expected, which explained why my line had not floated to the surface – the fish was still attached! The poor creature hardly needed any more playing and was wound in to an incredulous captor – all 10 oz (280 g) or so of it! I really cannot remember whether I returned that fish – I hope in retrospect that I did – but certainly it was singularly unfortunate ever to have been caught and landed.

Tight lines!

Index

AFTM line rating, 17–19
alder fly, 138
alevins, 44
angler's curse (*Caenis* spp.), 123, 124
algae, 48, 65, 74, 132–3
angling,
   general motivation, 7–12
   safety, 65, 112
antennae, 158
artificial flies,
   dressings, 159–66
   tying, 144–58

Baby Loch Ordie, 137, 163
Ballantine, Georgina, 7
Barbour waterproofs, 15
beaching, 88
beetles, 136–8
Berners, Dame Juliana, 7
Bibio (Hawthorn fly), 86
birds' nests *see* tangles
black gnat (*Bibio johannis*), 131
Black Pennell, 161
'blond' style winging, 76, 151, 166
bloodworm, 106, 126
boat fishing, 112–22
   drifting, 113–19
   from anchor, 119
   nymph fishing, 117, 121
   partners, 112, 115
   safety, 115–16
bob fly, 82–3, 87
Booby Nymph, 110–11
braided leaders, 20, 169
   loops, 169
   monofilament, 24
broadwing *see* angler's curse
Brown and Green Nymph, 128

brown trout, 41–2, 49, 54, 82
Butcher, 85, 164
buzzers, 46, 56, 100, 106, 125–7,
   155–6, 159, 160

caddis *see* sedges
casting, 30–9, 88, 127
   double-haul, 35–7
   roll cast, 31, 37–8
   simple overhead cast, 31–4
   to rising fish, 94
charr, 55
chenille, 91, 151
chironomids *see* buzzers
Clarke, Brian, 177
climatic responses, 49
close season, 176
clothing, 13–16, 119
Coch-y-bondhu, 137, 163
Corixa, 85, 104, 110
crane flies (daddies), 86, 96, 130

daddy long legs *see* crane flies
damselfly, 47, 108, 129–30
daphnia, 46, 48, 73, 99, 132
dead drift, 89, 119, 132
Dog Nobbler, 70
dragonflies (Odonata), 108, 129–30
drifting pattern, 114–15
drogue, 115–16
droppers, 82, 84, 168
Drumbeg Hotel, 179
dry flies, 93–8
duck fly *see* buzzer
dun, 124
Dunkeld, 91, 137

eclosion *see* emergence
emergence, 111, 124, 126
Ephemeroptera, 46, 85, 100, 105, 123–5
epilimnion, 53
Ethafoam, 108
evening rise, 97, 126
eye protection, 14, 71–2

Farson, Negley, 177
ferox trout, 54
Ferret, 73, 165
figure-of-eight retrieve, 103
fish, cooking, 172
  following, 71
  fry, 48, 74, 85, 135
  large, 50
  storage, 29, 171
fishing bags, 29
fishing depths, 63, 65, 71–2
fishing lines
  double taper, 23
  floating, 24, 71, 100–102
  running line, 22–3
  selection, 17–19
  shooting head, 23–4, 37
  shooting line (backing), 23–4, 39
  sinking, 51, 71, 92, 101, 118
  specific gravity, 24
  types (profiles), 21–5
  weight-forward, 22–3
fishing records, 174
fishing tackle, 16–29
fishing waistcoat, 16
flies, at surface, 93–4
floatant, 95
fly boxes, 29
fly tying, 139–58
  dubbing, 142
  hackling, 149
  whip finish, 142–3
  winging, 143, 147–9
fly tying tools,
  bobbin holder, 140
  dubbing needle, 141
  fly tying wax, 141
  hackle pliers, 141
  scissors, 141
  vice, 140

freshwater shrimp, 46, 85, 134

G & H Sedge, 98, 118, 132
General Representative, 162
Gink, 95, 109
Going Fishing, 177
Grafham Water, 11, 50, 157, 175
Grenadier, 91
greased leader, 90
Green Nymph, 128
Green Sedge Pupa, 161
Greenwell's Glory, 162

hair wing lures, 75–6, 151
Hanningfield, 56
hackles, tying in, 145–6
hackles, 'beard' style, 148–9
hackles, alternative to 'beard' style, 148, 150
half-blood knot, 167
  tucked, 167–8
hatching *see* emergence
hats, 14, 15–16
hatchery fish, 44–5
hawthorn fly (*Bibio marci*), 131
heather fly (*Bibio pomonae*), 131
Highland lochs, 54–5, 116, 137, 179
hook sharpening, 29
Hopper pattern, 111
hypolimnion, 52–3

imago *see* spinner
Invicta, 164
Ivens, Tom, 128, 176

Jezebel, 165
John Poole Deadly, 160

Kingfisher Butcher, 164
knots, 167–8
knotted dry flies, 95–6

lake olive (*Clöeon similie*), 123
landing fish, 170
landing nets, 28, 170
leaders, 19–21, 82, 87–8
  joining to fly line, 169
Leeda, LC reels, 28
lee boards, 50

lines *see* fishing lines
  control, 23, 32, 34
  retrieve, 71–2, 83, 90, 101
  tray, 39
loch style, 81, 86
Loch Torr, 137
loop-to-loop joining system, 20, 170
lure colours, 73
  fishing, 68–80
  sizes, 73
  tying, 150–3
lures, 18, 68–9, 130

marabou wings, 77, 152
Matuka dressing, 130
mayfly (*Ephemera danica*), 123
memorable fish, 178–80
memory, 21, 24
mending line, 102
Mini-Muddlers, 91, 166
moral issues, 177–8
moving round the water, 67
Mucilin, 24
Muddler Minnow, 76–9, 91, 129

nymphs, 99–111, 124
  fishing from boats, 117, 121
  Ivens Brown and Green, 160
  tying, 153–8
  weighted, 101, 104, 108
nymph fishing, tackle for, 100

Palmer dressing, 84, 137
parr, 44
Permaflote, 95, 98, 109
Peter Ross, 85
Pheasant-tail Nymph, 104, 154–5, 159
polarised sunglasses, 14, 71
pond olive (*Clöeon dipterum*)
polystyrene, 108
pupae, 99, 100, 106, 126

Olive Nymph, 159
Orange Sedge Pupa, 161

rainbow trout, 42–3, 47, 49, 55, 59–60, 94
reels, 27–8

reservoirs, 55–60, 86
roach, 175
rod selection, 17–19, 25–6
Rutland Water, 58, 73

salmon, 55
sea trout, 55–6
seal's fur and substitute, 91, 142, 151, 152
seasonal feeding patterns, 46, 123–8
sedges, 47, 84, 92, 96–8, 100, 106, 127
sedge pupa, 106–8, 128, 129, 156–8
Shipman's Buzzer, 109–110
shoaling, 47, 49–50, 60
shooting heads *see* fishing lines
shuck, 111
Silver Invicta, 163
sink and draw, 90
small flies, 18
small stillwaters, 59
snails, 131
snails, floating, 98, 118
Soldier Palmer, 137, 162
spawning, 43–5, 54
Spider dressing, 83
spinner, 124
squirrel tail, 151
steelhead trout, 42
Stick Fly, 107, 128, 160
Still Water Fly Fishing, 128, 176
stocking, 58–9
striking, 79, 95
sub-imago *see* dun
Sugg, Ray, 150
surrounding terrain, 63
Suspender Nymph, 109

tackling up, 66–7
Tadpole lure, 70, 130, 150, 164–165
Tadpole Muddler, 77–9, 130, 152, 166
take detection, 79, 90, 99–100, 103, 122
tangles, 88
Teal and Black, 134
Teal, Blue and Silver, 85, 163
terrestrial flies, 85, 130–1
The Compleat Anger, 7

The Pursuit of Stillwater Trout, 177
thermocline, 47, 53
throat hackle *see* beard hackle
torpedo taper *see* fishing lines,
    weight-forward
Traver, Robert, 177
Treatyse of Fishing with an Angle, 7
Trout Magic, 177

upwinged flies *see* Ephemeroptera

vest *see* fishing waistcoat

Walker, Richard, 97, 98
Walker's Skimming Sedge, 98, 129,
    162
Walton, Isaak, 7
water, oxygen content, 52–3, 64
    acid/peaty, 54
    alkaline, 57

water boatman *see* Corixa
water coverage, 72
water knot, 168
water movement, 52–3, 63, 65
water flea *see* Daphnia
water louse, 46, 134
water stratification, 52–3
waterproof clothing, 14–16
weighted lures, 70
wet flies, 81–92
Whillock, Albert, 133
Whisky Fly, 133
Wickham's Fancy, 164
William's Favourite, 144–7, 161
wind direction etc, 62, 102, 113
wind knots, 20, 38–9, 89
wind lanes, 117
winged wet flies, 85
winging, 149